W9-AVC-727

The Age of Rights

Louis Henkin

The Age of Rights

 Columbia University Press   New York

COLUMBIA UNIVERSITY PRESS
NEW YORK   OXFORD

Copyright © 1990 Columbia University Press

Library of Congress Cataloging-in-Publication Data

Henkin, Louis.
  The age of rights/Louis Henkin.
    p. cm.
  Bibliography: p.
  Includes index.
  ISBN 0–231–0644–6
  1. Civil rights—United States—History. 2. Human rights—History. 3. Human rights—
United States—History. 4. United States—Foreign relations—1945–   I. Title.
KF4749.H46 1989
342.73'085—dc20   89-35555
[347.30258]CIP

Casebound editions of Columbia University Press books are Smyth-sewn
and printed on permanent and durable acid-free paper
∞

Book design by Charles Hames

Printed in the United States of America

c 10 9 8 7 6 5 4 3 2

For Alice
human rights champion

Contents

Preface

THIS volume bears the title I had used for lectures honoring Thomas Jefferson. One might well designate Jefferson's time as the Age of Rights—decades marked by the Declaration of Independence, the Virginia, Massachusetts, and the United States Bills of Rights, the French Declaration of the Rights of Man and of the Citizen, and heralded by Thomas Paine's *The Rights of Man*. In fact, my title refers not to Jefferson's age but to ours.

Ours is the age of rights. Human rights is the idea of our time, the only political-moral idea that has received universal acceptance. The Universal Declaration of Human Rights, adopted by the United Nations General Assembly in 1948, has been approved by virtually all governments representing all societies. Human rights are enshrined in the constitutions of virtually every one of today's 170 states—old states and new; religious, secular, and atheist; Western and Eastern; democratic, authoritarian, and totalitarian; market economy, socialist, and mixed; rich and poor, developed, developing, and less developed. Human rights is the subject of numerous international agreements, the daily grist of the mills of international politics, and a bone of continuing contention among superpowers.

Despite this universal consensus, as all know, the condition of human rights differs widely among countries, and leaves more-or-less to be desired everywhere. This may suggest that the consensus I have described is at best formal, nominal, perhaps even hypocritical, cynical. If it be so, it is nonetheless significant that it is *this* idea that has commanded universal nominal acceptance, not

(as in the past) the divine right of kings or the omnipotent state, not the
inferiority of races or women, not even socialism. Even if it be hypocrisy, it is
significant—since hypocrisy, we know, is the homage that vice pays to virtue—
that human rights is today the single, paramount virtue to which vice pays
homage, that governments today do not feel free to preach what they may persist
in practicing. It is significant that all states and societies have been prepared to
accept human rights as the norm, rendering deviations abnormal, and requiring
governments to conceal and deny, or show cause, lest they stand condemned.
Even if half or more of the world lives in a state of emergency with rights
suspended, that situation is conceded, indeed proclaimed, to be abnormal, and
the suspension of rights is the touchstone and measure of abnormality.

A more troubling challenge insists that in a world of wide and deep cultural
and ideological diversities there is no one single idea of human rights. There can
be agreement only if the idea of rights is sufficiently broad and vague, an
abstraction suspended high over real differences; only if universal declarations of
rights are sufficiently general and ambiguous to permit different societies to read
them as they will. In large measure this challenge too is misconceived. Language
is ambiguous but it is not wholly, fatally ambiguous and the language of international human rights instruments is less ambiguous than most (less, some
might insist, than that of the United States Bill of Rights). International texts
were indeed promulgated by diverse authors and designed for diverse societies,
but the framers sought not to build an umbrella large enough to encompass
everyone, but rather to respond to a sensed common moral intuition and to
identify a small core of common values. The Universal Declaration they have
proclaimed reflects general commitment to ideas that have proved contagious
and difficult to quarantine and that have become part of our zeitgeist; to conceptions of individual and societal needs that are widely recognized; and to notions
of decency and fairness that are universal and that surely no one denies. There
are however, as we know, differences among societies in their conception of
rights, and there are conceptions of the good society that have little room for the
idea of rights. How does the idea of human rights respond to competing ideas?

For Americans—our common usurpation for the inhabitants of the United
States—the idea of rights is an old friend, and we tend to think of it—with
some arrogating exaggeration—as our contribution to mankind. In 1976, we
celebrated the bicentennial of our famous expression of that idea in the Declaration of Independence. From 1987 through 1991 we celebrate the bicentennial of
the realization of that idea in the United States Constitution and the Bill of
Rights. There are libraries on United States constitutional rights, but only a
little has been written about the theory of rights in the United States, about the
relevance of theory for contemporary issues, about the development of rights in
the United States during two centuries.

For Americans, the internationalization of human rights may come as a
compliment, but it also suggests questions to be explored. How different is the
international human rights idea from the one proclaimed by Thomas Jefferson
and from what is reflected in the Bill of Rights? How has the United States
responded to these differences, notably to the contemporary insistence on "eco-

nomic and social rights" as human rights? What is the significance of the internationalization of human rights for the United States? What have other nations done with the concept of rights?

These and related questions are addressed by the essays gathered in this volume. Prepared at different times and for different occasions, some of the essays have required minor updating or invited a footnote on intervening events, all have profited from coordination and cross-referencing, the elimination of repetition, and additional reflection and editing. Some have been previously published and are included here with the permission of the copyright owners.

The essays have been grouped, ordered and loosely linked. The idea of human rights has been universally accepted as well as internationalized (see essays 1 and 2). International concern with the condition of rights within every state has stirred questions about the relevance of state borders to that concern (see essays 3 and 4). Human rights have entered the foreign policy of states, notably that of the United States (see essays 4 and 5). The international law of human rights has had to be fit into a political system of nation-states, leaving international human rights norms to depend on national laws and institutions. International concern with human rights, whether reflected in the bilateral diplomacy of states or the multilateral diplomacy of international organizations, continues to meet resistance from ingrained conceptions of state sovereignty and the embedded attitude that the way a state treats its own inhabitants is not anyone else's business. For the United States, the internationalization of human rights has induced self-examination, promoted thinking about individual rights under the United States Constitution (see essays 6, 7 and 8), and prompted comparison of constitutional rights with international human rights, and of rights in the United States with rights elsewhere (see essays 9 and 10). In the end, I conclude, the idea of rights has established itself against (and with) competing ideas, old and new, as essential to human dignity in our age (see Epilogue).

Four of the essays in this volume (Introduction, essays 3 and 6, and Epilogue) were prepared for presentation at the University of Pennsylvania Law School in 1983 in inauguration of the Thomas Jefferson Lectures. Most of essay 5 was the Irvine Lecture at the Cornell Law School in 1986. Essay 7 was prepared for a meeting on the Bicentennial of the United States Constitution in Birmingham, England in 1987. Essay 8 was the Cutler Lecture at the Marshall-Wythe School of Law, College of William and Mary in 1985. Essay 9 was the Biddle Lecture presented at the Harvard Law School in 1978 and revised and presented as a University Lecture at Columbia University in 1979. Essay 10 derives from the Sherrill Lecture presented at the Yale Law School in 1981. In am grateful to those who created those occasions, and to Columbia University, the Guggenheim Foundation, and the Luce Foundation for supporting research and reflection that contributed to these lectures.

I am grateful also to generations of law students who assisted me in the preparation of these essays, and, most recently, Grace Shelton, J.D. 1969 Columbia Law School, and to Elizabeth Martin, B.A. 1989 Columbia University, who helped put this volume together.

The Age of Rights

Introduction:
The Human Rights Idea

THE contemporary idea of human rights was formulated and given content during the Second World War and its aftermath. During the War, the Allied powers had proclaimed that assuring respect for human rights was their war aim. In 1945, at Nüremberg, the Allies included crimes against humanity among the charges on which Nazi leaders were tried. The United Nations Charter declared that promoting respect for human rights was a principal purpose of the United Nations Organization. The human rights idea found its contemporary expression in the Universal Declaration of Human Rights adopted by the United Nations General Assembly in 1948, and in the numerous covenants and conventions derived from it.

"Rights" have figured prominently in moral, legal, and political theory. The idea of rights is related to theories of "the good," of "the right," of "justice," and to conceptions of "the good society." In contemporary philosophical literature the idea of rights is often considered an alternative to various brands of utilitarianism.

Individual rights as a political idea draws on natural law and its offspring, natural rights. In its modern manifestation that idea is traced to John Locke, to famous articulations in the American Declaration of Independence and in the French Declaration of the Rights of Man and of the Citizen, and to realizations of the idea in the United States Constitution and its Bill of Rights and in the constitutions and laws of modern states.

For this Introduction, I draw on my book, *The Rights of Man Today* (1978), ch 1.

The idea of human rights that has received currency and universal (if nominal) acceptance in our day owes much to these antecedents but it is discrete and different from them. The contemporary version does not ground or justify itself in natural law, in social contract, or in any other political theory. In international instruments representatives of states declare and recognize human rights, define their content, and ordain their consequences within political societies and in the system of nation-states. The justification of human rights is rhetorical, not philosophical. Human rights are self-evident, implied in other ideas that are commonly intuited and accepted. Human rights are derived from accepted principles, or are required by accepted ends—societal ends such as peace and justice; individual ends such as human dignity, happiness, fulfillment.

What the pattern of declared norms amounts to, the idea it reflects, is nowhere articulated. I attempt to do so here, not as a philosophical construct, but as a distillation of what underlies national and international instruments.

Human rights are rights of individuals in society. Every human being has, or is entitled to have, "rights"—legitimate, valid, justified claims—upon his or her society; claims to various "goods" and benefits. Human rights are not some abstract, inchoate "good";* they are defined, particular claims listed in international instruments such as the Universal Declaration of Human Rights and the major covenants and conventions. They are those benefits deemed essential for individual well-being, dignity, and fulfillment, and that reflect a common sense of justice, fairness, and decency. In the constitutional jurisprudence of the United States, as we shall see, individual rights have long been thought of as consisting only of "immunities," as limitations on what government might do *to* the individual. Human rights, on the other hand, include not only these negative "immunity claims" but also positive "resource claims," claims to what society is deemed required to do *for* the individual. They include liberties—freedom *from* (for example, detention, torture), and freedom *to* (speak, assemble); they include also the right to food, housing, and other basic human needs.

Human rights are universal: they belong to every human being in every human society. They do not differ with geography or history, culture or ideology, political or economic system, or stage of societal development. To call them "human" implies that all human beings have them, equally and in equal measure, by virtue of their humanity—regardless of sex, race, age; regardless of high or low "birth," social class, national origin, ethnic or tribal affiliation; regardless of

---

*Human rights are not equivalent to, or interchangeable with, "justice," although some conceptions of justice—commutative, distributive, or retributive justice, or justice as fairness—are reflected in human dignity and in the particular rights human dignity requires. Human rights are not equivalent to, or interchangeable with, "democracy." The contemporary articulation of the idea of rights includes some democracy, declaring that the will of the people is the foundation of government, and that every human being has the right to authentic participation in his or her government. But democracy thus defined is one human right of many. The will of the people, surely the will of the majority, is subject to the human rights of the individual, although in some respects rights are limited by the common interest in security, public order, health, and general welfare as democratically determined.

wealth or poverty, occupation, talent, merit, religion, ideology, or other commitment.* Implied in one's humanity, human rights are inalienable and imprescriptible: they cannot be transferred, forfeited, or waived; they cannot be lost by having been usurped, or by one's failure to exercise or assert them.

Human rights are *rights;* they are not merely aspirations, or assertions of the good. To call them rights is not to assert, merely, that the benefits indicated are desirable or necessary; or, merely, that it is "right" that the individual shall enjoy these goods; or even, merely, that it is the duty of society to respect the immunity or provide the benefits. To call them "rights" implies that they are claims "as of right," not by appeal to grace, or charity, or brotherhood, or love; they need not be earned or deserved. The idea of rights implies entitlement on the part of the holder in some order under some applicable norm; the idea of human rights implies entitlement in a moral order under a moral law, to be translated into and confirmed as legal entitlement in the legal order of a political society. When a society recognizes that a person has a right, it affirms, legitimates, and justifies that entitlement, and incorporates and establishes it in the society's system of values, giving it important weight in competition with other societal values.

Human rights imply the obligation of society to satisfy those claims. The state must develop institutions and procedures, must plan, must mobilize resources as necessary to meet those claims. Political and civil rights require laws, institutions, procedures, and other safeguards against tyranny, against corrupt, immoral, and inefficient agencies or officials. Economic and social rights in modern society require taxation and spending and a network of agencies for social welfare. The idea of human rights implies also that society must provide some system of remedies to which individuals may resort to obtain the benefits to which they are entitled or be compensated for their loss.† Together, the affirmation of entitlement, the recognition by society of an obligation to mobilize itself to discharge it, and the implication of remedy, all enhance the likelihood that the right will be realized, that individuals will actually enjoy the benefits to which they are entitled.

Human rights are claims upon society. These claims may derive from moral principles governing relations between persons, but it is society that bears the obligation to satisfy the claims. Of course, the official representatives of society must themselves respect individual freedoms and immunities; political society must also act to protect the individual's rights against private invasion. As regards claims to economic and social benefits, society must act as insurer to provide them if individuals cannot provide them for themselves. Thus, government must protect me from assault by my neighbor, or from wolves, and must ensure that I have bread or hospitalization; in human rights terms my rights are

---

*A person may have additional rights in a given society by virtue of such extraneous qualities, or of others, such as citizenship, residence, or having been elected to office, but those are not everybody's "human rights."

†In some circumstances the idea of rights may also legitimate some measure of "self-help" to realize one's entitlement, for example, by resisting repressive behavior when no effective societal protection or remedy is available.

against the state, not against the neighbor or the wolves, the baker, or the hospital. The state may arrange to satisfy my claims by maintaining domestic laws and institutions that give me, say, rights and remedies in tort against my neighbor, or administrative remedies against a corrupt, misguided, or inefficient bureaucrat, or access to public schools or health services. Those legal rights and remedies against individuals or agencies within society give effect to my human rights claims upon society.

The idea of human rights has implications for the relation of the individual's rights to other public goods. It is commonly said that human rights are "fundamental." That means that they are important, that life, dignity, and other important human values depend on them; it does not mean that they are "absolute," that they may never be abridged for any purpose in any circumstances. Human rights enjoy a prima facie, presumptive inviolability, and will often "trump"[1] other public goods. Government may not do some things, and must do others, even though the authorities are persuaded that it is in the society's interest (and perhaps even in the individual's own interest) to do otherwise; individual human rights cannot be lightly sacrificed even for the good of the greatest number, even for the general good of all. But if human rights do not bow lightly to public concerns, they may be sacrificed if countervailing societal interests are important enough, in particular circumstances, for limited times and purposes, to the extent strictly necessary. The Universal Declaration recognizes that rights are subject to limitations determined by law "for the purpose of securing due recognition and respect for the rights and freedoms of others and of meeting the just requirements of morality, public order, and the general welfare in a democratic society" (Art. 29[2]).

The idea of rights accepts that some limitations on rights are permissible but the limitations are themselves strictly limited. Public emergency, national security, public order are weighty terms, bespeaking important societal interests, but they are not to be lightly or loosely invoked, and the conception of national security or public order cannot be so large as to swallow the right. Derogations are permitted only in time of a public emergency that threatens the life of the nation, not as a response to fears (warranted or paranoid) for other values, or for the security of a particular regime. Even in an authentic emergency, a society may derogate from rights only to the extent strictly required by the exigencies of the situation, and even such necessary derogations must not involve invidious inequalities, and may not derogate from basic rights: they must not invade the right to life, or involve torture or cruel, inhuman punishment, slavery or servitude, conviction of crime under ex post facto laws, denial of rights as a person before the law, or violate freedom of thought, conscience, or religion. Moreover, considerations of public emergency permitting derogations, or of national security or public order permitting limitations on certain rights, refer to a universal standard, monitored by external scrutiny and judgment.

In sum, the idea of human rights is that the individual counts—independent of and in addition to his or her part in the common good. Autonomy and liberty must be respected, and the individual's basic economic-social needs realized, as a matter of entitlement, not of grace or discretion (even by wise and benevolent authority, or even by "the people"). The individual has obligations to others and to the community, and society may ask all individuals to give up some of their rights for the rights of others and for the common good, but there is a core of individuality that cannot be invaded or sacrificed. And all individuals count equally. An individual's right can be sacrificed to another's right only when choice is inevitable, and only according to some principle of choice reflecting the comparative value of each right. No particular individual can be singled out for particular sacrifice, except at random or by some other "neutral principle," consistent with the spirit of equal protection of the laws.

I have referred to rights as claims *upon* society, not *against* society. In the ideology of rights, human rights are not "against society," against the interest of society; on the contrary, the good society is one in which individual rights flourish, and the promotion and protection of every individual's rights are a public good. There is an aura of conflict between individual and society only in that individual rights are asserted against government, against those who represent society officially, and because the human rights idea often requires that an individual's right be preferred to some other public good. But this apparent conflict between individual and society is specious; in the longer, deeper view, the society is better if the individual's rights are respected.

Human rights, as conceived by and specified in the Universal Declaration and other international instruments, are the rights of individuals. They include the individual's right to associate with others and to form groups of varying character for various purposes. The individual has the right to marry and create a family, to join a religious community and to pursue religious, cultural, or social activities with them, to identify with an ethnic or other group and to pursue their common interests, to join a political party or trade union. But the essential human rights idea addresses the rights of the individual, not of any group or collectivity.

Groups may have rights in domestic legal systems but, at least at its origin, the human rights movement did not address them. Later, the principal international human rights covenants declared the rights of "peoples" to self-determination and to sovereignty over their natural resources,[2] but those provisions were an exceptional addition to the general conception in the covenants that human rights are claims of a person upon his or her own society.* There has been a movement to recognize other "generations of rights"—a right to peace, to development, to a healthy environment—but none of these has been incorporated into any legally binding human rights agreement.

---

* Western states resisted those provisions on the ground that they dealt with matters that were not individual rights.

POLITICAL AND MORAL UNDERPINNINGS

The idea of rights here distilled from contemporary international instruments responds, I believe, to common moral intuitions and accepted political principles. Those intuitions and principles have not been authoritatively articulated. Developed during the decades following the Second World War, international human rights are not the work of philosophers, but of politicians and citizens, and philosophers have only begun to try to build conceptual justifications for them. The international expressions of rights themselves claim no philosophical foundation, nor do they reflect any clear philosophical assumptions; they articulate no particular moral principles or any single, comprehensive theory of the relation of the individual to society. That there are "fundamental human rights" was a declared article of faith, "reaffirmed" by "the peoples of the United Nations" in the United Nations Charter. The Universal Declaration of Human Rights, striving for a pronouncement that would appeal to diverse political systems governing diverse peoples, built on that faith and shunned philosophical exploration. Because of that faith—and of political and ideological forces—governments accepted the concept of human rights, agreed that they were properly matters for international concern, cooperated to define them, assumed international obligations to respect them, and submitted to some international scrutiny as to their compliance with these obligations.

International human rights derive from natural rights theories and systems, harking back through English, American, and French constitutionalism to John Locke et al., and earlier natural rights and natural law theory. In its American version, that constitutionalism included concepts of original individual autonomy translated into popular sovereignty; of a social compact providing for continued self-government through accountable representatives; of limited government for limited purposes; and retained, inalienable, individual rights (see essay 7). But the profound influence of that constitutionalism on international acceptance of human rights did not depend on, or take with it, commitment to all the underlying theory. International human rights reflect no comprehensive political theory of the relation of individual to society, only what is implied in the idea of individual rights against society. Human rights are "inherent" but not necessarily "retained" from any hypothetical state of nature anteceding government. There is a nod to popular sovereignty, but nothing of social compact or of continuing consent of the governed. Retained rights are not the condition of government, and violating them does not necessarily give rise to a right to undo government by revolution. Inevitably, international human rights also implicate the purposes for which governments are created, but they surely do not imply a commitment to government for limited purposes only. Born after various forms of socialism were established and spreading, and commitment to welfare economics and the welfare state was nearly universal, international human rights implied rather a conception of government as designed for all purposes and seasons. The rights deemed to be fundamental included not only limitations precluding government from invading civil and political rights, but positive obligations for government to promote economic and social well-being, implying government that is activist, intervening, planning, committed to economic-social programs for the society that would translate into economic-social rights for the individual (see essay 1).

Those who built international human rights perhaps saw these rights as "natural," but in a contemporary sense; human rights correspond to the nature of human beings and of human society, to *his* or *her* psychology and *its* sociology. Rights (to quote from the principal international instruments) "derive from the inherent dignity of the human person."[3] "Recognition . . . of the equal and inalienable rights of all members of the human family is the foundation of freedom, justice and peace in the world."[4] Respect for, and observance of, human rights will help create "conditions of stability and well-being which are necessary for peaceful and friendly relations among nations."[5] We are not told what theory justifies "human dignity" as the source of rights, or how human dignity is defined or its needs determined. We are not told what conception of justice is reflected in human rights, or how preserving human rights will promote peace in the world.

Necessarily, however, the idea of rights reflected in the instruments, the particular rights recognized, and the consequent responsibilities for political societies, imply particular political ideas and moral principles. International human rights does not hint at any theory of social contract, but it is committed to popular sovereignty. "The will of the people shall be the basis of the authority of government" and is to "be expressed in periodic and genuine elections which shall be by universal and equal suffrage."[6] It is not required that government based on the will of the people take any particular form. Presumably, Western-style presidential or parliamentary systems and communist "democratic central-ism" might both be equally consistent with the international standard—provided the people in fact have control over how they are governed, provided they have the freedom and the means to inform their governors of their wishes, provided the governors are accountable in fact and the people can replace them at frequent, regular intervals. In any system, government by bureaucracy is presumably not government by the people if, although political authority is conceived and couched in legal forms and decorated with occasional formal votes, arbitrary power in fact prevails, without meaningful accountability and meaningful opportunity for the people to terminate or control the exercise of such power. The will of the people is not the basis of the authority of government if the people are not free to change their form of government or their political and economic system, for instance, to move toward—or away from—socialism or a market economy.*

International human rights has no commitment to any particular economic system, and a society is free to choose between a market economy and socialism and among the various gradations and combinations of each. Some of the human

---

* Of course, even the will of the people does not justify government in violating the rights of individuals or minority groups.

rights recognized, however, imply commitment to some political-economic principles. Every person has a right to own property and not to be arbitrarily
deprived of it;[7] the right to work and be free to choose employment;[8] to enjoy
trade union protection against a powerful employer, private or public; and to be
protected against unemployment or its consequences.[9]

International human rights imply a broad conception of the purposes and
responsibilities of government. The obligation of society to ensure rights may
require government to plan, to regulate, to tax and to spend. Perhaps civil and
political rights can be respected—in a fortunate society—by a civilized citizenry,
and a minimal, honest, and benign officialdom, without any special societal
interventions. But if citizen civility and official self-restraint are insufficient, the
society must intervene, by civil rights acts and other laws, by institutions and
remedies governing the behavior of citizen and official. Economic and social
rights (food, shelter, work, health, and education) can perhaps be secured—in a
fortunate society—by private initiative and means, by market forces, by employment contracts, by private insurance. But society must ensure these rights, must
act as "insurer" for them; it must do what is necessary to see that such rights are
in fact enjoyed, whether by improving the performance of private agencies or by
supplementing or replacing these efforts by official programs.

Beneath the responsibilities of government for individual rights are political
principles governing the relation of the individual to political authority, and
beneath those political principles appear to be moral principles governing relations between individual human beings. If government responds to the will of
the governed, the undertaking by governments to respect and ensure individual
rights implies that the governed recognize these rights for each of them, and
assume responsibility for these rights even when other interests, including other
common interests, compete. The individual must recognize the obligation, both
as an individual and as a member of the sovereign people (the majority), to
respect and ensure those rights, to support the laws and institutions and the
costs necessary to make the agreed-upon rights secure.

Political-moral principles are implied both in the idea of rights and in the
particular rights recognized. Of course, a commitment to fair trial in the criminal
process reflects a common sense of justice requiring that a person—not only I,
but any other person—not be found guilty and deprived of freedom if he or
she is innocent. Political-moral principles are implied in the fact that individuals
not only demand for themselves, but also recognize for others equally, the
autonomy, the physical integrity and freedom, the rights to due process, to
property, to privacy, to "personhood," to liberties, as well as to basic human
needs and other economic and social rights.

Less obvious are the moral assumptions underlying the other dispositions of
the idea of rights. In general, what government may not do are those things we
may not do to each other, and the reason why officials may not do them—say,
deprive us of our life, liberty, privacy, or property—is because ordinarily no
individual may do that to another. Human dignity requires respect from my
neighbor as well as from the state. Under the international instruments the state

is required not only to respect but to ensure rights, that is, ensure respect for them by private persons. By what moral calculus, then, are officials permitted to do to an individual what his neighbor may not?

Implicit political-moral principles accept limitations on individual rights for the common good—to protect society against external enemies and internal disorder, or to regulate individual activity for the benefit of others and for the common welfare. Therefore, the state is permitted to take away my freedom through the criminal law, at least when imprisonment is designed to prevent and rehabilitate, probably also if it aims to deter, and perhaps even when the purpose is to express moral judgment by societal retribution. It is permissible to take away my property through taxation in order to provide for the common defense and the public welfare. From some perspectives at least, it may be assumed that these limitations on the individual are acceptable because the individual consents to them, or consented to them, in principle and in advance, by living in society and thereby submitting to government by democratic process. Individuals consent *a priori,* it can be argued, even to the possibility that they might be sent to their deaths for the common cause, on the assumption, or hope, that the need will not arise, and the sacrifice not prove necessary; that if someone will have to be sacrificed it will be someone else; that others submit to the same risk for one's own welfare, and that the selection will be by lot or chance or at least according to some rational, neutral principle. Whether such consent to the sacrifice of one's rights is authentic, whether an individual is really free to leave society so that his or her continuing consent can be assumed, is debatable and may differ from society to society, time to time, context to context, individual to individual. Or, perhaps—without insisting on consent and contract as the basis for rights and for limitations on rights—limitations on individual liberty or property are to be justified on notions of equity and practicability and some uncertain blend of the rights idea with utilitarian dedication to the "general welfare" or to maximum total happiness.*

The commitment in the human rights idea to the welfare society may imply other political-moral principles or assumptions. It implies, I think, that the basic human needs of those unable to provide for themselves are the responsibility of all, and that it is permissible if not obligatory to take from those who have (as by taxation) to provide for those who have not. Such moral obligation has been supported on various grounds:

- In the twentieth century, societies and political institutions are created and maintained for road purposes; not only for security against one's neighbor and against external aggression, but to assure the welfare of all and each. The social contract includes agreement to create a welfare state.
- In a society with a complex, integrated economy, the economically disadvantaged—for example, the unemployed—are victims of deficiencies in the economic system, often of policies that purposefully maintain such

---

*The rights idea, however, rejects the extreme utilitarian position that would justify even the complete sacrifice of individuals if it would increase total happiness.

disadvantages for systemic ends. Those who benefit from the system are therefore morally obligated to help those who suffer from it, at least to the extent of assuring their basic human needs.

- We are all members of a community that benefits all. Community and communality imply obligations, and high among them is the obligation to assure basic human needs for those who cannot satisfy their own.
- We have moved away from the moral intuitions of the Anglo-Saxon tradition which saw the Good Samaritan as acting from charity, not from moral obligation. Today, we are coming to believe, one is morally obligated to save a person in danger, at least if it can be done without undue risk or cost to oneself. There is, then, a moral obligation, for one who can, to save another from death or serious injury, as by starvation. If, in the case of the hungry in the community, that obligation is indeterminate in that the moral obligation to save any one person does not ordinarily attach to any other particular person, it attaches to all members of the community collectively. The collective obligation can be met by any collective action but effectively falls on the political authorities of society to meet by public action with public funds.

The moral foundations for human rights within society apply to all societies, and perhaps also between societies, as economies and polities become interdependent and community and communality expand. The idea of human rights, born in the West, has spread and, nominally at least, been universally accepted. Sovereign states continue to resist, but the implementation of the human rights idea has been "internationalized," and become the concern of the international community of states (see essay 1).

PART ONE

International Human Rights

1

The Internationalization
of Human Rights

RIGHTS, human rights, have long been the province of philosophy and law, and have been prominent in political theory and constitutional jurisprudence. Until our times, they did not concern students of international relations, international politics, or international law, and how individuals fared in countries other than their own did not seriously engage government officials or diplomats. Today, human rights are ever on the international conscience and never far from international consciousness. They are the stuff of international relations, appear on every international agenda and are the preoccupation of powers and superpowers; they are the subject of a growing body of international law and international agreements. Yet the myth that the condition of human rights in any country is its own affair, not international business, still persists even at high levels of many governments. There remain deep tensions between the traditional internal autonomy of states (sovereignty) and international concern for individual welfare, tensions that pervade both the law and the politics of international human rights and embarrass the international effort to improve the condition of individual human beings everywhere.

ANTECEDENTS

The internationalization of human rights, the transformation of the idea of constitutional rights in a few countries to a universal conception and a staple of international politics and law, is a phenomenon of the middle of our century. But it did not spring full-blown.

Historically, how a state treated persons in its territory was indeed its own affair, implicit in its territorial sovereignty. International law developed one early exception when it recognized that how a country treats a national of another state is the proper concern of that state.[1] That exception might be seen as essentially political, not humanitarian, in motivation: if a citizen of the United States is abused elsewhere, the United States is offended. It was widely accepted, therefore, that injustice to a stateless person was not a violation of international law since no state was offended thereby; surely, there was no state that could invoke a remedy for such injustice. But assuming that the doctrine developed because the offended state was concerned for its own rather than for human dignity, it is significant that governments were offended by violations of the "human rights" of their nationals.

In order to determine whether a state could properly claim that its national had been denied "justice," international law developed an international standard of justice. There was no accepted philosophical foundation for such a standard, and no agreed definition of its content; doubtless, it was redolent of "natural rights" and tantamount to a notion of "fairness." Whatever its underpinnings, whatever its substance, the standard for the treatment of foreign nationals that was invoked by their governments and acquiesced in by host governments was often higher than that—if any—applied by these countries to their own citizens at home. The international standard, then, was not a universal human standard, and governments that invoked or accepted it did not suggest that it applied also to how governments treated their own citizens. The treatment accorded by a state to its own citizens was not the concern of international law or the business of other governments, and in fact governments rarely concerned themselves with domestic injustice elsewhere. The few major-power intercessions—for example, that of the United States in the nineteenth century in response to Russian pogroms—did not invoke international law and occurred only when violations were egregious and dramatic. This was usually the case when there was a demand for intercession by a domestic constituency with special affinity for the victims in the other country (as in the United States, for example, the Irish, the Jews, and others).

International political considerations inspired other exceptions to the principle that how a government acts toward individuals at home is a matter of domestic concern only. Beginning in the seventeenth century, Catholic and Protestant princes (and others) concluded agreements according freedom of worship and wider toleration to each other's coreligionists.[2] Later, governments assumed international obligations to respect freedoms for ethnic minorities, even those who as a matter of law were nationals of the country in which they lived; in the late nineteenth and early twentieth century, such minority treaties were virtually imposed by the major powers on smaller ones in Central and Eastern Europe because it was believed that violation of minority rights led to intervention by countries that identified with them, and thus to war. Again, the basis for international concern in these cases was some special affinity on the part of some government for some inhabitants of other countries, and concern for international peace, not concern by governments generally for the basic dignity of all human beings, including their own inhabitants. In a different context, the mandate system of the League of Nations following World War I required a commitment by the mandatory power to promote the welfare of the local population. It has been argued that such clauses, too, did not reflect bona fide concern for human rights but were only a "sop" to justify keeping "the natives" in continued tutelage in disregard of commitments to the principle of self-determination. There were authentic humanitarian motivations in the development of "humanitarian law" to mitigate the horrors of war by outlawing certain weapons, protecting the sick and wounded and prisoners of war, and safeguarding civilian populations,[3] but that humanitarian law probably derived from concern by states for their own soldiers and citizens, not for all human beings equally.

The International Labor Organization was an early and noteworthy contributor to international human rights. The ILO was organized after World War I to promote common basic standards of labor and social welfare. In the intervening seventy years, the ILO has promulgated more than a hundred international conventions, which have been widely adhered to and fairly well observed. Again, some might find political-economic rather than humanitarian motivations for what the ILO achieved. The ILO, it is said, was the West's fearful answer to socialism, which had gained its first bridgehead in the USSR; perhaps the conventions reflected also a desire by developed states to reduce "unfair competition" from countries with substandard labor conditions.

A less ambiguous example of early international concern for human rights was the movement in the nineteenth century, after major powers abolished slavery in their countries, to outlaw slavery and slave trade by international agreement. Perhaps slavery was sufficiently egregious that no state could be allowed to claim to contain it within its domestic jurisdiction. Moreover, the products of slave labor were sold abroad at a competitive advantage with goods produced by societies that had abolished slavery. Slave trade, surely, was not an internal matter only, involving as it did international trade and colonial competition.

In all, international relations before our time were not impervious to the human condition inside countries, but concern for individual welfare was framed and confined within the state system. That concern could not spill over state borders except in ways and by means that were consistent with the assumptions of that system, that is, when a state identified with inhabitants of other states on recognized grounds, and that identification threatened international order; when the condition of individuals inside a country impinged on the economic interests of other countries. Whatever the reasons, primitive human rights provisions appeared in international instruments, and the seeds of international human rights were planted.

THE INTERNATIONAL HUMAN RIGHTS MOVEMENT

"International human rights" is a term used with varying degrees of precision (or imprecision) and with different connotations in different contexts. In wide usage it corresponds to the "international human rights movement," born during the Second World War out of a spreading conviction that how human beings are treated anywhere concerns everyone, everywhere. That attitude itself perhaps blended several different "statements": an assertion of fact about human psychology and emotion, that human beings cannot close their minds and hearts to mistreatment or suffering of other human beings; a moral statement that mistreatment or suffering of human beings violates a common morality (perhaps also natural law or divine law) and that all human beings are morally obligated to do something about such mistreatment or suffering, both individually and through their political and social institutions; an international political statement that governments will attend to such mistreatment or suffering in other countries through international institutions and will take account of them also in their relations with other states. These three kinds of statements combined to support a concept of "human rights" and a program to promote their enjoyment, as implied in declarations like President Franklin Roosevelt's Four Freedoms message,[4] in various articulations of the war aims of the Allies in the Second World War, and in their plans for the postwar world.

The end of the war saw wide acceptance of human rights reflected in two forms. Human rights appeared in the constitutions and laws of virtually all states. Victors in the war, for instance, the United States, wrote human rights into law for occupied countries, as for Germany and Japan. Later, departing colonial powers sometimes required a commitment to human rights of newborn states as part of the price of independence; many new states wrote them into their constitutions as their own commitment. Older states, responding to the Zeitgeist, also emphasized human rights in new constitutions and other national documents.

The human rights movement also took a second transnational form. Human rights were prominent in the new postwar international order: in treaties imposed upon vanquished nations, for example, Italy and Rumania;[5] in the Nüremberg Charter[6] and the UN Charter; in numerous resolutions and declarations of the new international institutions, notably, the United Nations, and of regional institutions in Latin America and Europe and, later, in Africa. In the United Nations, human rights were on every agenda, and the dedicated efforts of individuals and of some governments resulted in important international political and legal instruments, beginning with the Universal Declaration of Human Rights and the Convention on the Prevention and Punishment of the Crime of Genocide, both adopted without dissent in 1948.* There followed a series of

---

*When the Universal Declaration was adopted, "the Communist bloc" (then including Yugoslavia, but not China) abstained, as did Saudi Arabia and South Africa. The European

other resolutions and declarations and an impressive array of other international covenants and conventions, principally the International Covenant on Civil and Political Rights and the International Covenant on Economic, Social and Cultural Rights, both completed in 1966 and in force since 1976. Europe and Latin America also developed important regional human rights laws and institutions. The African Charter on Human and Peoples' Rights came into effect in 1987. At Helsinki, in 1975, in the Final Act of the Conference on Security and Cooperation in Europe, 35 countries from Eastern and Western Europe, as well as the United States and Canada, made an important political bargain in which Western states accepted the political status quo in Europe and the Communist states committed themselves to respect human rights.*

I stress—and distinguish—those two different manifestations of general, worldwide concern with human rights. "Universalization" has brought acceptance, at least in principle and rhetoric, of the concept of individual human rights by all societies and governments and is reflected in national constitutions and law. "Internationalization" has brought agreement, at least in political-legal principle and in rhetoric, that individual human rights are of "international concern" and a proper subject for diplomacy, international institutions, and international law.

Strictly, "international human rights," that is, human rights as a subject of international law and politics, are to be distinguished from individual rights in national societies under national legal systems, but the two are not unrelated in law or in politics. The international movement accepts human rights as rights that, according to agreed-upon moral principles, the individual should enjoy under the constitutional-legal system of his or her society. But national protections for accepted human rights are often deficient; international human rights were designed to induce states to remedy those deficiencies. That would be done by establishing a common international standard by which to judge national rights systems, and by inducing states to undertake international obligations to abide by those standards and to submit to international "machinery" that would monitor compliance. The law, politics, and institutions of international human rights, then, do not replace national laws and institutions; they provide additional international protections for rights under national law. The international law of human rights is implemented largely by national law and institutions; it is satisfied when national laws and institutions are sufficient.

The international law of human rights differs little in content from many national systems of human rights law. Ambiguities in the content or scope of international rights are resolved (at least in the first instance) by national governments, in the light of national standards. When there are differences between

communist states have since accepted the Declaration in various ways, formally by explicit reference in the Final Act of the Conference on Security and Cooperation in Europe, Helsinki 1975. Spokesmen for the People's Republic of China have also invoked the Declaration in the United Nations.

*These are undertakings that the parties agreed would not have binding legal character but are nonetheless important "political obligations." See generally Thomas Buergenthal, ed., *Human Rights, International Law, and the Helsinki Accord* (Montclair, N.J.: Allanheld, Osmun, 1977).

national and international standards, international rights supplement national rights. Thus, if the United States adhered to the International Covenant on Civil and Political Rights, courts in the United States would give effect to the limitations on capital punishment contained in the covenant,* as well as to those imposed by United States constitutional jurisprudence.[7]

In peripheral respects, there may be conflict between the conceptions of rights, or between particular rights, in the two systems. Again, for example, the International Covenant (Article 20) requires states to enact law prohibiting propaganda for war, but in some states the courts might declare such a law unconstitutional as abridging the freedom of expression, placing the state in violation of its international obligation under the Covenant.

An important change took place during the process by which the idea of rights became universal as well as international. Individual human rights as a political idea derives both conceptually and historically from Euro-American ideas, rooted in individual autonomy and supported by conceptions of popular sovereignty and social contract. The rights implied in those ideas were rights of autonomy and freedom, limitations on government, immunities from undue, unreasonable exercises of authority. But in the nineteenth century there began to grow another sense of right, rooted not in individual autonomy but in community, adding to liberty and equality the implications of fraternity. The various socialisms and the burgeoning welfare-state ideology began to accept a broader view of the obligations of society and the purposes of government—not only to maintain security and protect life, liberty, and property, but also to guarantee and if necessary provide basic human needs. What began in Europe crossed the Atlantic during the New Deal. In his Four Freedoms message, Franklin Roosevelt articulated the new conception, wrapped—perhaps disguised—in the language of freedom, when he added freedom from want to eighteenth-century liberties. When, in the postwar years, individual rights became universal and international, they did so in their broader conception. The Universal Declaration of Human Rights contains not only rights to life, liberty, and property, but also rights to social security, declaring that everyone is entitled to the realization "of economic, social and cultural rights indispensable for his dignity and the free development of his personality" (Art. 22). Specified, in addition, are the right to work, to rest and leisure, to a standard of living adequate for health and well being, and to education.

THE INTERNATIONAL LAW OF HUMAN RIGHTS

Those who wrote the Nüremberg Charter found in customary international law principles outlawing "crimes against humanity." The United Nations Charter,

---

*Article 6 of the International Covenant prohibits the imposition of capital punishment on pregnant women, or for offences committed by persons under 18 years of age.

an international treaty to which almost all states have adhered, declared it to be a purpose of the United Nations to promote universal respect for human rights, and all members pledged themselves to take action to achieve that purpose. It continues to be debated whether a violation of human rights by a member of the United Nations is a violation of the Charter pledge, but egregious violations such as apartheid have been authoritatively declared to be violations of the principles of the Charter.

In 1948, the United Nations General Assembly adopted the Universal Declaration of Human Rights. The Universal Declaration is not an international treaty. In form it is a declaration, not an agreement to be signed and ratified and designed to have the binding character of a treaty. It was proclaimed as a

> common standard of achievement . . . to the end that every individual and every organ of society . . . shall strive by teaching and education to promote respect for these rights and freedoms and by progressive measures, national and international, to secure their universal and effective recognition and observance.

At the time, surely, few saw its provisions as international norms or even as contributing to law. It was a "common standard of achievement" and it was hoped and expected that it would influence states to behave accordingly at home.

The Declaration has proved to be a giant step in the internationalization of human rights. But it was only a step. Some thought that the United Nations should stop with the Declaration and devote itself to programs of education and promotion. But the dominant mood was to press on to establish legally binding norms of human rights.

With time, the Universal Declaration has itself acquired significant legal status. Some see it as having given content to the Charter pledges, partaking therefore of the binding character of the Charter as an international treaty. Others see both the Charter and the Declaration as contributing to the development of a customary law of human rights binding on all states. Few claim that any state that violates any provision of the Declaration has violated international law. Almost all would agree that some violations of the Declaration are violations of international law.

The international law of human rights derives principally from contemporary international agreements in which states undertake to recognize, respect, and ensure specific rights for the inhabitants of their own countries. The older obligations in international law not to "deny justice" to nationals of other states are extended and supplemented—not superseded—by the new human rights law that applies to nationals and aliens alike. The older international agreements devoted to specific conditions—the antislavery conventions, the ILO conventions on labor and social conditions—continue in effect, and give special and strong emphasis to particular rights, but the benefit they brought to individuals are now subsumed in larger conceptions. Antislavery, for example, is not only state policy reflected in a willingness to assume international obligations to abolish the practice. Freedom from slavery is a right, an entitlement for every individual, one of an array of individual rights that in their sum reflect a conception of the minimum implications and needs of human dignity that states have come to recognize and to which they are obliged to give effect.

The international law of human rights is contained principally in the International Covenant on Civil and Political Rights and the International Covenant on Economic, Social and Cultural Rights, which together legislate essentially what the Universal Declaration had declared. In the Covenant on Civil and Political Rights, states undertake to respect and ensure rights to life and physical and psychological integrity of the person, to due process of law and a humane penal system; freedom to travel within as well as outside one's country; freedom of expression, religion, and conscience; cultural and linguistic rights for minority groups; the right to participate in government (including a right to vote in genuine free elections); the right to marry and found a family; and the right to equality and freedom from discrimination—a dominant theme in international human rights. Most, but not all, rights are subject to derogation "to the extent strictly required" in "time of public emergency which threatens the life of the nation and the existence of which is officially proclaimed" (Art. 4[1]). Public emergency apart, some rights—freedom of movement, assembly, association— may be curtailed by law as necessary to protect national security, public order, health or morals, or the rights and freedoms of others (Arts. 12, 21, 22).

In the Covenant on Economic, Social and Cultural Rights, states undertake to "take steps," "to the maximum of available resources," "with a view to achieving progressively the full realization" of designated rights (Art. 2[1]). These include the right to work, to enjoy just and favorable conditions of work, and to join trade unions; the right to social security, to protection for the family, for mothers and children; the right to be "free from hunger," to have an adequate standard of living, including adequate food, clothing, and housing, and the continuous improvement of living conditions; the right to the highest attainable standards of physical and mental health; the right to education; the right to take part in cultural life. In this Covenant, too, equality and nondiscrimination are a pervasive theme. Derogations and limitations by law are permitted if they are compatible with the nature of these rights and are solely for the purpose of promoting the general welfare in a democratic society. Some rights—e.g., trade union freedoms—are subject only to limitations "necessary in a democratic society in the interests of national security or public order or for the protection of the rights and freedoms of others" (Art. 8 [1][c]). Many have called the economic-social benefits recognized by this Covenant aspirations at best, but the Covenant uses the language of rights and of binding legal commitment by states to realize them. The undertaking is to achieve these benefits "progressively" and within the limits of available resources, but it is a legal obligation subject to international interpretation and scrutiny.*

---

*It has been suggested that states parties to that Covenant may have undertaken also to help other states insure the economic-social rights of their inhabitants. See Article 2 of the Covenant on Economic, Social and Cultural Rights. That apart, the international acceptance of human rights is seen in the context of the state system, with obligations only upon an individual's own society.

The International Covenants and other conventions dealing with specific rights, such as the Convention on the Prevention and Punishment of the Crime of Genocide and the Convention on the Elimination of All Forms of Racial Discrimination, create obligations binding on the states party to those agreements. But forty years of international human rights activity have engendered some universal human rights law binding on all states, whether as interpretations of the general human rights pledges in the United Nations Charter, or as customary law established by the practice of states. The precise contours and content of this customary law are uncertain, but it is widely accepted that it is now a violation of international law for any state to practice or condone genocide, slavery or slave trade, killing or causing the disappearance of persons, torture, prolonged arbitrary detention, comprehensive and systematic racial discrimination, and perhaps other consistent patterns of gross violations of internationally recognized rights.*

INTERNATIONAL REMEDIES

International human rights standards are high and compare favorably with those articulated in enlightened national constitutions and laws. States have been prepared to accept these international standards, and many have assumed legal obligations to abide by them. States have been far less willing to submit to international scrutiny of their compliance with those standards and, with some exceptions, have been reluctant to scrutinize compliance by others.

International remedies for state violations of human rights are still developing. In principle the remedies for a violation of international human rights obligations are the same as for violations of other international obligations (see essay 2). A state party to an international agreement can make claim for a violation of the agreement by another party and seek redress through diplomatic channels or by agreed-upon international "machinery," or, in some limited respects, by self-help. In a human rights agreement, every state's undertakings are promises to every other state party to the agreement, but the true beneficiaries of the agreement are individuals, the inhabitants of the states that adhered to the agreement. That the state promisees are not the true beneficiaries of the agreement does not detract from the right of any state party to seek observance of the agreement by others, but states have been reluctant to expend political capital and good will and jeopardize friendly relations to vindicate the human rights of nationals of other countries against their own governments.

Particular conventions provide additional "enforcement machinery." Under the Covenant on Civil and Political Rights, all states parties are required to

---

*Human rights might come into international law in yet another way, as "general principles of law recognized by civilized nations." Because national legal systems now generally outlaw the enumerated practices, arguably these practices may be deemed prohibited by international law as "general principles." Statute of the International Court of Justice, Article 38. See generally *Restatement,* note 1, § 702.

report to a Human Rights Committee. The Committee is composed of independent experts but, as in other bodies of international experts, some are not
independent in fact but are subject to substantial control by their governments.
States parties are required to report to the Committee within a year of adherence
and thereafter as requested (Art. 40), but many such reports are skimpy and
almost all of them are self-serving and concealing rather than revealing inadequacies in compliance. The Committee has been torn between those who wish to
scrutinize and challenge these reports and those who tend to consider such
scrutiny to be intrusive and not what the parties contemplated. The Committee
can only make "general comments," not specific charges or findings of violations.
Even as regards this modest Committee, the Covenant leaves it optional whether
states parties will agree to have other states bring charges against them before
the Committee. Submitting to private complaints before the Committee is also
optional, indeed the subject of a separate protocol.* Under the Covenant on
Economic, Social and Cultural Rights, states are required to report on their
compliance to the UN Economic and Social Council, which may transmit the
reports to the UN Commission on Human Rights "for study and general recom-
mendation," and "may submit from time to time to the General Assembly
reports with recommendations of a general nature" (Arts. 16, 19, 21). In 1985,
the Economic and Social Council established a Committee on Economic, Social
and Cultural Rights, parallel to the Human Rights Committee, to receive and to
consider reports by states parties on their compliance with the Economic-Social
Covenant.

HUMAN RIGHTS AND
INTERNATIONAL INSTITUTIONS

The machinery established by the International Covenant on Civil and Political Rights did not contemplate sanctions against violators of the Covenant. The
"general comments" by the Committee, reflecting its consideration of state reports, do not identify violators and their effect to deter or to modify state behavior
is small. "Views" expressed pursuant to private complaints against states that
accepted the Protocol do have some influence, but the major organs, the General
Assembly and the Security Council, have not been available to add weight to the
Committee's findings.

The Covenants are agreements by the states parties only; they do not speak
to violations of human rights by states not parties. Of course, virtually all states
are parties to the UN Charter but it seems clear that sanctions against violators

*A state may submit to interstate complaints by a declaration under Article 41, and to
private complaints by adherence to the optional protocol to the Covenant. As of May 1, 1989,
87 states had adhered to the Covenant on Civil and Political Rights; 23 had declared under
Article 41; 43 had adhered to the Optional Protocol to the International Covenant on Civil and
Political Rights.

of human rights were not contemplated by the Charter, except perhaps where violations threaten international peace and security.[8]

United Nations bodies, however, are political organs, and from the beginning those who could command majorities did not resist using that command. Early, Western states sought to use the United Nations to press the USSR to allow Russian wives of foreign nationals to emigrate. The General Assembly acted on complaints of discrimination by persons of Indian origin in South Africa. But, in general, states resisted United Nations involvement and thousands of human rights complaints received by the United Nations in effect went unattended.[9]

Perhaps it was the frustration of Black Africa in the face of apartheid in South Africa that moved United Nations organs to begin to consider complaints of violations in particular countries. For that purpose African states and others built on the UN Charter. All states were parties to the Charter and bound by its terms and by what can be read into them. The inchoate, undefined human rights pledges they contain soon began to serve as legal bases for dealing with at least some gross violations of human rights, and states that had avoided adhering to any of the new human rights agreements found themselves considered bound by some human rights law by virtue of the Charter commitments. Building on the purposes and pledges in the Charter, a modest procedure whereby a working group of a subcommission of the UN Human Rights Commission might consider private complaints began with complaints against apartheid and was extended to other "consistent patterns of gross violations."[10] Then the Assembly began a long series of resolutions calling for economic sanctions against South Africa.[11] In time, under pressure of Third World solidarity, the UN General Assembly could not resist public attacks on Chile and on Israel's activities in the West Bank.

For a time, the United Nations addressed human rights violations principally in a few countries that were in effect on a United Nations blacklist. "Selective targeting" has not ended, but in time other targets were swept into the process. Efforts to "depoliticize" the process, to have UN bodies address gross violations impartially, independently of other political considerations, began to succeed more often. Politicization tends to be in direct relation to the size and prominence of a particular body. In the General Assembly, Third World solidarity supports selective targeting and resists attention to the atrocities of Third World states, for a long time even the atrocities of Idi Amin. The Human Rights Commission, less prominent, can be pressed to widen its net, to report on disappearances in Argentina, on repression in Poland and in an increasing number of assorted states.*

International enforcement can claim dramatic successes in the European human rights system.[12] The European human rights system has a more complex and more exigent system of remedies, combining an active European Commission of Human Rights (which receives petitions also from individuals and non-

---

*The establishment of even a "toothless" office such as a UN High Commissioner for Human Rights has been strenuously (and to date successfully) resisted.

governmental organizations), a Committee of Ministers, and a Court of Human Rights to which cases may be brought by the Commission or by states. The Commission and the Court have decided many cases involving important rights —claims of torture and inhumane treatment, of unlawful detention, violation of freedom of the press, of the right of privacy claimed by homosexuals, denial of parental rights, of rights to marry, rights to peaceful enjoyment of possession of property, the right to education. States found guilty of violations have provided reparation and other remedies and have changed their laws and their ways.

The American human rights system is younger than the European but has already had some successes. The Organization of American States has also had an active Commission, which acquired a role in the implementation the American Convention on Human Rights. The American Court of Human Rights has a large jurisdiction to issue advisory opinions, as well as authority to hear cases at the behest of states.* The Court has now had several years of experience and has delivered opinions that promise active and imaginative support for human rights.[13] The African Commission provided for in the Charter on Human and Peoples' Rights was established in 1988. The African system is as yet untried but is promising.[14]

The influence of United Nations bodies, and of the committees established under the International Covenants and conventions, to induce compliance by states generally with international human rights standards is difficult to appraise. The fact is that the condition of human rights leaves much to be desired in many countries, including many that are party to international covenants and are subject to international enforcement. To date, the need for stronger implementation of international standards has not led to stronger international institutions. In part as a consequence of those inadequacies, particular governments, notably the United States, have sought to exert influence to end or deter violations. Much of the task of enforcing international standards has fallen to nongovernmental organizations—Amnesty International, the International League for Human Rights, the International Commission of Jurists, Human Rights Watch, the Lawyers Committee for Human Rights, and others. Domestic nongovernmental organizations—legal aid societies, civil liberties unions, legal defense funds, bodies with religious affiliation—have contributed to the development of rights under domestic law by influencing the public, legislatures, and courts. But domestic organizations generally supplement governmental institutions and help make them effective; international nongovernmental organizations often act to fill a void left by inadequate governmental and intergovernmental institutions. The international press has sometimes helped end violations by exposing them and has perhaps deterred others by the threat of exposing them.

---

*Submission to the jurisdiction of the Court is optional but most parties to the Convention have done so.

HUMAN RIGHTS IN
INTERNATIONAL POLITICS

The internationalization of human rights has not been limited to drafting impressive international agreements and building institutions to monitor them; human rights have permeated international politics. Human rights affect relations between states, between liberal and authoritarian governments, between every state and gross violators of human rights such as South Africa. Human rights permeate the foreign policy of some states, in particular, the United States, Canada, Western Europe. Human rights are on every agenda of the United Nations and other international organizations. Particularly offensive violations, such as apartheid in South Africa, have evoked repeated and universal condemnation and various sanctions. Many other violations are also cited and condemned. The biennial Helsinki review meetings have provided major occasions for challenging human rights violations, particularly violations by the USSR, and are credited with some influence for improving the conditions of rights.

But if human rights are part of international politics they are also subject to the laws of international politics. The international human rights movement has not fundamentally altered the character of the international system as a system of states, without any central authority, and with each state responsible for matters —and individuals—within its territory. States differ widely in political, economic, social, and cultural development and in the place they give to the individual and to human rights in their hierarchy of national values; they differ too in their perceptions as to how promoting human rights at home or elsewhere affects their national interests in relation to other states.

The state system is not necessarily hostile to the growth of human rights within countries, or to transnational support for their development. Long ago, the Peace of Westphalia led to diversity among states and to pluralism and toleration within states. International concern to protect foreign nationals helped develop an international standard of justice that inevitably commended itself for state behavior toward its own nationals. Minorities treaties, mandates, humanitarian laws of war, postwar peace treaties, Nüremberg, and the United Nations Charter and organization all had their influence in establishing and spreading the idea of human rights and common international norms. Influential states with an ideological bent for human rights; states with special links to inhabitants of other countries; states in strong communication with the outside world through electronic and other media that bring human rights violations into the homes of their citizens—such states and others have concerned themselves with the condition of human rights in other countries.

But there are limits to such political influence. The habits of thought and the rhetoric of state sovereignty are deeply ingrained. The state system itself helps suggest that the state is an ultimate good, if only as a carrier of values, and the perceived needs of state survival are often a basis for derogating from human rights (as the international human rights instruments themselves provide). Concern for survival sometimes brings paranoia, renders human rights at home secondary if not marginal, and limits concern for human rights elsewhere. State boundaries bring a sense of distance, of differentiation rather than identification, weakening concern for rights in other countries. There is inevitable ignorance as to what goes on elsewhere, and there is skepticism as to the effectiveness of particular measures to improve the condition of human rights in unknown countries. The weapons of international power are generally not appropriate for promoting human rights. International institutions have not been developed sufficiently to enable them to exercise a decisive influence in favor of human rights. In the international organizations in which states address human rights formally and prominently, states tend to see human rights issues in the light of their own political concerns and interests, and human rights concerns are ever in the shadows of world politics. The "politicization" of human rights, and, in particular, their subordination to ideological conflict and to Third World solidarity, have resulted in more concern with human rights violations in some countries than in others, and human rights are the text, or the pretext, for attacks on particular states. Even when all states are prepared to declare that apartheid in South Africa is an abomination, they differ as to what they are willing to do about it. Inevitably, politicized scrutiny attenuates the influence of the United Nations and distorts the human rights movement.

The internationalization of human rights was a new development in international relations and inevitably created tensions between the new transnational concern with the rights of individuals in all countries and ingrained assumptions and habits of state autonomy. States have differed as to the extent to which they were prepared to share or submit to this international concern. Virtually all states have been prepared to adopt the general exhortations and make the general pledges of the UN Charter, and to declare themselves committed to the Universal Declaration. Many have accepted covenants and conventions as international norms. Some have submitted their compliance with those norms to international monitoring. Only a few have been prepared to accept intensive, "intrusive" scrutiny. As regards economic and social rights, there has been little disposition to take even small steps to redistribute resources between states so as to help poor states assure their inhabitants the enjoyment of those rights.*

RETROSPECT: RHETORIC AND REALITY

What have been the results of forty years of the international human rights movement? Human rights are in the constitution of virtually every state. All states have recognized the idea of human rights and have accepted their articulation in the Universal Declaration; most states are parties to some of the principal international instruments, and at least half of the world's states (including most

---

*There has been no disposition to monitor whether states are spending available resources on other things—e.g., armaments—rather than on the basic human needs of their inhabitants.

of the major powers, but not the United States) are parties to the principal, comprehensive covenants. Although the UN human rights program is still politicized, its human rights bodies—the Human Rights Commission and its Subcommission on Discrimination and its working group—increasingly consider charges of violation by more countries and seek to bring about improvement. Regional human rights systems, in Europe and also in Latin America, are at work and have contributed to significant ameliorations in the condition of human rights in various countries. And yet, after forty years of worldwide, pervasive and incessant activity, there is a common impression that international human rights are all rhetoric and exhortation. Government spokesmen still commonly feel, sometimes say, and often act on the premise, that what a country does to its own is its own business.

The impression that the issue of human rights is essentially domestic, not international, is patently mistaken. That which is the subject of international law is ipso facto not domestic. What is more, human rights have in fact been deeply implicated in the realities of international politics. Colonialism was once a "domestic affair"; now colonialism (at least in its traditional form) is in effect illegal and self-determination is the first article in both international human rights covenants. The United Nations system has for many years asserted authority to concern itself, if only in a still, small way, with any "consistent pattern of gross violations" of human rights. The Republic of South Africa is virtually alone in believing that apartheid is no one else's business. At Helsinki, a "realpolitik" Secretary of State in a Republican Administration in the United States followed the lead of "realist" Western Europeans to exact human rights commitments from the Soviet Bloc in exchange for important political concessions. For years human rights were prominent in the ideological conflict of the Cold War, and they have been again in its latter-day versions and during periods of détente. In a different way, the Third World insists that some local human rights conditions —e.g., hunger—are not only the business of other states but the obligation of other states to alleviate. The politicization of international human rights only confirms their international character, and human rights have become important counters in international politics.

A different question is whether the internationalization of human rights is authentic. Skeptics have insisted that international acceptance of human rights is at best nominal, even hypocritical. Indeed, how can it be otherwise since, they say, human rights is a Western idea, foreign to most of the world, and internationalization just another form of imperialism? In any event, one hears, human rights is not an appropriate international concern. States are not prepared to submit conditions at home to external standards and scrutiny. States are not prepared to subject conditions in other countries to such scrutiny, at the expense of other interests, at cost to friendly relations and other foreign policy interests. The extended, complex, international human rights network is expensive in effort and resources, ineffectual, and disruptive of the proper business of international relations.

That bill of indictment is weighty but not, I think, compelling. The idea of rights as a political principle in a political theory prescribing relations between individual and society may have been articulated by some Western philosophers, but is not more congenial to Western societies than to others. Few Western societies accepted and adopted it before our day, and some (Hitler's Germany is only the most infamous example) explicitly rejected and flouted it. Respect for human rights today does not come more naturally to the West, and some of the most ineffable violations were committed in Western countries. Moreover, if the human rights idea is Western, so are most other political ideas that are today universal. Ancient traditions and cultures had no recognizable conception of political society (see Epilogue); today every society has political forms that necessarily implicate relations between individual and society. For the modern polity human rights is no more foreign than are statehood, sovereignty, international law, plebiscites, or various forms of socialism. In any event, if the idea of rights is modern and Western, the values inherent in the conception of human rights and in the particular rights that have been recognized are not Western. That a human being ought to live, should not suffer torture, arbitrary detention, or fake trials, and should not be allowed to die of hunger, is not an idea exclusive to the West.

The decision to internationalize human rights, made under the impetus of World War II and the Holocaust, has been continually reaffirmed not only by the states that made that decision in 1945, but also by more than a hundred new states since. International concern with human rights has required redefinition of what lies within each state's domestic jurisdiction and what is of international concern. The international community of states has, with virtual unanimity, agreed on that redefinition, and although the precise boundaries between domestic and international domains are often blurry and controverted, their general outlines are clear. Like other matters of international concern in a world of states, international human rights activities create tensions between state autonomy and international "intervention." These tensions are no doubt more acute in respect of human rights which engage the relation of the individual to society and which have been subject to international concern only during recent decades. The tensions are inevitable, and we must learn to live with them. Americans in particular will recall how, in the United States, we have learned to live with similar tensions resulting from the nationalization of individual rights which had been essentially the domestic concern of the individual states of the Union. As in the United States, so in the world of states, the result has not been fatal to the autonomy of states, and it has helped make human rights flourish.

In response to pressures and influences both domestic and external, all kinds of political systems, all kinds of governments have accepted the idea of rights, have written rights into constitutions, and have undertaken obligations to respect them. No doubt the commitment of many countries to human rights is less than authentic and whole-hearted. Yet the fact of the commitment, that it is enshrined in a constitution, and that it is confirmed in an international instrument, are not to be dismissed lightly. Even hypocrisy may sometimes deserve one cheer for it confirms the value of the idea, and limits the scope and blatancy of violations (see Preface). A constitution is at least a promise to the people at home and an assertion to the world at large. It responds to and generates forces that induce compliance, and it cannot long be maintained in the face of blatant noncompliance. A promise abroad provides grounds for scrutiny and criticism that inevitably have some force to induce compliance.

That human rights are not of authentic international interest and ought not be of diplomatic concern may still be asserted by some students and practitioners of diplomacy, but it is not in fact a view asserted by any government. Countries accepted that human rights are of international concern when they wrote (or adhered to) the UN Charter, the Declaration and the covenants and conventions, and do so when they all vote, repeatedly, to condemn apartheid or even less-deserving targets. Every country has at one time or another made human rights in some other country its own business, and has thereby accepted that human rights at home are someone else's business.

Whether the international human rights program has been effective is a more difficult question. There are some violations of human rights in every country, and gross violations in too many countries. There are forces that lead to violation of rights everywhere, and the institutions that enhance respect for human rights are weak in many countries. It requires more than international instruments and primitive international institutions to supply domestic deficiencies. It may be that the international community could not abandon or desist from pursuing an international human rights program even if doubts as to its efficacy were over-whelming. The fact is, however, that faith in it continues. No one is prepared to say that human rights would be better without the forces for compliance generated by the human rights movement. There is some deterrent influence in the very idea of rights, in the fact of making a commitment in a constitution or in an international instrument, in continuing participation in human rights discussions. The existence of commitments and institutions renders violations illegitimate, requiring concealment or false denials. It provides basis for protest both within countries and from the outside, by international organizations, nongovernmental organizations, the press, and individuals whose voices are heard. The national and international commitment to human rights has been an influence against authoritarian behavior. It helped remove Idi Amin of Uganda, Bokassa of Equatorial Africa, and the military junta in Argentina. It is a constant pressure for return to civilian government wherever military juntas control, and to more popular government wherever authoritarian regimes reign. Even totalitarian governments are compelled to respond or take account of it.

The international human rights movement has established the idea of human rights, and that idea is not likely to be superseded. In modern, industrial urbanized societies that idea and the forms into which it has been poured remain essential for human dignity.

2

International Human Rights as "Rights"

INTERNATIONAL human rights is now a common subject for intellectual as well as popular discourse, but few have written about it in relation to the massive literature on "rights." Are "international human rights" "rights," and what is the source and basis of their authority? Are they moral rights? Are they legal rights and, if so, in what legal universe? Whose rights are they? Are there correlative duties and if so upon whom? What remedies are there when the rights are violated? Are the remedies necessary and adequate to support their quality as rights?

Like international law generally, the international law of human rights creates legal rights and obligations within the international legal system. But international discourse, including international law, refers repeatedly to "human rights" apparently as preexisting in some other universe. The individual had human rights before the international system took notice of them and would continue to have them if the international law of human rights were repealed and the international system turned its back on them. One may properly inquire how seriously the word "rights" is to be taken in the frequent reference to human rights in international discourse. Some will argue that it carries no philosophical "rights" implications at all but is essentially rhetorical. It suggests an affirmative value, a "good," that is universal, fundamental, overriding. Particular reference,

From 1 *Cardozo L. Rev.* 425 (1979) and Pennock and Chapman, eds., *Human Rights,* NOMOS XXIII (1981).

too—say, to a "right to education"—means only that it is desirable and important, indeed very highly desirable and important, that every human being be educated.

International reference to human rights commonly indicates also, however, a positive attitude to the concept of individual rights vis-à-vis national societies and largely also to the content of such rights, generally as set forth in international documents. Indeed, international discourse insists that these human rights exist and that they are rights, although it is not clear what kind of rights they are and in what universe.

Independently of any international law on human rights, international discourse seems to see human rights in one or more of the following ways:

a. as "goods," desiderata, that are not rights but that might be translated into legal rights in domestic or international law;
b. as moral rights in an accepted moral order (or under some natural law), the individual having "claims" to freedoms and basic needs, seen perhaps as claims upon the moral order, or the universe, or God;
c. as moral (or natural law) claims by every individual upon his society; or
d. as legal claims upon his society under its constitutional system and law.

These rights are human in that they are universal, for all persons in all societies. Some rights—to form a trade union, or to enjoy vacation with pay— of course apply only to workers in industrialized societies, but these too are universal in that they apply to all to whom they are relevant. Perhaps they are human rights, too, in the sense that they are particular expressions of an overall, *a priori,* universal moral principle, that a human being is entitled to what he or she requires for "human dignity."

The purpose of international political and legal preoccupation with human rights, and of recognizing their quality as rights of some order, is to help obtain for them the quality of legal rights in domestic societies and to enhance the likelihood that they will be enjoyed in fact.

The international law of human rights builds on faith in the validity and desirability of human rights, but it largely avoids the philosophical uncertainties that trouble human rights discourse generally. Whatever the status and character of human rights in the moral order or in some other legal order, for international law human rights are positive law, conventional or customary.*

The positive character of international legal human rights disposes of one part of the debate about economic and social rights. Maurice Cranston[1] can properly ask whether one can have a right to two weeks vacation with pay, and whether that is a human right, and he and others (including the governments of the West) argued against treating social and economic aspirations as rights and

---

*The positive law may incorporate some morality or natural law by reference, as in phrases such as "cruel, inhuman or degrading treatment or punishment," or "arbitrary arrest or detention," or treatment "with humanity and with respect for the inherent dignity of the human person."

giving them status as law.* But the majority of states did not heed those admonitions, and the Covenant on Economic, Social and Cultural Rights is now in force.

There are, of course, important differences between that covenant and the Covenant on Civil and Political Rights. The latter is designed for full and immediate realization; the former requires steps only "to the maximum of [a state's] available resources," and with a view to achieving the full realization of rights "progressively." There is even a subtle but conscious and pervasive difference in tone and in the terms of legal prescription. The Covenant on Civil and Political Rights speaks throughout in terms of the rights which the individual has: "Every human being has the inherent right to life"; "No one shall be held in slavery"; "Everyone shall be free to leave any country, including his own"; "Everyone shall have the right to hold opinions without interference." The Covenant on Economic, Social and Cultural Rights, on the other hand, is couched in terms of the state's action (or obligation), not the individual's right: "The states-parties to the present covenant recognize the right to work"; "the states . . . undertake to ensure . . . the right of everyone to form trade unions"; "the states . . . recognize the right of everyone to social security," "to an adequate standard of living," "to education." There are also important political and practical differences between the two sets of rights, especially in that the economic-social rights tend to be collective, and to depend on national planning and policies, and on their success. As a matter of law, however, I do not think any of these differences critical. The Convention on Economic, Social and Cultural Rights uses language of obligation, not merely of aspiration or hope. An undertaking to do something "to the maximum of its available resources" and to achieve "progressively" creates a clear and firm legal obligation, subject to those limitations. That a state "recognizes the right to an education" is not different, legally, from "everyone shall have a right to an education." Both create a legal claim against the state for failure to provide what was promised or for not insuring it against interruption ("to the maximum of its available resources").[2] A state's failure to perform its undertakings gives rise to the same kind of remedies as do other international agreements. (see essay 4).

---

*The argument for treating economic-social benefits as rights is not countered persuasively by ridiculing "vacation-with-pay" as a human right. That may only suggest that this particular benefit is not "right-worthy." Adequate food and other necessities, however, are surely fundamental, and essential to human dignity. The argument against treating them as rights was that they depended on available resources and large national policies and could not be enforced by the means available for enforcing civil-political rights. Treating them as rights, therefore, would only dilute international efforts to obtain respect for civil and political rights. These fears have been realized to some extent, although perhaps in forms different from those anticipated: Many states have asserted the priority of long-term economic and social development (even as against present economic-social rights), and the need to sacrifice or defer civil and political rights. Compare UNGA Res. 32/130, Dec. 16, 1977.

RIGHTS UNDER INTERNATIONAL HUMAN RIGHTS LAW

What has international law done to human rights *qua* rights? What new legal rights have the international legal instruments created?

According to the common view, one has a legal right only against some other; to say one has a legal right against another is to say that one has a valid legal claim upon him and that the addressee has a corresponding legal obligation in the relevant legal system. Commonly, it is deemed to imply also that the system provides a recognized and institutionalized legal remedy to the right-holder to compel the performance of the obligation or otherwise vindicate the right. That one has a right may imply also that the right claimed is, in fact, commonly enjoyed (and "as of right," not by grace), and the corresponding duty is, in fact, generally carried out (and from a sense of legal obligation).

To examine the international law of human rights from the perspective of rights theory, it helps to keep in mind special characteristics of international law and of the international legal system. Because international law is made by states assuming legal obligations, the states parties to international human rights instruments might be seen in two different roles. Acting together, the states parties are legislators, making law. As a result of that legislation, every state party is an "obligor," having obligations, duties, to respect and ensure what are designated as the "human rights" of its inhabitants. After the agreement comes into force, the state as legislator largely disappears (except in the sense that lawmaking continues by interpretation and application); only the state as obligor remains.

Because the international law of human rights is made by states assuming obligations (the state as legislator), the international instruments focus at first on the state's obligations: it is the state's undertaking that creates the law. But under that law after it is in effect, the focus shifts sharply. The instruments are designated as dealing with the rights of individuals, and there is reference to individual rights in every article.[3] But the state's obligation and the individual's right are not necessarily correlative, or even in the same legal order. There are different possible perspectives on the relation between them:

1. The simple, undaring view sees international human rights agreements essentially, if not exclusively, in interstate terms. The agreements constitute undertakings by each state party to every other state party, creating rights and obligations between them. For violations of the agreement, as for other international agreements, there are "horizontal" interstate remedies: the victim state can make diplomatic claims upon the violator, request redress and reparation, sometimes may (lawfully) resort to "self-help." Insofar as the victim state has a legal right and pursues legal remedies, the violating state has correlative duties, including the duty, after violation, to provide redress and reparation, and even to accept the victim state's self-help where it is appropriate. The human rights agreements contemplate also special remedies, and a victim state—or the agreed

international body—has the right to invoke those remedies and the violating state has a duty to submit to them.*

In this perspective, the only rights and duties created by international human rights are the duty of every state party to act as it had promised, and the right of every other state party to have that promise to it kept. The individual has no international legal rights; he is only the "incidental beneficiary" of rights and duties between the state parties. The individual has no international remedies; he is only the incidental beneficiary of the remedies available between states parties. He stands no better even as regards states that have adhered to the Optional Protocol to the Civil and Political Rights Covenant. A state party to the protocol "recognizes the competence of the [Human Rights] Committee to receive and consider communications from individuals subject to its jurisdiction who claim to be victims of a violation by that State Party of any of the rights set forth in the Covenant" (Protocol, Article 1). That, it will be argued, does not establish a private remedy for violation of a private right, but only an additional mechanism for enforcing the rights and duties of the states under the covenant, by providing the committee with evidence as to whether those rights and duties have been honored. If a party to the Protocol should interfere with an individual's attempt to transmit a communication to the committee, or with the committee's action upon that communication, the state is violating its duty to other parties to the protocol, not any right of the individual, and the only remedies for that violation, too, are interstate remedies.

A *fortiori*, there are no individual legal rights under the Covenant on Economic, Social and Cultural Rights. The obligations assumed are by states to other states and even these are collective, long-term; the individual is not only an incidental beneficiary but a contingent and remote one and has no remedies whatever.

From this perspective, I stress, there are no international legal rights for the individual. When international law speaks of "human rights," it does not refer to, establish, or recognize them as international legal rights in the international legal system. By establishing interstate rights and duties in regard to "human rights," international law indicates its adherence to the morality and moral values that underlie them and strengthens the consensus in regard to that morality; it encourages societies to convert those moral principles into legal rights in their domestic legal order; it creates international legal remedies and promotes other forces to induce states to make such "rights" effective in the domestic legal system; it does not, however, make them international legal rights for individuals in the international legal order.

2. A second perspective would see the international agreements, while creating rights and duties for the states parties, as also giving the individual rights

---

*The parties have analogous rights and duties also under the Covenant on Economic, Social and Cultural Rights. Every state party assumes legal obligations and is also the "addressee" of such obligations by the others. There are the usual international remedies as well as the additional remedies provided by the Covenant, that is, requirements of reporting to the UN Economic and Social Council, reports and recommendations by the Council.

against his state under international law (in addition to any rights he has under his national constitutional-legal system).* The language of the agreements clearly declares these individual rights in every clause: "Every human being has the inherent right to life"; "No one shall be held in slavery"; "Everyone shall be free to leave any country, including his own." The individual has these international legal rights even though they are enforceable only by interstate remedies, by governments or international bodies acting in his or her behalf. Under the Optional Protocol to the Covenant on Civil and Political Rights providing for consideration by the Human Rights Committee of individual complaints, or under the provision in the European Convention that the European Commission "may receive petitions" from any person claiming to be the victim of a violation, the individual enforces his own right by his own remedy.

The same argument might apply even to economic and social rights. In the Covenant on Economic, Social and Cultural Rights, the covenant speaks of rights for the individual in every article. In principle, surely, one can have a legal right to an education, or even to a vacation with pay, and the states assumed obligations to accord these, thereby giving the individual a right—a valid, legal claim—to them. That there are no individual remedies provided, that even the international remedies hardly guarantee that the individual will enjoy the indicated rights presently, may weaken the real enjoyment of these rights but does not derogate from their quality as rights. Every individual has a legal right under international law to have his or her society "take steps . . . to the maximum of its available resources with a view to achieving" all the enumerated rights.

3. A third perspective, which is independent of but might be combined with either of the two set forth, would suggest that the states parties, as legislators, have legislated "human rights" into international law giving them status as affirmative independent values. That status is supported and furthered by the rights and duties that were established, whether the rights be those of states or of individuals. It is unusual for international law to create status or values,

---

*Individuals are entitled to have the state protect their rights against private interference, but the entitlement under international law is against the state only, not against the would-be interferer. A different question is whether the international agreement serves to create (or confirm) legal rights and remedies for individuals under their society's national law. The "preferred view" would have it that although the state is obliged by international law to accord such legal rights, it remains master of its domestic legal system, but a state's failure to accord such rights in the domestic legal order would, of course, violate its duties under international law.

Somewhat similarly, the Covenant on Civil and Political Rights, in Article 20(2), provides that any propaganda for war, or advocacy of national, racial, or religious hatred, shall be prohibited. The covenant creates an international legal duty upon the state to prohibit, and a right in other states parties to the agreement to have the prohibition enacted; there is no international legal duty upon any individual not to publish. Compare American constitutional theory, which also sees constitutional rights as only against the state. For example, the freedom of speech is freedom from official interference. The state is not even constitutionally obligated to protect my freedom from private interference. If it does so, by tort or criminal law, I acquire rights against the interferer and he duties to me, but these are not constitutional rights or duties. See essay 9.

On the "monist-dualist" debate as to the relation of national to international law, see *Restatement, Third, Foreign Relations Law* §703, Comment *a*.

independent of rights and duties,[4] since law is made wholly by way of states assuming obligations. But one can say, perhaps, that every state party assumes two different kinds of obligations corresponding to the two roles I have described. Acting with other states (the state as legislator), each state agrees to recognize and give legal status in the international system to "human rights" as claims that every individual has—or should have—upon his or her own society. In addition, each state (the state as obligor) undertakes to respect and ensure these values for its own citizens, thereby also creating rights in other states, and perhaps in individuals.

Rights, Remedies, and Enjoyment

The different perspectives I have suggested depend, of course, on different conceptions of rights. Immediately, whether the individual can be said to have legal rights in the international legal system depends in large part on the subtleties of "third-party beneficiary." At common law a third-party beneficiary generally had no remedy and had to depend on the remedy of the promisee. The third party was the "true beneficiary" of a binding legal promise; the promise was likely to be kept, and the threat of a remedy by the promisee helped make it even more likely. Did the third party nonetheless have no "right" because he himself had no remedy that he could initiate in his own name? Later, American states began to give the third-party beneficiary a remedy; did that convert a nonright into a right?

International law has moved to recognize a *ius tertii* for another state when the parties intend to accord it.[5] In our context the beneficiary is not a third state, but a mass of individuals. The individual's relation to the promise is not the same as that of third-party beneficiaries generally. The law declares that there is an individual "right." The individual is the true beneficiary, perhaps even the exclusive beneficiary (although one can find indirect "benefits" to the states impelling them to adhere to these agreements). The remedies are state to state and international, but individuals or nongovernmental organizations and other forces in their behalf often activate those remedies in fact. Under the Optional Protocol—even more so under the European Convention—the individual himself can formally activate the principal international machinery. As a matter of fact, and as regards some rights also as a matter of law, the individual can waive the obligations and rights created by the international agreements. Can that add up to an individual "right" under international law?

To me, these questions about the rights of individual third-party beneficiaries are aspects of larger issues about rights. What do we achieve by characterizing some claims as "legal rights"? What determines our definition of rights and the elements we require to satisfy it? Why do we ordinarily insist that a legal right must have a formal, institutional, legal remedy and that the remedy must be in the "right-holder"?

Of course, one can define a legal right *a priori* as a valid legal claim supported by a formal remedy that lies with the right-holder. I would suggest, however, that the concept and definition of "right" are not arbitrary but serve a social purpose. In part, the concept of right is descriptive: jurisprudence (and language) developed it to describe legal relations, implying special entitlement, respected by the society with a sense of obligation, and generally enjoyed by the right-holder in fact. In large part, the concept of right is normative: a society develops the notion that someone has a legal right to something in order to assure, or at least enhance the likelihood, that he or she will enjoy it in fact. Recognizing that a claim is valid, giving it legal status as a right, itself contributes to the likelihood that it will be enjoyed in fact. Usually, however, it is not sufficient. An institutionalized remedy not only enhances the legal quality of the right and its contribution to the likelihood of enjoyment but creates practical "machinery" to help bring about enjoyment. The remedy is more likely to be used, and therefore to bring about enjoyment, if it is controlled by the right-holder.

If the definition of "right" has a purpose, if it is intimately related to probability of enjoyment, one must ask how the requirement of remedy fits that purpose. Even in domestic law, the relation of right to remedy to enjoyment is not simple or perfect. We do not insist that a remedy for violation of a right assure its prompt and full enjoyment. A promise by A to sell B a book is often said to give B the legal right to have that promise performed, but for breach of the correlative obligation the available legal remedy does not assure enjoyment of the book, but only compensation for its value, and only much later. Even when domestic law gives B the remedy of "specific performance," he obtains the object only much later, often after a long proceeding. The remedy for vindicating other legal rights is not necessarily more prompt, adequate, and effective; even when B takes a book that A owns and possesses, the remedy will bring prompt and effective enjoyment of it only in rare cases where a policeman is present or A can exercise "self-help." As a practical matter, of course, the real purpose of an available remedy is to deter violation of the right, and often it will be not the right-holder's remedy but the state's penal "remedy" that will serve as the effective deterrent and make enjoyment of the right highly probable.

Some rights in domestic law are even further removed from remedy. Except perhaps for some strict Austinians,[6] constitutional rights in the United States are surely legal rights, yet the principal remedy for violations is judicial review, a limited remedy at best: it may prevent future violations but does not undo the past; for many violations there is not even compensation to the victim (see essay 7). Some constitutional rights moreover have no judicial remedy at all: they raise "political questions," not justiciable ones.[7] Judicial review is accepted as an adequate remedy, moreover, although it has unarmed judges dictating to powerful executives, because "it works": rights are in fact vindicated. If so, why not other remedies, other institutions, other forces, that enhance the likelihood that rights will be enjoyed, bringing about some repair or compensation and deterring violators.

A legal right, I suggest, is a claim that the law recognizes as valid, as to which it recognizes a legal obligation on the addressee, and whose benefit the legal system renders likely to be enjoyed. Ordinarily that likelihood depends on the availability of legal remedies in the hands of the right-holder. But in special contexts and circumstances it can be supplied as well by other remedies or other forces—criminal penalties, advisory opinions by judges, an ombudsman, even effective public accountability and other societal deterrents.

Again, except to the eye of some strict Austinians, the international legal system creates legal rights and duties, generally between states. The right-holding state has valid legal claims, but the remedy for its violation often consists only of the right to make the claim, infrequently also to assert it in some judicial or arbitral forum. Yet the remedy "works" to achieve probability of enjoyment because it is supported by political-systemic forces, the general desire to keep the system going, and the particular "right" and power of the victim state to respond in ways the violator would not like.* In a word, the sense of legal obligation exists, and although institutional remedies are few and infrequent, there are inducements to comply, creating a likelihood of enjoyment and thereby warranting the character of legal rights and duties.

As regards the international law of human rights too, even the rights and duties of states under the conventions depend on institutional "remedies" that are at best no stronger than those operating in international law generally. But there are, ever waiting in the wings, other forces inducing compliance—political criticism by other states and international bodies (and sometimes stronger reaction, sanctions as in regard to apartheid); criticism by nongovernmental organizations including various activist organizations, and world-press available to mobilize hostile opinion. Might these qualify as well, or in addition, as "remedies" that support the quality of international legal rights because they enhance the likelihood that the rights will be enjoyed in fact?

From this perspective, it may not matter whether one sees the rights created by international human rights law as rights of states or rights of individuals. But seeing them as individual rights may in fact help make it more likely that they will be enjoyed in fact. And especially if the states do not act to vindicate their rights, so that their rights lack effective "remedies" (i.e., effective inducements to comply), it becomes desirable to see the rights as those of the individual so he can mobilize whatever remedies (inducements to comply) are available to him or to nongovernmental organizations in his behalf.

Rights in Theory and in Fact

The relation of rights to remedies to enjoyment raises other questions for the international law of human rights. In principle, whether the human rights

---

*Those who insist that there can be no right without a formal, institutional remedy, might even question whether the state promisees have rights under the covenants. The only expressed remedies are reporting to and "follow-up" by the Human Rights Committee (or by the Economic and Social Council). A provision that the Committee might consider interstate complaints is optional (Art. 41).

agreements are being honored, whether the individuals are in fact enjoying the human rights promised, is not immediately relevant legally (or philosophically). For the short term, at least, failure of one or more states to carry out their international human rights undertakings does not vitiate the character of the undertakings as legal obligations, or the rights and duties they create. But if international human rights obligations fail to make any difference in fact over an extended time; if the states that undertook these obligations act continuously and consistently as though they had not, or as if these were not legal obligations; if the promisee states do not seek to have the undertakings enforced, and otherwise acquiesce in violations and act as though no obligations exist—then one would have to consider whether there are legal obligations and consequent rights and duties. One might then ask whether, despite the legal forms followed and the legal words used, legal obligations were intended and were consummated; or, perhaps, whether despite original intentions to make law, the obligations were ended by implied mutual agreement or acquiescence, or lapsed from "desuetude." (In regard to economic-social rights, in particular, the future may provide evidence belying the assumption that legal obligations were intended.)

A different question is whether the derogations and limitations permitted by the agreements are so large as to render the undertakings illusory, especially since they are, in the first instance at least, interpreted and applied by every acting state for itself. I do not think these and other "loopholes" render the undertakings illusory or derogate from the quality of any rights created. In my view, the derogation clauses are not destructive of the obligations (or the rights) so long as they are in fact interpreted and applied as written and intended, and other states and the international bodies scrutinize their interpretation and application. Similarly, I do not consider undertakings to realize economic, social, and cultural rights "progressively" as essentially illusory. The economic-social undertakings were made legal obligations in order to establish the idea of economic-social benefits as rights and to increase the likelihood of their enjoyment; it was not clear what else was expected to flow from making them legal obligations. Even those purposes may be sufficient to support law and rights; the future may show whether there are in fact other purposes and consequences for seeing, and continuing to see, the covenant as law and as creating rights.

I have written about rights and duties and remedies, formally conceived, but have felt impelled to allude to a prevalent skepticism about their reality and effectiveness. If questions of reality are philosophically relevant, they cut both ways. The formal edifice of rights, duties, and remedies is not wholly realistic; in particular, to date the state promisees do not commonly assert their rights or invoke their remedies; these may not therefore meaningfully contribute to the probability of enjoyment. On the other hand, there is a network of other forces, including some formal machinery, notably the international committees, and some domestic machinery, whether courts, ombudsmen or something else; and there are informal influences, both international and domestic—the influence of norms themselves, intergovernmental intercessions, "activist" nongovernmental organizations, the effects of publicity by media of information—which combine to achieve substantial respect for the international obligations to different extents in different countries. Some students of law and of politics have learned to ask not only what are the formal rights and remedies and who enforces legal rights but what are the inducements to comply with them and are they respected in fact.[8] If judicial remedies make rights, why not ombudsmen, whether initiated by the individual or self-initiated? And internationally, why not a Human Rights Committee, or—some day—a UN human rights commissioner, especially if they "work" and induce compliance? Does not philosophy have place for these "realities" in its conception of remedies for rights?

3

Rights in a World of States

THE idea of rights has addressed the individual's relation to society as though that society were the only society in the universe, or heremetically sealed off from other societies. In our age, the age of rights, the idea of rights has leaped from society to society, disregarding state boundaries and eroding the separateness and independence of states in significant respects. Human rights have been "internationalized" and are a staple of international law and international politics.

Nevertheless, the "sovereignty" of states, and the underdeveloped character of the international political-legal system, have shaped the content of internationally recognized human rights and limited the means available for their implementation. Some human rights, moreover—for example, the human rights of refugees—have effectively fallen between states, no state assuming responsibility for ensuring them. And some rights for some persons in some states, notably economic rights of the poor in poor countries, cannot be effectively ensured unless other states assume some responsibility to help realize them. Is there any moral, political or legal basis for extending rights beyond a state's jurisdiction and across state boundaries?

RIGHTS AS CLAIMS UPON ONE'S SOCIETY

Under the International Covenant on Civil and Political Rights, a state party undertakes to respect and ensure the recognized human rights "to all individuals within its territory and subject to its jurisdiction" (Article 2 [1]). The International Covenant on Economic, Social and Cultural Rights and other human rights conventions also clearly imply that a state's obligations are to its own inhabitants.[1]

That rights are seen as claims upon one's own society reflects both the traditional theoretical foundations of the idea of rights and practical considerations in realizing that idea. The various justifications of the idea of human rights derive from moral rights and obligations between persons in a society, or between such persons and the political authorities of that society; none of these justifications considers whether there may be moral rights and obligations between a person in one society and a person in another society; none of them seems to suggest rights and obligations between a person and a state other than his or her own. Neither do they suggest any political or legal rights and obligations between states in support of each state's responsibility for the human rights of persons subject to its jurisdiction.

The failure of the international human rights movement to address the responsibility of a state for human rights of persons in other states may reflect only the realities of the state system. States are not ordinarily in a position either to violate or to support the rights of persons in other states. States are reluctant to submit their human rights behavior to scrutiny by other states; states are reluctant to scrutinize the behavior of other states in respect of their own inhabitants; surely, states are reluctant to incur heavy costs for the sake of the rights of persons in other countries. The political system is unwilling to encourage or even tolerate a state's intervention by force or by other strong sanctions to ensure human rights in another state. Therefore, human rights in another state are not the explicit concern of international human rights law.

CIVIL AND POLITICAL RIGHTS AND STATE BOUNDARIES

State boundaries, however, are not definitive for human rights purposes. State boundaries do not define the moral obligations and rights that underlie human rights. Surely, a person in one state has a moral obligation to respect the life, liberty or property of persons elsewhere; it is immoral for a person standing in his own territory purposely to do injury to persons or property in another state, whether by shooting weapons or sending pollutants across state lines. Similarly, states are required to respect the rights of persons in other states. A state that intrudes in another state to violate the rights of persons there is guilty of a violation of human rights law (as well as of other international norms). Also, a state must not assist or encourage another state to violate the rights of its inhabitants. A state must not train the police of another state in techniques of torture or mistreatment or sell it weapons that are primarily designed or are likely to be used for such purposes. A state must not harbor persons who committed gross violations of human rights (such as genocide) in another state.[2] Although a state need not admit persons seeking to leave another state, neither may it conspire with that state to help it deny its inhabitants the right to leave their country and seek refuge elsewhere.[3]

A state's obligation to respect—to refrain from violating—the civil and political rights of individuals, then, applies in principle to all individuals wherever they are.[4] Human rights law does not ordinarily address that obligation expressly, only because the character of the state system and general principles of international law ordinarily preclude such violations. Similarly, because a state may not ordinarily exercise authority in the territory of another state, there is no obligation upon it to act to ensure respect for human rights there, whether by the government of that state or by private persons. A state is not internationally responsible for another state's failure to respect or ensure respect for rights.

In sum, a state must itself respect the human rights of inhabitants of other states; it is not required to ensure that human rights are respected and ensured there. The distinction reflects the overriding imperatives of a world of independent states and governments.* Such interventions are to be discouraged if not outlawed since they are incompatible with the assumptions of territorial sovereignty and are dangerous to international peace and order.

ECONOMIC AND SOCIAL RIGHTS AND STATE BOUNDARIES

In the Universal Declaration of Human Rights, and in the Covenant on Economic, Social and Cultural Rights deriving from it, rights to food, housing, education, health care, and other forms of social welfare are recognized as claims on one's own society, and as obligations on the political authorities of that society. Again, although these instruments expressly impose obligations on states only in respect of their own inhabitants, there are some obligations that cross state lines. As in the case of civil and political rights, a state may not act purposefully to deprive persons in another state of their economic and social rights, say by cutting off their food supply. A state may not assist or encourage the government of another state to deny such rights to its inhabitants. A state need not, probably may not, intervene forcibly in another state to meet the economic-social rights of the people of that state or to compel their government to do so. As is not the case with civil-political rights, however, another state can help give effect to some economic-social rights—the right to food, education, health care and an adequate standard of living—without forcible intervention, merely by financial aid to the local government. Is there an obligation to give such aid?

---

*Behind that distinction may also be moral assumptions, not yet wholly abandoned. In the past, at least, it was assumed that a person is not morally obligated to come to the aid of another, even if he or she can do so without undue risk or cost; surely, then, a state is not obligated to come to the aid of persons in another state. See Introduction.

Economic and social rights, like political and civil rights, also seek their justification in political and moral principles (see Introduction). Accepting the idea of economic and social rights implies the common acceptance that in the twentieth century (if not in the eighteenth) governments are responsible not only for protecting a person against neighbors (or against external aggression) but are obligated to help all members of the society meet their basic human needs. And society, through its political institutions, may—must—obtain resources for that purpose if necessary by taxing those who have, as it does for internal police or for defense against external threat.

This view of the purposes of government also reflects moral assumptions. If such programs of social welfare were deemed only a benefit voluntarily conferred by society as an act of charity, taking my property (by taxation) for the benefit of others would presumably be justified on the ground that I have consented, that I have agreed to be charitable. But if the beneficiary has economic and social rights "as of right," such entitlement, and the responsibility of society to respond to it and to do so by taxing others, are presumably justified on the basis of some moral obligation upon other members of society to provide for those needs.

It has been suggested that such moral obligations might be supported on the ground that they are in fact implied in the contemporary social compact; that community implies moral obligations as well as rights; that in an integrated interdependent economy those who benefit are obligated to those who suffer; that at least when we can save life without undue cost or risk, there is a moral obligation to be a Good Samaritan. In different degrees some of these moral justifications for economic and social rights within a society suggest also obligation across state boundaries. It is not only a national economy but the world economy that is interdependent, and, as the Third World has insisted in its campaign for a New International Economic Order, the prosperity of some in fact derives from and feeds on the misery of others; wealthy states are therefore morally obligated and should be legally obligated to help the poorer states. Community and communality as a source of obligation are also matters of perspective and are not necessarily coterminous with state boundaries.

In particular, the indeterminate obligation of human beings to help those in danger or need is not obviously limited by state boundaries. Applying our contemporary moral intuitions to a hypothetical state of nature, one might say that before, or in the absence of, societies and states, the obligation of persons to each other knew no boundaries, although consanguinity, ethnicity, or proximity might suggest a basis for preference and priority where resources were insufficient for all. Today, if all societies merged, if all states joined in world government, presumably all persons would have their underlying moral obligations vis-à-vis all others. The preexisting, underlying human rights and obligations of persons should not change because they become identified and separated by the organization of a state and the creation of other states.*

---

*The suggested moral obligations to feed the hungry might be extended to all basic needs —to clothing and housing, perhaps even basic education and health care. It is a different

But if, in moral principle, economic interdependence, communality, and interpersonal obligations are not eliminated by the emergence of states and state boundaries, they are inevitably modified by them. Identification with one's own society brings lack of identification with, even estrangement from, others, and political forms and institutions harden both the identification and the estrangement, strengthening the sense of moral obligation to one's own, weakening any sense of obligation to "foreigners." Moreover, since there is no single world society to assume the indeterminate obligation to feed the needy wherever they may be, every society can disclaim its particular obligation. Morally as well as politically, the responsibility for feeding the hungry is primarily that of the home state, which alone has the authority to tax and spend and regulate to that end. The indeterminate obligation of states other than the home state to feed the hungry is not readily accepted, not easily allocated, in a world of states.

What is lacking, in particular, is the justification in social contract. By hypothesis, persons forming a society accept political-legal obligations to each other, not to persons in other societies. One might argue that individuals forming societies and establishing political institutions might also address their relations with other societies and with their members, that rational people behind John Rawls' veil of ignorance as to their particular endowments, prospects and fates, might well recognize and accept obligations of mutual support in case of need in relation to all persons in all societies. But there is missing the concomitant, indeed underlying agreement, to create and accept political institutions to carry out any such undertakings.

The lack of agreement to create larger political entities and universal institutions—the fractionalization that is implicit in multiple states and state boundaries—suggests a different kind of obstacle to the recognition of an obligation to provide basic needs in other states. The insistence of states and their peoples on their sovereignty, on their political independence and on their right to be let alone and to do their things in their own way, is itself a valued good and it tends to belie the interdependence they might claim as the basis for obligating others to assist them in meeting their basic needs. The citizen of State A who claims that citizens of State B have an obligation to help feed him, does not consider himself responsible for other kinds of problems in B, does not share in political responsibility to pay taxes for the solution of B's problems, say for defending B against an aggressive State C. State B cannot even assure that State A will do all it can to meet the needs for which it claims B's help—say, by raising taxes, cutting other expenses, working harder, improving efficiency, eliminating waste, or controlling its population growth. And so, even if one accepted moral obligation regardless of state boundaries, political boundaries and their implications interfere in fact and may modify those obligations even in principle. Short of world government, which would eliminate state boundaries, the recognition and effective implementation of moral obligations across state lines would seem to

---

argument to claim a moral right to "distributive justice," to economic equalization or at least to a narrower gap between rich and poor.

require some accommodation and agreement between the two states in question to reduce the relevance of state boundaries at least ad hoc. But it may make all the difference, in principle and in result, if one begins by recognizing moral obligations regardless of state boundaries and then attends to the political accommodations, rather than denying all obligation and relegating all such foreign assistance to the realm of charity or to considerations of national interest for the donor state.

PERSONS BETWEEN STATES: THE RIGHTS OF REFUGEES

The claims upon one's society that have been recognized as human rights include some that address the basic relationship between individual and society. A society cannot terminate the individual's rights by terminating the relationship, that is, by exiling or expelling a citizen, or refusing to let him return from abroad. On the other hand, "Everyone has the right to leave any country, including his own,"[5] and may do so permanently, for any reason or no reason, and that state has a corresponding obligation to permit his departure.

The individual, then, has the right to terminate his "social contract" by leaving his society. He can enter into a new social contract with any other willing society. But although a right to a nationality, to a "social contract," may be a fundamental human right (Article 15[1]), in a world of states the individual has no right to the nationality of his choice, or to live in a country of his choice; he has no right to join another society unless it is willing to have him. Even the refugee from persecution has only "the right to *seek* and to enjoy" asylum in another country (Article 14[1]), but there is no obligation on any other state to grant him asylum; there is no recognized right for anyone, refugee or other emigrant, to immigrate permanently to another country and to acquire a new nationality making him party to the local social contract.

The right to leave one's country, then, even for one who must leave it because of persecution, is only half a right, or less. Having exercised it definitively, the individual may even jeopardize the right to return and lose other human rights. A state may not reach out to exercise jurisdiction over him in ways that violate his civil-political rights, but he has no claim on any other society to admit him, and no claim on any other society for anything else—even food and shelter— unless he is admitted or otherwise finds his way into its jurisdiction. The refugee falls in the interstices of state boundaries.

In a world of states, then, international human rights give preference to the "right" of the state (and its inhabitants) to exclude new residents over any claim of an "outsider" to join them. Therefore, a state may protect its borders against uninvited immigrants, even against refugees from oppression (though the latter may not be thrown back to their oppressors).[6] But, surely, the fact that a state need not admit would-be immigrants does not justify it in interfering with the person's established right to leave his country, or in violating his other rights. Thus, the United States is entitled to close its borders and its ports to would-be immigrants from Mexico, or El Salvador, or Haiti. But was the United States justified in entering into an agreement with Haiti under which the United States would board United States or Haitian vessels on the high seas and interrogate the passengers, arguably in violation of their rights of privacy? In providing the passengers with at most a perfunctory opportunity to assert a claim that they are refugees? In not merely refusing to allow passengers to come to the United States, but compelling them to return to Haiti? To compel a person to return to his previous home state, even if he is not a refugee from oppression, is to become an accomplice in denying the human right "to leave any country, including his own."[7] Similarly, the "right" of a state to refuse admission to someone who has left his country does not justify the state in keeping a person who has succeeded in entering its territory in indefinite detention, even if no other state will accept him.[8]

The age of rights is also the age of refugees. Many millions of people have been displaced since the Second World War, and at every time since then many millions continue to be in refugee status, not permanently resettled in some other state. States that have recognized the human rights of their own inhabitants have not been willing to recognize a right of persons not in their territory to be admitted and settled there, even if their lives depend on it. And the human rights idea, limited to persons subject to some state's jurisdiction and permanently entitled to be there by the state's law, has found no way to provide human rights for the many millions of human beings who become refugees.

In a world of states it has been impossible to persuade states to recognize a refugee's right to be admitted, or even a shared moral obligation to provide the refugee a new home and a new social contract. If there is a moral obligation to feed the starving in another country there is no less obligation, surely, to feed the starving who are without a country. Perhaps the same moral obligation extends to providing a home, at least to those who do not have one involuntarily, through no fault of their own, as for victims of persecution, war or natural disaster. Again, the obligation to do so being indeterminate, falling on no particular society, it can perhaps be attributed to those in a position or in the best position to do so.

In respect of refugees—as in respect of feeding the starving around the world —the human rights idea is underdeveloped, and its development is frustrated by political boundaries and their political-legal implications. But if our moral intuitions were sufficiently sensitive to accept a moral obligation to resettle the refugee (or feed the hungry in other countries), the allocation of responsibility for meeting that obligation should not be beyond us. Unlike feeding the needy at their home, which requires cooperation between the home state and others to carry out a common obligation, the home state (often the state morally responsible for the creation of refugees) is not involved in the solution (unless one can get it to change its ways). For the rest, in general, the obligation would best be treated as indeterminate, the responsibility of the "community of nations" as a whole. Whether through existing institutions or by ad hoc arrangements, the obligation to resettle refugees, and to care for them pending resettlement, has to be accepted as the common responsibility to be met by common action. Principles or guidelines for allocation might be developed. What requires funds can be allocated on "progressive-tax" principles. Allocation of people for resettlement can be based on population needs, space availability, capabilities for economic absorption. And those who have no population needs or capacity to absorb can be required to contribute funds to support resettlement elsewhere.

The human rights of refugees and the human rights of the needy come together in respect of so-called economic refugees, those who seek to settle elsewhere to escape a sorry economic condition. Here the communal obligation can perhaps be allocated, and satisfied, by more complicated formulae involving contribution in various forms: some states can accept some poor of other countries for resettlement, or provide financial assistance for their resettlement in third countries; some can bring some poor as temporary workers; some can provide financial assistance to the home state to develop economic opportunities at home so as to discourage emigration. But it matters whether the world of states sees the plight of poverty everywhere as the responsibility of all, and can overcome the fractionalization implicit in state sovereignty to organize themselves to help discharge that responsibility equitably. Most societies, however, have not yet accepted the moral responsibility of all their inhabitants for the needy of their own society and have not organized themselves effectively to discharge such a responsibility; embedded habits of thought reflecting notions of separate state sovereignty make it substantially more difficult to persuade governments and citizens that there is communal responsibility for the poor of all states and to organize themselves internationally for that charge.

The world of states has internationalized human rights, recognizing human rights and international concern for their fulfillment. But it remains a world of states, with international concern stopping short of accepting international responsibility. Contemporary moral intuitions are still underdeveloped and political will to create even primitive political institutions is less developed still.

It would not be impossible to prepare a blueprint for a moral, humane system, reflecting international responsibility for economic-social rights; it would not be impossible to prepare an analogous plan reflecting international responsibility for refugees. Except in unusual circumstances, where some particular state bears special responsibility for some situation of hunger in (or a flow of refugees from) another state, one might develop principles and guidelines of general applicability. One might suggest special responsibility for particular states—regional members, special trading partners, other allies. For the rest, other formulae for allocation, on principles akin to progressive taxation, are not beyond international capacity or imagination—if the moral obligation were accepted and backed by international political will.

4

Human Rights and "Domestic Jurisdiction"

C HARGES that various parties to the Helsinki Final Act have not been complying with its human rights provisions have, of course, evoked denials as well as countercharges against other participants. Some accused governments have also insisted, however, that, regardless of Helsinki, how they treat their own inhabitants is a matter within their domestic jurisdiction, and that scrutiny and censure by other governments constitute intervention and are unlawful.

"Domestic jurisdiction" and its counterpart "nonintervention" have confused and bedeviled international human rights activities since their inception. Volumes of official debate and scholarly comment have been devoted to these terms, particularly as regards the human rights activities of the United Nations,[1] in the light of Article 2(7) of the U.N. Charter.* Before and since Helsinki, even statements by high government officials have reflected fundamental misunderstanding of the concepts, their import, and their limitations.

Much of the confusion about these terms derives from the tendency in international diplomatic life to confound legal concepts with political rhetoric, particularly as regards concepts that speak to the essential tension between national

From *Human Rights, International Law, and the Helsinki Accord*, T. Buergenthal ed., American Society of International Law, 1977.

* "Nothing contained in the present Charter shall authorize the United Nations to intervene in matters which are essentially within the domestic jurisdiction of any state or shall require the Members to submit such matters to settlement under the present Charter; but this principle shall not prejudice the application of enforcement measures under Chapter VII."

autonomy and international accountability. Confusion results, too, from the fact that, while domestic jurisdiction and nonintervention are legal terms used in legal documents, there is hardly agreement on the boundaries between domestic and international jurisdiction, or on what constitutes intervention or other impermissible interference.

For all their heavy freight of rhetoric and their penumbra of uncertainty, as legal terms both domestic jurisdiction and nonintervention have hard cores of agreed meaning. Domestic jurisdiction is that which is not a proper subject of foreign or international concern,[2] what is not, in plain words, anyone else's business.* That which is governed by international law or agreement is ipso facto and by definition not a matter of domestic jurisdiction.[3] Short of direct legal obligation, moreover, many domestic matters are only defeasibly domestic, and may become legitimate subjects of international attention because a state had submitted to international or foreign jurisdiction by some general undertaking, for example, the UN Charter establishing the jurisdiction of United Nations organs.

"Intervention" is an effort to bring influence to bear on other governments by particular means. Although there are occasional references to "unlawful intervention" and some circumstances where intervention is said to be justified, strictly intervention is better defined as unlawful interference; and what by definition constitutes intervention is ipso facto unlawful. Treaties and declarations, and the Final Act at Helsinki itself, forbid intervention (not merely unlawful intervention).

International law forbids intervention in matters that are within the domestic jurisdiction of another state. If a matter is not within the domestic jurisdiction of another state, external or international concern with it cannot be intervention. Beyond dispute or doubt, it is not intervention or other improper interference for one state to respond to violations by another of her obligations under international law or agreement, though some forms of external or international reaction may be barred by other legal doctrine, e.g., the unilateral use of force under Article 2(4) of the UN Charter. It is not intervention for an international body to consider a matter † within its granted jurisdiction.[4]

Strictly, moreover, intervention means dictatorial interference by force or threat of force. Lesser forms of interference may be bad (diplomatic) manners, and some may roil friendly relations, but generally do not violate any principle

* Political as well as legal writing have often treated domestic jurisdiction and international concern as mutually exclusive. Domestic jurisdiction has become a legal concept (as in Article 2(7) of the UN Charter), but international concern is less clearly so except when used as meaning strictly "not a matter of domestic jurisdiction." The phrase is here used in that sense, but for convenience it is sometimes used colloquially also, without having legal significance attributed to it.

† In general, United Nations practice reflects the view that international discussion, perhaps even declarations, recommendations, and judgments of the General Assembly, are not interventions by the United Nations forbidden by Article 2(7). In practice, too, United Nations bodies have asserted authority to determine whether a UN action would be intervention contrary to that article.

of international law. It is not intervention, or other interference forbidden by law, for a government to express views about, or even to criticize publicly, the actions of other governments that are distasteful to it, for example, the political ideology guiding another government or its economic and social system. Surely, in the absence of agreement to the contrary, it is not intervention or other improper interference for one state to shape its own policies (say, on trade), or the warmth of its relations, on the basis of taste or distaste for actions of another government, even as regards matters that are strictly that government's own affair and even if done to influence that government's behavior in these matters.

As blanket objections to international concern with human rights, the claims of domestic jurisdiction and nonintervention have been long dead.[5] Surely, there are some circumstances in which the condition of human rights is a legitimate concern of and a basis for appropriate action by other states or international organizations. Surely, there are some responses that international organizations or individual states can make to infringements of human rights that are not interventions or other unlawful interferences in the affairs of the violating state. If human rights were always a matter of domestic jurisdiction and never a proper subject of external attention in any form, provisions of the UN Charter, the Universal Declaration of Human Rights, the various international covenants and conventions, and countless activities, resolutions, and actions of the United Nations and other international bodies would be *ultra vires;* every government would be guilty of meddling and some also of intervention; and numerous nongovernmental organizations and millions of individuals would have labored egregiously and in vain for decades. Helsinki itself assumed that human rights are a proper subject of international attention. Human rights were on the international agenda for consideration at the highest levels of government; human rights undertakings were exchanged among many governments for undertakings about international security and trade, and the Final Act includes respect for human rights as one of the Principles Guiding Relations between Participating States. Any suggestions that the human rights "Basket" of Helsinki is not of legitimate concern to other parties would vitiate all the other understandings and undertakings that depended on it and would nullify the entire accord.

The domestic jurisdiction objection to external attention to human rights is worthy of any legal (or political) notice only if asserted narrowly and precisely. One might consider the following arguments.

1. How a state treats its own nationals is not a matter of international concern unless the state has assumed international legal obligations governing such treatment. There is no customary international law of human rights and no international agreement to which all states are party. While almost all states have adhered to the UN Charter, they did not thereby assume any binding normative obligation to respect the human rights of their own citizens. The Universal Declaration of Human Rights, too, did not create any legal obligation for any state. The Final Act at Helsinki, not being legally binding, created no human rights obligations for the participants.

2. While states party to an international agreement (e.g., the International

Covenant on Civil and Political Rights or the Convention on the Elimination of All Forms of Racial Discrimination) undertake to comply with its provisions, they do not thereby submit to any scrutiny or censure nor to any procedures, remedies, or claims for violations other than those expressly provided for in the agreement. In particular, unless agreed otherwise, such agreements do not create legal obligations by one party toward another and do not give one party any legal interest in compliance by other parties or any right to enforce the agreement and invoke legal remedies against other parties.

3. The Helsinki Accord cannot be the basis for any response or remedy by another state because its provisions do not constitute legal obligations. In any event, the Final Act does not authorize claims, complaints, criticisms, or any other recourse by one participating state against another for alleged violations of human rights generally or of any particular provision in the Final Act. The part of the Final Act titled "Follow Up to the Conference" provides only for negotiation and exchange of views and for further meetings. And the Final Act declares that "the participating States will refrain from any intervention, direct or indirect, individual or collective, in the internal or external affairs falling within the domestic jurisdiction of another participating State, regardless of their mutual relations."

4. Except as otherwise expressly provided in some international agreement, a criticism or protest by one state that another is violating human rights, even that it is violating international obligations to respect human rights, constitutes intervention or is otherwise impermissible. It is impermissible for one government to deal directly with, support or encourage nationals of another state in their attempt to seek redress, even if they allege that they are victims of human rights violations. It is impermissible for one state to attempt to coerce another to modify its domestic policies on human rights, e.g., by manipulating trade arrangements or offers of aid or by criticism and unfriendly statements.

These arguments are generally misconceived and ill-founded. My thesis may be briefly stated:

1. Virtually all states are now subject to some international law and obligation as regards at least some human rights of their inhabitants. To that extent their actions in regard to such human rights are, of course, not within their domestic jurisdiction; and external scrutiny and efforts to bring about compliance with the human rights obligations are not intervention or other improper interference in domestic affairs.

2. Unless the agreement provides otherwise, any party to an international agreement on human rights has, against another party who has violated the agreement, the remedies and recourses available generally for breach of an international agreement. Unless the agreement provides otherwise, any special machinery provided for implementing its human rights obligations does not replace but merely supplements the usual remedies for breach of international aggreement.

3. That the Helsinki Accord is not legally binding means that there are no legal remedies for its violation; adherence to the Accord is nonetheless an international undertaking and violation of its provisions is a proper basis for interna-

tional (nonlegal) recourse and remedy by other participants. Insistence by other adherents that the accords be honored and the peaceful means that they might use to induce compliance with these international undertakings are not interventions or other impermissible interferences in domestic affairs, but rather the proper and normal means and methods of the international system.

4. Intervention forbidden by international law signifies dictatorial interference. A state's expression of criticism or distaste or its policies modifying relations of trade, aid, or other intercourse with governments because they violate human rights are not interventions but legitimate acts of self-interest that are a state's own affair and within its own domestic jurisdiction.

INTERNATIONAL HUMAN RIGHTS OBLIGATIONS

There are now numerous international agreements dealing in whole or in part with human rights. Matters covered by these human rights undertakings are, of course, not within the domestic jurisdiction of the states party to them.

The Human Rights Obligations of United Nations Members

Almost all states are parties to the UN Charter and bound by its human rights provisions. By adhering to the UN Charter, states expressly "pledge themselves to take joint and separate action in cooperation with" the United Nations organization to promote "universal respect for, and observance of, human rights and fundamental freedoms for all without distinction as to race, sex, language, or religion" (Articles 55, 56).

That states "pledge themselves" imports legal obligation; but there has not been agreement among governments, or among commentators, as to the import and content of that obligation. While some governments and commentators have considered it only a general requirement of cooperation that has no normative content, others have urged that important infringements of generally-agreed human rights are violations of Articles 55 and 56. Some have argued that, while the undertakings in the UN Charter were inchoate and general, they were realized and particularized in the Universal Declaration of Human Rights, so that all parties to the UN Charter are legally obligated to abide by the provisions in the Universal Declaration. Yet another view has it that the UN Charter, the Universal Declaration, the various international conventions, resolutions of United Nations organs and other multilateral bodies, and the practices of states have combined to create customary, or a blend of customary and conventional, legal obligations upon all states to respect at least some human rights norms.

There has been no resolution of these diverse views and no authoritative definition of the human rights obligations of states under the UN Charter and under legal developments since the UN Charter. United Nations practice since 1945, including numerous resolutions, one or more of which was supported by almost every state, clearly reflects a prevailing view that the UN Charter has at least some normative import and content.[6] Repeated resolutions have declared that apartheid in South Africa is contrary to the UN Charter.[7] In its advisory opinion on Namibia, the International Court of Justice declared the extension and continuation of apartheid in Namibia to be "a flagrant violation of the purposes and principles of the Charter."[8] In 1967, by an overwhelming vote, the Economic and Social Council (ECOSOC) extended the interpretation of the UN Charter to reach beyond racial discrimination, authorizing the Commission on Human Rights to study "situations which reveal a consistent pattern of violations of human rights, as exemplified by the policy of apartheid. . . ."[9] In 1970 ECOSOC approved a procedure for considering private communications "which appear to reveal a consistent pattern of gross and reliably attested violations of human rights and fundamental freedoms. . . ."[10] Even states (e.g., the USSR) that had opposed this procedure and the interpretation of the UN Charter it implied later joined in action by the Commission on Human Rights, approved by the General Assembly, to investigate alleged violations of human rights in Chile.[11] In its opinion in the *Barcelona Traction Case,* the International Court of Justice said that there are universal obligations deriving "for example, in contemporary international law, from the outlawing of acts of aggression, and of genocide, as also from the principles and rules concerning the basic rights of the human person, including protection from slavery and racial discrimination."[12] In the commentary to its draft articles of state responsibility, the International Law Commission concluded that "international law now in force" includes obligations of "essential importance for safe-guarding the human being, such as those prohibiting slavery, genocide and apartheid."[13]

It is difficult to avoid the conclusion that some violations of human rights (e.g., apartheid and other forms of racial discrimination, genocide, slavery, or torture), in addition to being violations of particular conventions if committed by parties to such conventions, are violations of the UN Charter for any United Nations member, if not of customary international law binding on all states. The generality of states have supported the view that "a consistent pattern of gross violations of human rights" is now a violation of international law and obligation if practiced by any party to the UN Charter and even, perhaps, by nonmembers.[14]

Such violations surely are not a matter of domestic jurisdiction. Whether an alleged infringement is such a violation is a question of international law, not one for an accused state to determine finally.

Parties to Particular Conventions

Some parties to the Helsinki Final Act have adhered also to particular international agreements on human rights, e.g., the Convention on the Prevention and Punishment of the Crime of Genocide, the International Convention on the Elimination of All Forms of Racial Discrimination, the International Covenant on Civil and Political Rights and its Protocol, and the International Covenant on Economic, Social and Cultural Rights. No state party can invoke domestic jurisdiction as regards matters covered by any convention.

Human Rights Undertakings at Helsinki

At the Conference on Security and Cooperation in Europe the participating states agreed to discuss human rights together with other matters relating to security and cooperation. In the Final Act, the participants declared it to be among the principles guiding relations between them that they would respect human rights and fundamental freedoms and promote and encourage their effective exercise. In addition:

> In the field of human rights and fundamental freedoms, the participating States will act in conformity with the purposes and principles of the Charter of the United Nations and with the Universal Declaration of Human Rights. They will also fulfill their obligations as set forth in the international declarations and agreements in this field, including inter alia the International Covenants on Human Rights, by which they may be bound. (1(a)VII)

They also agreed to fulfill in good faith obligations under international law generally (1(a)X). Later in the act (Basket III) the participating states "make it their aim," "declare their readiness," and "express their intention" to implement cooperation in humanitarian and other fields, including human contacts, information, and cooperation and exchange in culture and in education. These human rights provisions were the condition and the price of other provisions of great political importance desired by other participants. Western participants saw them as the condition of and an integral aspect of détente at which the whole Final Act aimed.

While Helsinki was not intended to be a legally binding agreement, and does not add legally binding human rights obligations, it clearly precludes any suggestion that matters it deals with are within domestic jurisdiction and beyond the reach of appropriate inquiry and recourse. Gentlemen's agreements and other nonbinding political and moral undertakings are established instruments in international relations, and their violation brings important political and moral consequences. Speaking of nonbinding international agreements, Professor Oscar Schachter said recently:

> The fact that the states have entered into mutual engagements confers an entitlement on each party to make representations to the other on the execution of those engagements. It becomes immaterial whether the conduct in question was previously regarded as entirely discretionary or within the reserved domain of domestic jurisdiction. By entering into an international pact with other

states, a party may be presumed to have agreed that the matters covered are no longer exclusively within its concerns.[15]

RESPONSE TO VIOLATION OF HUMAN RIGHTS OBLIGATIONS

Breach of a human rights obligation, like violation of any international legal obligation, is an international wrongful act for which the international legal system provides remedies. It has been suggested, however, that the only remedies for the violation of a human rights agreement are those specified in the agreement. In particular, unless expressly so provided, one party does not have a remedy against another for failure to live up to the agreement. That view is ill-founded.

The duty to carry out international obligations is the heart of the international legal system; and that prime duty implies an ancillary duty to cease and desist from violation and to give other satisfaction to the state or states to which the obligation was due. The injured state may seek reparation and ask that the violator take measures to prevent repetition, offer an apology, punish the persons who committed the violation, pay a symbolic sum of money, or afford other relief.[16]

Except for the few universal obligations, enforceable perhaps by any state (in a kind of *actio popularis*),[17] a breach of an international obligation is a wrong to the particular state or states to which that obligation is due, and only such state or states may enforce that obligation and seek a remedy for its violation. An international agreement creates obligations between parties and gives each party a legal interest in having it carried out; it may be enforced by one party against another even if it is an agreement for the benefit of a third entity not party to the agreement. Of course, parties may modify these general principles in particular cases. Thus, expressly or by clear implication from the nature of the agreement or from some of its provisions, a multilateral agreement may contemplate enforcement of the agreement only by a party directly aggrieved, not by all parties. (Some multilateral treaties are essentially a series of bilateral arrangements, so that a violation affecting only a particular other party is to be enforced only by that party.) A multilateral agreement will frequently establish special remedies for violation, and may expressly or by implication provide that these shall replace (rather than supplement) traditional interstate remedies.

The argument that human rights agreements are not directly enforceable between the parties is not based on any notion that the subject matter is in the domestic jurisdiction of the parties. It does not deny that human rights agreements create legal obligations or that the law provides remedies for violation of these obligations as for others. The argument seems to be based, rather, on the view that, as a matter of interpretation, human rights agreements in general contemplate no remedies between parties, but only whatever remedies are expressly provided. It is assumed that states are willing to enter into agreements about human rights but are unwilling to have them enforced among the parties; the quest for special enforcement machinery, it is said, also reflects the intention that ordinary interstate remedies be excluded.

These arguments are not persuasive. International human rights agreements are like other international agreements, creating legal obligations between the parties and international responsibility for their violation. They are essentially mutual undertakings among states for the benefit of third parties (the inhabitants of the countries party to the agreement) and in principle are enforceable by the promisees, that is, the other parties to the agreement. Prima facie, surely, and in the absence of any expressed or clearly implied intention to supersede them, the usual remedies for breach of an international obligation are available here.

Because violation by a state of the rights of its own inhabitants does not directly injure other states party to the agreement, it was recognized that other parties may be reluctant to seem officious and incur the political onus of calling a violator to account. It was thought, too, that such protection by another party might often not be an effective remedy for violations. Hence, the continuing efforts to develop special machinery to implement human rights obligations. But there is nothing in the character of human rights obligations, or in the principal human rights agreements, that suggests that such machinery is exclusive and is intended to replace the ordinary remedies available to any party to an agreement for breach by another party. The draftsmen of multilateral agreements recognized that other parties may be reluctant to enforce the agreement, but there is no evidence that they intended to deny parties the legal right to do so and to eliminate the ordinary legal consequences of international undertakings and the ordinary remedies for their violation.

The effort to create an international law of human rights has been largely a struggle to develop effective machinery to implement agreed norms. Arduous effort has not brought forth machinery of notable effectiveness. It would be ironic if the meager successes in establishing such machinery should become the basis for interpreting the agreements as excluding other traditional means of enforcement where they are most needed, and for denying them to states willing to use them. That the true beneficiaries of these agreements, the individuals inhabiting the territories of the parties, are usually not afforded an effective remedy (or any remedy at all) argues rather against finding that the other parties, the promisees, have no remedy either.

No human rights agreements, even those that establish elaborate enforcement machinery, expressly or by clear implication exclude the ordinary interstate remedies. In fact, the principal human rights agreements clearly imply the contrary: that every party to the agreement has a legal interest in having it observed by other parties and can invoke ordinary legal remedies to enforce it.[18] The first postwar, universal human rights agreement, the Genocide Convention, provides:

> Disputes between the Contracting Parties relating to the interpretation, appli-
> cation or fulfilment of the present Convention, including those relating to the
> responsibility of a State for genocide or for any of the other acts enumerated in

Article III, shall be submitted to the International Court of Justice at the request of any of the parties to the dispute. (Article IX)

Providing jurisdiction for the International Court of Justice clearly recognizes that every party retains legal interest in having other parties live up to their obligations under the Genocide Convention and might wish to resort to the usual legal remedies to vindicate that interest.

In later human rights agreements, special concern for human rights and the desire to provide additional incentives for states to comply with human rights obligations led to the establishment of special enforcement machinery; for example, the special committees to see to the implementation of the International Convention on the Elimination of All Forms of Racial Discrimination and the International Covenant on Civil and Political Rights, or the more elaborate enforcement system under the European Convention on Human Rights. Such special enforcement arrangements, however, were clearly intended to supplement not to supplant general remedies available to one party against violation by another. The International Covenant on Civil and Political Rights, for example, makes this plain:

The provisions for the implementation of the present Covenant . . . shall not prevent the States Parties to the present Covenant from having recourse to other procedures for settling a dispute in accordance with general or special international agreements in force between them. (Article 44)[19]

Again, the preservation of other procedures for settling disputes can only imply that the parties had legal interests in the enforcement of the agreement, interests which they might seek to vindicate by such alternative procedures.[20]

In other agreements, too, the normal rights and remedies of parties to human rights agreements are implied. Having established elaborate enforcement machinery, the European Convention provided:

The High Contracting Parties agree that, except by special agreement, they will not avail themselves of treaties, conventions or declarations in force between them for the purpose of submitting, by way of petition, a dispute arising out of the interpretation or application of this Convention to a means of settlement other than those provided for in this Convention. (Article 62)

There is no suggestion here, I note, that the human rights of all individuals everywhere can be protected by all states. Human rights agreements generally do not create universal legal interests for all states: they create legal interests for the parties to the agreement by virtue of the legal obligations assumed by them *inter sese*.[21] A different rule would apply to principles of customary law of human rights, which are *erga omnes,* and which can be invoked by any state against any other state. The remedies to be invoked are not by way of some extraordinary *actio popularis;* they are the ordinary remedies available to parties to an agreement against violation by another party. The distinction is fundamental and clear. In the *South West Africa Cases,* for example, the majority denied the standing of Ethiopia and Liberia to enforce the human rights provisions of the mandate because they "were not parties to them. . . . Not being parties to the instruments of mandate, they could draw from them only such rights as are unequivocally conferred."[22] The implication is that, even for the majority of the Court, had the petitioners been parties to the mandate agreement they would have had a legal interest to enforce it and could have availed themselves of the usual remedies for vindicating that interest.

The suggestion that human rights agreements are generally not enforceable by the parties apparently reflects a fear that parties may resort to reprisal and other forcible remedies. But, in general, the unilateral use of force in response to human rights violations is forbidden by the UN Charter. The danger that diplomatic protection, hitherto available only to a state's nationals against foreign governments, would now be provided by all governments party to a convention to all the inhabitants of any other party state, is also greatly exaggerated. States will not lightly risk their relations with another on behalf of the human rights of the latter's inhabitants. No doubt such responses would be used with prudence and infrequently, at most when there is "a serious breach on a widespread scale" of important provisions or a "consistent pattern of gross violations."[23] But as a matter of law, such protection is available, the consequence of a breach of international human rights obligations.[24]

Responses by Participants at Helsinki

Most of the participants at Helsinki are parties to the UN Charter and bound by its human rights provisions. Some of the participants are also parties to particular conventions, e.g., on genocide, racial discrimination, civil and political rights. These participants are entitled to monitor and take legal recourse against violations of those agreements by other participants party to them.

At Helsinki the participants made compliance with their undertakings to respect human rights and to carry out human rights undertakings in legally binding international agreements the proper concern of all other Helsinki parties. Respect for human rights was one of the principles as to which the participants:

Declare their determination to respect and put into practice each of them in its relations with all other participating States, irrespective of their political, economic or social systems as well as of their size, geographical location or level of economic development, the following principles, which all are of primary significance, guiding their mutual relations. . . . The participating States recognize the universal significance of human rights and fundamental freedoms, respect for which is an essential factor for the peace, justice and well-being necessary to ensure the development of friendly relations and cooperation among themselves as among all States.

The participants also declared their resolve, in the period following the conference, to pay due regard to and implement the provisions of the Final Act, unilaterally, bilaterally, and multilaterally; and to continue the multilateral process by a thorough exchange of views on implementation of the Final Act and by multilateral meetings to that end, the first of which was held in Belgrade in 1977, with others in Madrid (1979) and in Vienna (1986).

Respect *vel non* for human rights, then, is a proper subject for discussion "bilaterally, by negotiation with other participating states"; for discussion "multilaterally, by meetings of experts of the participating states, and also within the framework of existing international organizations . . ."; and for a "thorough exchange of views on [their] implementation" at meetings such as the review meetings that have been held. Surely, there is no obstacle, indeed there would seem to be an affirmative political and moral commitment, for all participants to monitor the behavior of all other participants on human rights matters covered by the Final Act and to engage in bilateral and multilateral discussions about the implementation of the political and moral undertakings in the Final Act and of any antecedent legal undertakings that the Final Act incorporates by reference. What is provided as follow-up would seem to include the ordinary remedies available to one party for breach of political and moral undertakings by another; surely, there is nothing in the Final Act (or in international law) that precludes such peaceful bilateral responses.

NONINTERVENTION

The confusions and uncertainties of nonintervention are also largely irrelevant here. Whether in its traditional unwritten conception, in the principles of the United Nations Declaration on Friendly Relations, or in the principles adopted at Helsinki (which derive from the Declaration on Friendly Relations), the obligation not to intervene applies only to matters within a state's domestic jurisdiction. By virtue of the UN Charter and its aftermath, of particular conventions, or of Helsinki itself, human rights are not a matter of domestic jurisdiction and concern with them cannot be intervention or other impermissible interference.[25]

Surely it is not intervention, or any other improper interference, for a state party to an international agreement to have legal recourse or to react in other accepted lawful ways to violations of the agreement by others. Any member of the United Nations, therefore, may properly respond to violations of Charter norms, at least to a "consistent pattern of gross violations" of human rights.[26] Any party to a particular convention, in addition to invoking special remedies provided by the agreement, may have legal recourse or respond in other accepted lawful ways to any violation of any provision in the agreement. Any participant at Helsinki may monitor the behavior of all other participants in regard to any undertaking in the Final Act and may have appropriate political recourse in response to violations of those political commitments. In addition, Helsinki provides for other bilateral and multilateral follow-up.

None of these responses and remedies is in any way precluded by the guiding principle on Non-Intervention in Internal Affairs included in the Final Act:

> The participating States will refrain from any intervention, direct or indirect, individual or collective, in the internal or external affairs falling within the domestic jurisdiction of another participating State, regardless of their mutual relations. [1(a)VI]

To the extent covered by the UN Charter, by particular conventions, or the Helsinki Accord, human rights are not "within the domestic jurisdiction of another participating State."[27] All the other clauses in that principle also apply only as regards matters within a state's domestic jurisdiction, not, therefore, to its human rights undertakings.[28] Efforts by one participant to induce compliance by another with the human rights undertakings of the Final Act cannot be an act of "coercion designed to subordinate to their own interest the exercise by another participating State of the rights inherent in its sovereignty. . . ."[I(a)VI]

The principle of nonintervention is also irrelevant to common forms of external concern with human rights for other reasons. As a legal concept, intervention signifies "dictatorial interference." It "must either be forcible or backed by threat of force."[29] Scrutiny, criticism, or even encouragement or support to victims of human rights violations is not intervention (and would not be intervention even if human rights had remained a matter of domestic jurisdiction) even if it is designed to modify the target government's behavior in regard to human rights.

Neither, it should be clear, is it intervention or other impermissible interference for one state to shape its own policies in ways that will influence the behavior of other governments on human rights. Every state is free to shape its policies to bring about corresponding change in the behavior of others. Such influence, no matter how effective, is implicit in voluntary relations between nations, and is the foundation of all agreements between them whether tacit or expressed. In the absence of international agreement to the contrary, a state's policies in regard to foreign trade or aid or other forms of international intercourse and relationship are her own affair, a matter of her own domestic jurisdiction. No state is legally required to be more friendly than it wishes to be with another state that violates human rights.

At Helsinki, the West paid in valuable political coin for political and moral undertakings in regard to human rights. In effect, the Final Act confirms that respect for human rights by all is indispensable to détente and is an integral aspect of détente, as are security, refraining from the use of force, territorial integrity, and inviolability of frontiers. Each party agreed to "respect each other's right freely to choose and develop its political, social, economic, and cultural systems as well as its rights to determine its law and regulations"; but made it clear that requesting compliance with human rights obligations was not an intrusion upon sovereignty. They agreed not to intervene in matters falling within each other's domestic jurisdiction, but made it clear that human rights were not a matter of domestic jurisdiction and that calling a state to account for violating human rights was not intervention. In fact, they agreed to build into détente mutual monitoring, negotiation, peaceful exertions of influence, pursuit of legal remedies, and requests for satisfaction in regard to each participant's observance of human rights, as much as to its respect for the interests of others in security or trade.

5

Human Rights and
United States Foreign Policy

IN the process that achieved the universalization and internationalization of
human rights, the United States has played a major part. Yet the significance
of international human rights in the policy of the United States has hardly been
understood either abroad or at home, and indeed it has been riddled with
apparent contradictions.

The United States is commonly acknowledged to be a principal ancestor of
the contemporary idea of rights. Individual rights dominate its constitutional
jurisprudence, and are the pride of its people, their banner to the world. President Franklin Roosevelt proclaimed human rights to be an aim of the Second
World War; Eleanor Roosevelt was a major force in the development of the
Universal Declaration of Human Rights. Other Americans labored for eighteen
years to help conclude the human rights covenants as well as other human rights
conventions; United States spokesmen continue to be prominent in all United
Nations bodies addressing international human rights issues. The United States
is party to the Helsinki Accord and has been most insistent on invoking its
human rights provisions. United States laws forbid arms sales and foreign aid to
nations guilty of gross violations of internationally recognized human rights.[1]
The United States Department of State has a human rights bureaucracy, sits in
judgment and publishes annual reports on the condition of human rights around
the world. President Carter made human rights a hallmark of his Administration. Congresses legislated and Presidents proclaimed human rights to be a
"central feature"—"a principal goal"—of United States foreign policy.

And yet: the United States is the only major power, and one of the very few countries generally, that has not adhered to any of the major international human rights conventions. The United States has opposed many attempts to impose international sanctions against violators of human rights. Among allies or friends of the United States are highly repressive regimes, and most recent Presidents, Secretaries of State, and United States diplomats have acted as though generally the condition of human rights in other countries is hardly the business of the United States.

What is the human rights policy of the United States and what is the place of human rights in United States foreign policy generally? I suggest that the confusion of United States policy reflects not only, or principally, different policies at different times by different administrations, but, rather, more than one policy at any time—a Congressional policy and a different executive policy; one policy in respect of international human rights in some countries and another policy for other countries; one policy abroad and another at home.

EXECUTIVE AMBIVALENCE

Presidents (and Congresses) in the nineteenth century sometimes addressed the human condition in other countries, but only spasmodically, when moved by some dramatic egregious event, and responding to strong domestic outcry. Human rights did not achieve a prominent place in United States foreign policy until the Second World War. President Roosevelt proclaimed the Four Freedoms for all mankind, and subsequent Allied statements in effect adopted them as war aims. Human rights were included in the planning for the postwar order, and, with active United States support, they appeared in the Nüremburg Charter, in the United Nations Charter, and in the Charter of the Organization of American States; the United States was in the forefront of the process that produced the Universal Declaration.

Ambivalence and tension in United States policy on human rights appeared early. Simply, one can attribute them to different influences in the foreign policy process, forces that combined to produce different "vectors" in different times and contexts. There were differences among the active, front-line participants in the process—within the executive branch, between the President (and his advisers) and the Department of State, and within the Department of State. There were differences between Executive and Congress in their attitudes toward human rights in other countries, and to international concern with human rights in the United States.

Human rights in other countries was the particular preoccupation of "liberal," "idealistic" elements which had come into the "foreign policy establishment" during the war, and remained when the war was over. Amateur, activist, less bound by diplomatic traditions and niceties, they pursued the promises of wartime rhetoric and favored United States leadership for international cooperation, including the development of international human rights standards and effective institutions and procedures for implementing them. They were prepared to have the United States press other governments to accept those standards as well as "machinery" for their enforcement, and to have the United States scrutinize and criticize the actions of governments that violated these standards. They saw no reasons why, in order to further those ends, the United States should not subject itself to the same standards and the same scrutiny.

On the other hand, leading members of the traditional foreign policy establishment, notably the career foreign service, tended to find the new international human rights movement "unsophisticated," and at best a nuisance. They were inclined to consider human rights conditions in any other country that country's business, and active concern with those conditions by the United States, or by international institutions, to be meddlesome, officious, unprofessional, disturbing of "friendly relations" and disruptive of sound diplomacy. During war, they had seen no reason to resist rhetorical declarations that served the needs of morale and psychological warfare, but they looked with growing concern when the wartime spirit and the influence of its amateur supporters continued in the postwar years. They were skeptical of international institutions generally, and resisted particularly their involvement in the internal affairs of states, such as human rights.

"Idealists" and "realists" served the United States side-by-side, but they looked in different directions and saw United States interests differently. As the glow of victory and the "spirit of the United Nations" waned, the influence of the human rights contingent receded and traditional diplomats again dominated. They concerned themselves with other important things: security, alignments, military bases, trade. But the human rights movement continued to command wide support from church and other "do-good" bodies, and from particular ethnic constituencies, and therefore some support in Congress and even in the White House. It was a continuing activity of international organizations and therefore of those who represented the United States in those bodies, principally part-time citizen-diplomats at periodic meetings, and of the newfangled bureaus of the State Department. On the United Nations sidetrack, the United States joined and often led the human rights bandwagon. "Realists" in the State Department remained skeptical but were not disposed to challenge that program as long as it remained on the plane of rhetoric and was not allowed to disturb the sensibilities of particular states or roil relations with them. Therefore, they acquiesced or were indifferent when the United States supported multilateral programs that concentrated on developing standards and even implementing machinery; the Universal Declaration (the preoccupation of Eleanor Roosevelt, not of Dean Acheson), the Genocide Convention, the international human rights covenants and other conventions followed. But, under "realist" influence, the United States was disinclined to exert pressure on reluctant friendly foreign governments, sometimes even on less-friendly Communist governments; it resisted in particular "intrusive" scrutiny, criticism, and especially economic or military sanctions against governments for human rights violations.

CONGRESSIONAL HUMAN RIGHTS POLICY

In some respects the policies pursued by the executive branch reflected concern for Congressional opinion and anticipated Congressional reactions, particularly where international human rights policy had implications for United States trade or for life in the United States. For the most part, however, Congress did not attend seriously to the condition of human rights in other countries during the first twenty-five years of the postwar era and generally acquiesced in what the executive branch did. Congress had little occasion for formal involvement in the development of United States human rights policy. One or both Houses, at the behest of individual members responding particularly to constituencies sensitive to human rights violations in particular countries—the rights of Poles, of Greek minorities, of Soviet Jews, of Blacks in South Africa—sometimes expressed their sense of outrage or concern. Individual members of Congress occasionally participated in executive activities as members of delegations to international organizations and conferences. The Senate, whose advice and consent is constitutionally required to human rights treaties as to others,[2] had few occasions to consider agreements that aimed at the condition of rights in other countries. It consented to treaties that imposed human rights standards on defeated enemy countries in World War II.[3] It consented to the UN Charter, including the provisions wherein the United States pledged to take joint and separate action in cooperation with the United Nations Organization to promote respect for human rights (Arts. 55 and 56).

An independent Congressional initiative to shape United States human rights policy developed in the early 1970s. Under influence of concerned liberal members of the House of Representatives, and responding to inadequacies in United Nations and other multilateral responses to human rights violations, Congress enacted a series of statutes declaring the promotion of respect for human rights to be a principal goal of United States foreign policy, and denying foreign aid, military assistance, and the sale of agricultural commodities to states guilty of gross violations of internationally recognized human rights.[4] In addition, United States representatives were directed to act in international financial institutions so as to prevent or discourage loans to governments guilty of such violations.[5] Congress also established a human rights bureau in the Department of State, and directed the department to report annually on the condition of human rights in every country in the world.[6]

The Congressional program, it should be clear, was directed not at deviations from democratic governance as practiced by the United States (and by its European allies) but against "consistent patterns of gross violations of internationally recognized human rights," those that nations publicly decried and that none claimed the right to do or admitted doing. Congress specified clearly the violations at which it aimed—"torture or cruel, inhuman or degrading treatment or punishment, prolonged detention without charges, causing the disappearance of persons by the abduction and clandestine detention of those persons, or other flagrant denial of the right to life, liberty or the security of person."[7] Also, it should be clear, this general legislation was not aimed at Communism and the Communist states since they received neither arms nor aid from the United States, but at the non-Communist Third World.* In addition, Congress addressed human rights in particular countries, e.g., denying various aid to Chile, Argentina, South Africa, Uganda and others, when the condition of human rights in those countries was particularly egregious.[8] Later, Congress imposed various human rights conditions on assistance to particular countries in Central America.[9] In 1986, Congress enacted the Comprehensive Anti-Apartheid Act.[10]

The Congressional program was never popular with the executive branch (regardless of political party), particularly with those who reflected the dominant, traditional attitudes in the Department of State. That program limited executive autonomy in the conduct of foreign policy. It required embassies to collect information often critical of the countries in which they "lived"; it required the Department of State to publish information often critical of countries with which the United States had friendly relations. It injected into foreign policy elements that foreign governments, and many in the State Department, thought not to be United States business. It sometimes disturbed alliances and alignments, base agreements or trade arrangements, and friendly relations generally.

Congress made some concessions to executive branch resistance. It gave the Aid Administrator authority to disregard the statutory limitation when assistance "will directly benefit the needy people in such country."[11] It authorized security assistance to a country guilty of gross violations if the President certified that "extraordinary circumstances exist warranting provision of such assistance," or if the President finds that "such a significant improvement in its human rights record has occurred as to warrant lifting the prohibition on furnishing such assistance in the national interest of the United States."[12] United States representatives to international financial institutions were to oppose loans to gross violators "except where the President determines that the cause of international human rights is served more effectively by actions other than voting against such assistance or where the assistance is directed to programs that serve the basic needs of the impoverished majority of the country in question."[13] The Anti-Apartheid Act was enacted despite resistance from the Reagan administration, but its terms took account of some executive objections.

In the main, the tension between Congress and the executive branch reflected not partisan or political differences, but the different positions and perspectives of the two branches. Congress was closer to popular sentiment in the United States, which was responsive to the human condition in other countries, and wished to do something about it or at least to dissociate the United States from repressive regimes in general or in particular countries. The executive branch,

---

*In a special gesture, hoping to encourage Communist countries to allow Jewish emigration, Congress denied most favored nation treatment to Communist countries as long as they denied the freedom of emigration. The Jackson-Vanik Amendment to the Trade Act of 1974, §402, 19 U.S.C. §2432.

more removed from constituent influence in the United States, was closer to official sentiment in other countries with which it had to deal; it was not indifferent to, but less swayed by, moral concerns, more attuned to international political and diplomatic needs and mores. But these general differences between the two branches have not been impervious to political considerations. Congress, while sensing the need to induce a reluctant executive to attend to human rights, was also content to provide an avenue of escape from these restrictions in some cases if the President were prepared to assume the onus for taking it. For its part, the executive branch, or some elements in it, were often content to criticize or implement sanctions against human rights violators if they could attribute responsibility to Congress and could maintain executive helplessness to disregard the restrictions.

HUMAN RIGHTS UNDER PRESIDENTS CARTER AND REAGAN

I have described tensions within the executive branch and differences between the two branches. There have also been differences between Presidents and between presidential administrations, reflecting some partisan or ideological differences and some personal differences. One President, Jimmy Carter, chose to join Congress instead of resisting it. He made human rights a plank in his campaign platform. In office he spoke out against gross violations, and during his administration the State Department implemented the Congressional program, often with vigor, sometimes with enthusiasm. Even his administration, however, sometimes felt impelled to "trim" its human rights pronouncements and actions in response to perceived diplomatic necessities or other competing national interests. Perhaps that gave an appearance of inconsistency, but such inconsistency, he might have said, was inevitable and had been contemplated, even prescribed, by Congress.

Partisan criticism, especially during the campaign that led to President Carter's defeat in his quest for reelection, created an impression that the "Carter human rights policy" was a mistake and a failure. In my view, the attack on his human rights program was essentially misconceived and profoundly mistaken. Nonpartisan students of the period would, I believe, conclude that the program was remarkably successful. It helped the cause of human rights, causing some governments to terminate some violations of human rights and deterring many others, saving the lives or the freedom of many thousands of human beings in many countries. Governments generally knew that the United States cared and was watching, that it might speak out in criticism, that it might reduce aid or arms sales. The Carter program also helped United States foreign policy generally. If some governments resented criticism and called it "interference," most governments accepted it. People in many parts of the world responded to it. In the ideological competition that has dominated international politics in the post–

World War II era, the human rights program proclaimed the commitment of the United States to human values, and emphasized that it cared for other people and what happened to them. The people of the United States were pleased to be dissociated from particularly egregious violators.

In his first presidential campaign, Ronald Reagan took strong issue with the "Carter human rights program." (It was not noticed widely that "the Carter program" was essentially a Congressional program, enacted and expanded by Congress with strong bipartisan support during Republican administrations.) After Reagan was elected President, there were some in his administration who apparently hoped to persuade Congress to repeal its human rights program, but there was little support for such a move in Congress. Then the administration appeared to be attempting to subvert the program by appointing persons to administer it who were committed to "scuttling" it; that too met resistance, and the first person nominated could not be confirmed. In time, the Reagan administration developed its own policy. It too favored United States concern for human rights, but would implement that concern by "quiet diplomacy." Though quiet diplomacy is ordinarily, by hypothesis, not known, and one could not know whether it was taking place and whether it succeeded in furthering human rights, there is evidence that the Reagan administration successfully exerted some influence in particular cases of individual human rights violations.[14] In respect of most countries, however, the Reagan administration appeared reluctant to address systemic violations, "consistent patterns of gross violations" that could not be met merely by a gesture in a particular case.

That was, perhaps, because human rights policy, including quiet diplomacy and "case" work, was part of, and subservient to, larger United States policy concerns during the first Reagan administration. In its early years, surely, United States foreign policy acquired a strong ideological aura, at times reflecting a Manichean view of world affairs, with the United States representing the good and the USSR the forces of evil, in a confrontation that could brook no "neutrals." For the Reagan administration, the struggle between good and evil was itself a struggle for the values commonly associated with human rights. The overriding concern for the United States was to resist, contain, and defeat Communist expansion. That was not only seen as in the United States interest generally, but it furthered human rights since Communism was the epitome of disrespect for human rights, and where Communism was, or came, human rights were lost irretrievably. Opposition to Communism, including criticism of any new and particular human rights violations by Communist states (as when military rule came to Poland, or Sakharov was confined and mistreated), should be strong and loud and clear.

In the early Reagan years, United States foreign policy generally, including its human rights policy, had to serve the "war effort," the larger human rights struggle with Communism, and United States reactions to the condition of human rights in Third World countries had to be shaped accordingly. Non-Communist governments, no matter how repressive, were only "authoritarian," not "totalitarian." There was room for hope that they would improve, or even cease to be repressive. In the meanwhile, they had to be cultivated and be-friended, to keep them from going into the Communist fold or otherwise align-ing themselves with the Soviet Union. Sanctions, even criticism of their human rights violations, were not in the interest of the United States. If that meant tolerance of, even friendship with, a Marcos regime in the Philippines, or a murderous junta in Argentina, it was the unpleasant cost of the war against the prime evil, Communism.

Whatever the merits of that policy and the validity of its assumptions and implications, it was not the policy that Congress had enacted. Inevitably, the administration, committed to a different policy, chafed under Congressional limitations. Diplomats reported on violations in all countries, as required by law, but the administration sometimes shaped the reports a bit to suit its larger design, and it often did not allow what it reported to defeat its deeper concerns. Certification of "extraordinary circumstances" to justify disregarding Congres-sional limitations became routine; "significant improvement" in a country's hu-man rights record was readily found. Critics repeatedly charged that the Presi-dent was violating his constitutional duty to "take care that the Laws be faithfully executed." [15]

During the course of the Reagan administration, human rights policy contin-ued to evolve. After a few years, the administration committed itself to working for "democracy" in other countries as *the* human right, rejecting in principle not only military "juntas" but the many one-party states of Africa and Asia. Democ-racy, we know, was not the aim of the Congressional program; that was directed at ending torture, detention, killing, and other gross violations. Perhaps the Reagan administration's policy implied that if there were democracy there would be no gross violations of human rights. Critics of the new emphasis noted, however, that almost all countries claim to be democratic, and many states— including Communist states—provide for periodic elections; even where oppo-sition parties are tolerated, elections can be fraudulent and manipulated, as in the Philippines in 1986. Moreover, it was feared that the administration would be satisfied by elections, while governments confident of their popular support or able to control election results continued to pursue consistent patterns of gross human rights violations. In fact, however, even democracy was not consistently pursued. It is true that United States pressure contributed to the return of civilian rule in Guatemala in 1985, and to the departure of the dictator Duvalier from Haiti in 1986. The administration also criticized fraudulent elections in the Philippines, as well as apartheid and the exclusion of Blacks from political life in South Africa. But the United States continued friendship with regimes that were undemocratic as well as repressive. There was no reported reaction to gross violations by regimes allied to the United States such as those in South Korea and some in Central America.

In Central America, in particular, presidential and Congressional policies during the Reagan administration were in continuing tension. If many in Con-gress did not share the Reagan perspective on world affairs, they too were concerned that there be no expansion of Communist influence in Central America. Congress too did not want "another Cuba," or even "another Nicaragua"; surely it did not wish the blame if any such development occurred. At the same time, it was committed to seeing the condition of human rights improved, and it did not like to see its laws flouted. And members of Congress knew that many of the people of the United States were concerned for human rights, did not wish the United States associated with tyrants and murderous juntas; many indeed saw respect for human rights as an essential ingredient if stability and order were to be maintained and radical revolutions prevented. And so, when the President sought aid for El Salvador, or for Guatemala, forces in Congress insisted on signs of progress in respect for human rights.

But Congress, too, is hardly of one mind, and its dedication to human rights in other countries is uneven. The majority at the time the human rights legislation was enacted had been prepared to follow the lead of a dedicated few, but most members are not disposed to press for human rights in other countries against a popular President invoking the cause of fighting Communism. Congress, then, was not prepared to try to compel the President to carry out the law as it had been enacted, but neither was it willing to repeal or abandon that program. Some thought Congress was content with the ambiguities: a law on the books expressing a policy Congress favored, but that would not unduly hamper a President, who would then bear the onus of subverting the law while relieving Congress of the charge that insistence on its laws had helped spread Communism.

In sum, human rights legislation in the United States does not govern as other law does. Although gross violations of human rights are rampant in many countries, including some that are important beneficiaries of United States aid and arms trade, there have been virtually no cases in which military assistance or foreign aid was in fact cut off on human rights grounds. But the law is hardly a dead letter and Congress is not a toothless tiger. The existence of the law, the constitutional posture of Congress and President, establish a political context and generate a process that have important human rights consequences. Sometimes they deter Presidents from asking for aid for blatant violators, as in Guatemala. Sometimes they compel the President to press would-be beneficiary governments to act to improve the human rights condition in these countries, so that the President could certify to Congress at least significant improvement.* Law and process also cause human rights policy to respond to political events, to United States relations with particular countries, to degrees of human rights violations. By a kind of *pas de deux* of President and Congress, by a combination of promise and threat, United States human rights policy has achieved a spectrum of influence on the condition of human rights around the world.

---

* A certification might minimize violations or exaggerate improvements, but it is not easy to certify black as white to a Congress with at least some alert members, and in an open society.

INTERNATIONAL HUMAN RIGHTS IN THE UNITED STATES

From the beginning, the international human rights movement was conceived by the United States as designed to improve the condition of human rights in countries other than the United States (and a very few like-minded liberal states). United States participation in the movement was also to serve the cause of human rights in other countries. To that end, the United States promoted and actively engaged in establishing international standards and machinery. It did not strongly favor but it also did not resist the move to develop international agreements and international law, but, again, it saw them as designed for other states.

Inevitably, a policy so motivated created difficulties for the United States both abroad and at home. Other countries were not disposed to agree that human rights in the United States need no improvement, especially since racial discrimination was still a fact of American life if not of law, and economic and social rights had no constitutional sanction and sometimes failed in practice. Other countries were not pleased to admit and accept that they alone were underdeveloped in respect of human rights and that they alone were in need of improvement and monitoring. The failure of the United States to adhere to international human rights instruments was resented as arrogant and was decried as hypocritical when the United States sought to invoke international human rights against others.

Here it was the executive branch that tended to favor active United States participation in the human rights movement. It generally favored United States adherence to international human rights agreements and consequent participation in the bodies they created, that is, the Human Rights Committee under the Covenant on Civil and Political Rights, and the Committee on the Elimination of Racial Discrimination under the Convention on the Elimination of All Forms of Racial Discrimination. Here it was Congress that resisted, and its resistance determined United States policy.

Even during the heyday of "internationalism," prevailing forces in Congress tended to resist United States involvement in ways that had effect within the United States. For example, Congress had little interest in sanctions against countries violating human rights—even South Africa—that might have adverse effects on United States trade.* Congressional resistance was particularly strong and was decisive when international human rights threatened to come into the United States. It was in substantial measure from anticipation of Congressional resistance that human rights provisions of the UN Charter, which (unlike the

---

*The case of Rhodesia was exceptional and Congressional acquiescence in the boycott of Rhodesian products, imposed by the United Nations Security Council with United States participation, was reluctant and for some years refused. In Diggs v. Shultz, 470 F.2d 461 (D.C. Cir. 1972), cert. denied, 411 U.S. 931 (1973), the court upheld a statute permitting imports contrary to the United Nations Security Council embargo on Rhodesian products.

peace treaties containing human rights provisions) imposed obligations on the United States as well as on other countries, remained general, hortatory, aspirational, avoiding firm, clear and specific commitment.* Later, the United States was as insistent as were its European Allies or the USSR that the Universal Declaration was only a standard by which states ought to shape their national behavior, not a treaty having binding legal character (and requiring Senate consent). Efforts during 1953–55, led by Senator Bricker of Ohio, to amend the Constitution so as to make it impossible for the United States to adhere to international human rights agreements failed,[16] but elicited a commitment from President Eisenhower that the United States would not adhere to such agreements.

As promised by President Eisenhower, the United States has adhered to none of the major United Nations human rights conventions. Few countries have "dared" not to adhere to the Genocide Convention, the international community's monument to the Holocaust and the defeat of Hitlerism, but the Genocide Convention remained on the shelf of the United States Senate from 1949 to 1986. President Carter clearly abandoned the Eisenhower commitment when he signed and sent to the Senate for its consent four major international covenants, but suggested far-reaching reservations; even with all those proposed restrictions, there has been no move in the Senate to consider those agreements.

The Reagan administration has shown no interest in pressing for Senate consent. Its request in 1984 for Senate consent to ratification of the Genocide Convention was clearly a gesture to the Jewish community during an election campaign; the Senate finally consented and United States ratification finally took place in 1988, but there is no promise of action on other human rights agreements, notably the principal international covenants, the Convention on the Elimination of All Forms of Racial Discrimination, and the American Convention on Human Rights.†

Congressional resistance has not kept international human rights wholly out of United States law. Before the Genocide Convention, the Senate did consent and the United States has adhered to the Protocol on the Status of Refugees and the Convention on the Political Status of Women, and earlier to conventions outlawing slavery and slave trade. In addition, by the practice and acquiescence of states—in the United States, principally the acquiescence of the executive branch—a few human rights principles have entered the stream of customary international law: it is accepted that a state violates international law if as a matter of state policy it practices or condones genocide or slavery, killing or torture, prolonged arbitrary detention or systematic racial discrimination.[17] Since

---

*Even those general undertakings have been held to be "non-self-executing," i.e., not automatically incorporated into United States law, its obligations falling on the political branches, but not for the courts to apply. See *Restatement, Third, Foreign Relations Law of the United States,* § 111, Reporters' note 5.

†There has been particular distaste in Congress for "economic and social rights," which to some smacked of socialism, although in fact they originated in Western Europe and parallel social and welfare programs that are firmly established in the United States and in all Western states.

customary international law is automatically law of the United States, violations of these human rights might in appropriate cases be held to violate United States law deriving from international law [18] as well as the Constitution or other United States law of domestic origin. A United States court has applied international law to a gross violation by a foreign official.[19] Some courts have applied it to actions of the United States when the United States Constitution has proved deficient, to protect rights of would-be immigrants.[20] United States adherence to the Charter and United States acceptance of the Universal Declaration have also given human rights some status in United States jurisprudence if only as guides to the interpretation of general constitutional standards ("due process of law," "cruel and unusual punishment") or as national public policy to guide the discretion of courts.[21]

The failure of the United States to adhere to the principal international covenants and conventions remains particularly mystifying to other countries and troubling to many Americans. Some ninety nations have adhered to the principal United Nations covenants; the United States has not and there is no assurance that it will do so soon. To the world, the United States has not been a pillar of human rights, but a "flying buttress"—supporting them from the outside. For the United States, it has been charged, human rights have been a kind of "white man's burden"; international human rights have been "for export only." Congress has invoked international human rights standards only as a basis for sanctions against other countries. President Carter invoked human rights agreements in criticism of others. In a word, it is charged, Americans have not accepted international human rights for themselves, only for others.

The reasons why the United States has maintained its distance from the international human rights agreements are not obvious. At one time, some lawyers in the United States questioned the constitutional authority of the treaty makers to adhere to such agreements: it was said that the agreements dealt with matters that under the United States Constitution were reserved to the States; or were delegated exclusively to Congress; or were not a proper subject for a treaty because they were only of "domestic concern." Each of these legal objections was long ago refuted.[22] Thirty-five years ago some feared that United States adherence to international human rights agreements would threaten then-existing institutions and practices, such as racial segregation; now, Americans are happy to say, those practices are outlawed, independently of international agreements. Thirty-five years ago Senator Bricker's proposed constitutional amendment sought to prevent the use of treaties to "nationalize" human rights matters and to give Congress authority to deal with them.[23] Today, as a result of new constitutional interpretations, individual rights are already national, Congress already has power to legislate about them.

And yet, resistance to United States adherence remains strong. In some measure, resistance to United States participation builds on differences between constitutional rights and international human rights. In particular, American constitutional rights are individualistic and deeply democratic in their eighteenth-century conception. Self-government is the basic right on which all others depend: *Representative government is freedom,* Thomas Paine said.[24] In contemporary international human rights, on the other hand, popular sovereignty does not imply any particular system of government; individual participation in government is only one right among others, and the form of participation is not defined. Americans believe that societies that are not democratic violate the basic human rights on which all others depend. The Communist states, however, insist that their form of government is more democratic than that of the United States. Many Third World countries, too, are single-party states and claim a need for strong government to build a nation, and promote political, social, and economic development; these countries also insist that they are democratic and based on popular sovereignty, even if this support is expressed only in periodic plebiscites.

But the resistance in the United States is deeper. There is resistance to imposing national standards on some matters that have long been deemed "local"; even more, there is resistance to accepting international standards, and international scrutiny, on matters that have been for the United States to decide. A deep isolationism continues to motivate many Americans, even some who are eager to judge others as by interceding on behalf of human rights in other countries. Human rights in the United States, they believe, are alive and well. Americans, they believe, have nothing to learn, and do not need scrutiny from others, surely not from the many countries where human rights fare so badly. Moreover, they say, the United States would take human rights obligations seriously, as others governments do not; in the United States, courts and other institutions would give them effect, as does not happen in most other countries. The United States, they argue, ought not join in a human rights enterprise with countries that do not share its ideals, that will dilute American standards, and that will use United States adherence as a pretext to distort and criticize the human rights record of the United States.

Americans who favor United States participation in international human rights are not persuaded. They believe that the United States should join, not abandon, the arena of ideological competition. Even if authentic democracy cannot at present be the linchpin of international human rights, other rights are still worth striving for. Human rights are not "all-or-nothing." Without granting that single-party states satisfy the individual's right to self-government, one can insist that single-party states, and even totalitarian regimes, should refrain from torture, lawless detentions, disappearances, fake trials. They should accord due process of law, respect freedom of conscience and freedom of movement, and afford substantial freedom of expression. They should establish Freedom from Fear.[25]

One should not exaggerate the significance of the failure of the United States to adhere to international human rights instruments. Surely one should not exploit that failure to distort the human rights record of the United States. The international human rights movement is concerned primarily to assure that states respect human rights, and in that respect the record of the United States is as good as that of any state, and better than that of the overwhelming majority of them.* The United States serves the cause of human rights well by its example, as a society committed to the idea of human rights and living by that commitment with notable success. The failures of the United States to adhere to international human rights instruments, it should be clear, are not blemishes on its human rights record, but on its record of international cooperation and participation. Failures of cooperation in the international human rights movement are important failures, however, and disarm the United States and lessen its influence for human rights (see essay 9).

Many Americans agree that full United States participation in the international human rights movement is long overdue. United States adherence to the principal covenants would help maintain the universal standards of political and civil rights. Adherence would give the United States a voice in the institutions that are applying and monitoring these standards, would enable Americans to help resist those who would distort or dilute them. Adherence would support the political efforts of Congress and of the executive branch to dissociate the United States from, and to deter, gross violations of human rights in the world. It would help remove the ambiguities that mar the present national posture of the United States, making clear its commitment to equality and to the welfare rights Americans also value, and which are paramount in the eyes of others.

Human rights is not a United States invention but Americans believe that their society can justly lay claim to being one of its most loyal adherents and proponents. At the end of the twentieth century, in appearance to the world, in relations with other nations, thoughtful Americans know that it is not the wealth or power of the United States, its culture, or even its political system generally, but its commitment to human rights that is its just pride and the envy and aspiration of people everywhere. The United States is one of two superpowers; it has been generally acknowledged to be the superpower that is more committed to human dignity, that more consistently has a human face. That is the most valuable asset of the United States, its most potent weapon in any competition for the values of today and in its aspiration for the approval of history. How the United States behaves at home, how it chooses its friends, how it reacts to enemies of human rights are among its principal assets. The United States depreciates those assets by incidental inadequacies in constitutional appearance and by failures in international cooperation in support of human rights.

PROSPECT

The human rights policy of the United States is part of a larger foreign policy in the national interest broadly conceived. National interest is not a simple,

---

* Even in respect for economic and social rights. The United States is a rich country and its failures in meeting basic human needs for all its inhabitants are disgraceful and should be remedied, but those failures would not be remedied more effectively if the United States adhered to the Covenant on Economic, Social and Cultural Rights.

single concern, and United States foreign policy has often struggled with competing national interests. But the ambiguities, ambivalences, and contradictions of United States human rights policy have been particularly glaring. For those concerned with human rights, it is difficult to see any national interest, to see anything but outdated and unwarranted dogmatism, to explain the failure of the United States to give wholehearted support to the international human rights movement, to adhere to the international instruments and take its place in bodies that monitor them. It is not much easier to accept the failure of the United States to exercise leadership in multilateral bodies to shape the human rights agenda, to "depoliticize" their human rights activities, to strengthen their human rights organs.

The bilateral human rights policies of the United States will doubtless continue to trouble and divide the people of the United States. After fifteen years of Congressional policy, after two administrations with different human rights policies, some conclusions seem warranted. There are few voices now to insist that human rights elsewhere are not the business of the United States. President Carter proclaimed and made it so, and in different ways and with different emphasis, the Reagan administration confirmed that it is, originally only where Communism is or threatens, later elsewhere—in South Africa, and through pressures for democracy in Guatemala, Haiti, the Philippines.

No one in the United States suggests that the United States should end human rights violations in other countries by war and conquest; that would be a violation of international law and would bring more human suffering than it would cure. Some favor economic sanctions such as boycotts but most knowledgeable Americans recognize that such measures are generally ineffective and might damage other United States interests, though it may sometimes be necessary to make a political-moral statement as Congress did in enacting the Comprehensive Anti-Apartheid Act of 1986. But human rights advocates insist that the United States is fully entitled to withhold its foreign aid and deny arms to regimes that are guilty of consistent patterns of gross violations of human rights, as it has denied them to Communist countries. Even the Communist countries, they believe, can sometimes be induced to do better by human rights if the United States and others make it clear that they are concerned with gross violations and are not invoking human rights to threaten the Communist system or USSR hegemony in Eastern Europe. It is not beyond hope that, as at Helsinki and at other times in the past, the United States could successfully link Communist improvement in human rights to other issues between them. In many non-Communist countries, too, there is hope of inducing improvement in the condition of human rights; at the least, taking care that the Congressional program is faithfully executed would assure that the United States would not become associated with gross violations and violators in the mind of the victims and their countrymen, in the minds of people in third countries, and in the minds of the people of the United States.

Americans recognize that the condition of human rights in other countries is of concern to the United States; the human rights community recognizes that it is not the only national interest of the United States. Peace, security, trade are important national interests and they sometimes require that the United States deal with governments whose policies are anathema to the people of the United States. In a telling metaphor it was once suggested that if a person requires a blood transfusion and the only blood available is tainted with syphilis, one will take the transfusion. That is persuasive, but is not the whole of the matter. One might suggest that one should first make doubly sure that one really needs the transfusion; one should make doubly sure that there is no other blood available; and, finally, one should proceed immediately to treat the disease: one should not act as though syphilis is not so bad. Proponents of a human rights policy urge that the United States should make doubly sure that it really needs alliance or even lesser associations with any regime that is a gross violator of human rights; it must make doubly sure that there is no other association that could be substituted and would be less distasteful. If the association is really essential, the need is usually reciprocal; such associates need the United States at least as much as the United States needs them, and United States influence can be wielded to effect significant improvement in human rights. For the human rights community, moreover, no such association can be more than a temporary expedient. Relations may have to be correct, but they need not be cordial. There is no reason for any President of the United States to put his arm around a Shah or a Marcos and call him friend.

The tension between the autonomy of states and the international concern for human rights is particularly strong in its manifestations in United States policy. The United States is as concerned as any state for its own autonomy, as resistant to external legislation, intervention, scrutiny. But it is also as concerned as any state for the condition of human rights around the world. In the age of instant communication, interdependency, universal ideological competition, autonomy cannot demand either isolationism or unilateralism. For the United States, resolution of, or living with, tension requires a place for human rights in United States foreign policy that is supportive of its global interests but is also congenial to its ideology, an ideology in which respect for human rights is central.

PART TWO

Rights in
The United States

6

The Idea of Rights
and the United States Constitution

AMERICANS exalt their constitutional rights and consider them their particular invention, but few have inquired into their sources and theoretical foundations. Political and moral philosophers are currently preoccupied with justice and rights, but they have paid little attention to constitutional rights jurisprudence. Constitutional law and lawyers, for their part, have eschewed theory. Individual rights under the Constitution are the stuff of innumerable judicial decisions and of a luxuriant jurisprudence but these, too, hardly address the idea of rights or the political and moral principles that inspire that idea. Doubtless as the result of judicial neglect, law schools teach constitutional law as though the Constitution has no theory, and some students of the law may be surprised to learn—and some may deny—that it has one.

In this essay I set forth what seems to be the theory of constitutional rights and expose what seem to be its political and moral underpinnings. I suggest respects in which that theory has shaped constitutional development and other respects in which theory has apparently been neglected. I conclude that, perhaps, a few drops of theory would enrich and enlighten constitutional jurisprudence.

THE THEORY OF CONSTITUTIONAL RIGHTS

In the United States, we tend to see rights as constitutional protections, established by the framers or added later by formal constitutional amendment.

We know that constitutional rights have been shaped and defined by construction and interpretation, by Congress, by the President, as well as by the judiciary,
but all of them have based what they have done on the Constitution and have
disclaimed any authority to add, subtract or modify rights on any basis not
supported by the Constitution.[1]

Our rights, then, are rooted in the Constitution and are respected because
they are there, or deemed to be there. The Constitution is positive law, a higher
positive law, "the supreme law of the land" (Article VI). That the Constitution
is the source and the protector of individual rights, that it is binding and must
be accepted as higher law is assumed, not justified, not explained. For the
explanation and the justification I turn to Thomas Jefferson.

That may be surprising. We acclaim Jefferson as the author of the Declaration
of Independence, as the dominant spirit of 1776, but he was not in Philadelphia
that second time (1787), and has not been considered one of the constitutional
fathers. Indeed, it has long been commonplace to stress the differences in tone
and ideology between the Declaration of Independence and the Constitution,
and some have suggested that some of those differences are due to the dominance
of Jefferson at Philadelphia I and his absence from Philadelphia II.

These suggestions, I believe, are misleading if not mistaken. There are indeed
differences between a declaration of independence with its rhetoric of revolution,
and a constitutional blueprint designed for the sobrieties of governing. But
Jefferson based his bill of particular grievances justifying revolution on a theory
of government. That theory was in the intellectual and political air of the day—
it was "self-evident"—and it animated the constitutional framers. The ideas
declared by Jefferson in 1776 constitute, I believe, the theory of American
constitutionalism. Those ideas, however, found their early realization principally
in the state constitutions, which were the direct descendants of the Declaration
and were concerned with the principles of government. In Virginia, in Massachusetts, and elsewhere, our political ancestors wrote state constitutions according to their political faith as proclaimed by Jefferson.

The United States Constitution came later and had a limited purpose, "to
form a more perfect union," and those who framed that constitution did not feel
required to reaffirm or even address that faith.* But the United States Constitution was conceived in the same faith and reflected the same principles as did the
state constitutions. "The Constitution," the Supreme Court has said, "was conceived in largest part in the spirit of the Declaration of Independence."[2] It does
not depreciate the importance of economic, social, and political forces in the
shaping of the Constitution, it does not require overlooking the important
respects in which the Constitution deviated from theory and principle, to recognize that the United States Constitution reflects the political philosophy that
found its most famous articulation in the Declaration of Independence. I propose,
therefore, to take Jefferson seriously, and explore some of the implications of
doing so for constitutional jurisprudence.

Consider the words we all know:

* See essay 7. That may be an explanation and a small excuse for the later neglect of its
theory.

We hold these truths to be self-evident, that all men are created equal, that they are endowed by their Creator with certain unalienable Rights, that among these are Life, Liberty, and the pursuit of Happiness. That to secure these rights, Governments are instituted among Men, deriving their just powers from the consent of the governed. That whenever any form of Government becomes destructive of these ends, it is the Right of the People to alter or to abolish it, and to institute new Government, laying its foundation on such principles and organizing its powers in such form, as to them shall seem most likely to effect their Safety and Happiness.

Jeffersons' truths are rhetoric, "self-evident," not analytically derived, but their antecedents and underpinnings, I think, can be discerned and some of their implications can be readily developed. Jefferson played variations on a theme by John Locke. He took "natural rights" and made them secular, rational, universal, individualist, democratic, and radical. For Jefferson, the rights of man are not (or not necessarily) divinely conceived and ordained; they are God's gift in that they result from his creation. They are natural in the sense that nature (and nature's God) created and inspired man's reason and judgment; they are natural also in a different sense, in that they are man's in the "state of nature," and he brings them with him when, by contract—a social contract—he joins with others to form a political society and establish a government. The individual was autonomous, sovereign, before society was established, and he and other individuals taken together—"the people"—remain sovereign in any society and under any government they form, for their sovereignty is inalienable, and government is only by consent of the governed.* Sovereignty of the people implies self-government by the people, directly or through chosen representatives. But every individual retains some of his or her original autonomy as "rights" that are protected even against the people and their representatives.†

American constitutionalism, then, has two elements: representative government and individual rights. Both are confirmed by constitutional compact. The Constitution is a contract among all the people to create a political society and to establish and to submit to representative government. The contract among the people to form a polity implies, it would seem, ancillary contracts: every individual agrees to respect the rights of every other individual within the polity; the people, and every individual as a member of the people, agree that, through elected representatives, they will respect individual rights and maintain laws and institutions to protect them. The Constitution serves also as a contract between the people and their representatives, or better, as a bill of instructions by the people to their representatives, prescribing the terms and conditions of government. And high among these conditions is that government is responsible to the people and must respect individual rights. The government's responsibility to

* The leap from autonomy of the individual to the sovereignty of the people and majority rule was not commonly noted or explained; presumably that was agreed upon or deemed implicit in the social compact.

† Contrast Rousseau: By his social contract, "the surrender [of the individual to the community] is made without reserve." J. J. Rousseau, *The Social Contract* Book I, ch. VI in *The Essential Rousseau* (L. Blair trans. 1974).

the people, and its respect for individual rights, are the condition of the people's consent to be governed, and the basis of the government's legitimacy.

Individual rights, then, are "natural," inherent. They cannot be taken away, or even suspended. They are not a gift from society or from any government. They are not merely concessions extracted from, and limitations imposed on, preexisting established government, in the tradition of Magna Carta and subsequent English bills; rather, they are freedoms and entitlements of all men, everywhere, antecedent and superior to government. They do not derive from any constitution; they antecede all constitutions.[3] When, after 1776, the American people adopted state constitutions creating new governments, when in 1789 they ordained the United States Constitution, they retained substantial autonomy and freedoms, for themselves and for their descendants, as individual rights against government. Their "right" to rights was axiomatic, an *a priori* entitlement; the right to retain rights vis-a-vis their government, and the content of the rights they retained, were fixed by the contract.

The rights retained on entering society reflect conceptions of the good society, of justice, and of other values accepted as self-evident. Every human being is a person, entitled to the political, social and legal implications of personhood. The family is the natural unit. The individual is essentially autonomous, free to pursue his or her happiness. The good society is the liberal society in which individuals enjoy their antecedent freedoms—religion, speech, press, assembly, general autonomy—giving up only a little to the needs of society. They are entitled to property acquired honestly by labor, exchange, or inheritance. An individual accused of crime is entitled to a fair trial because it is unjust —obviously—to punish him, to deprive him of his liberty, without due process of law.

Neither the Declaration of Independence nor the early state constitutions describe fully the rights the people retained. The Declaration lists among the unalienable rights "life, liberty and the pursuit of happiness," but that was an elegant distillation, hardly intended to be an exhaustive list.* The Virginia Bill, other early state bills of rights, as well as the United States Bill of Rights, go on to enumerate important freedoms government must respect—political and religious liberty, privacy, procedural justice especially in respect of government's criminal process. They all refer, in addition and separately, to "liberty" generally, and the Bill of Rights that soon became part of the United States Constitution provides expressly that other rights not enumerated in the Constitution are also "retained by the people" (Amendment IX).

Of course, what the people retained is determined also by what they agreed to give up in creating a political society and establishing a government. Individ-

---

* Much has been made of the fact that in that triad "the pursuit of happiness" is substituted for "property" in John Locke's earlier enumeration, but, for present purposes at least, I would not exaggerate the significance of that change. Jefferson would surely have agreed that his formulation includes what was in his less-eloquent model, the Virginia Bill of Rights, which expressly included "the means of acquiring and possessing property," as well as "pursuing and obtaining happiness and safety."

uals pooled some of their autonomy when they formed "the people," subjecting themselves to majority rule; the people also gave up some of their autonomy to their government, retaining the rest as individual rights and freedoms under government.* The people gave to their representatives the authority they needed for governing, and gave up such rights, and submitted other rights to such limitations, as the purposes of government required. The authority granted to government was not particularized either, but its scope is defined by the purposes for which governments were formed, purposes commonly understood.

By implication, the purposes of government were central to the ancestral conception of rights that Jefferson articulated. Governments, he said, are instituted "to secure these rights," the rights of every individual to life, liberty and the pursuit of happiness, and the other rights they implied. Later, President Thomas Jefferson, in his First Inaugural Address, described the purposes of government as follows:

> Still one thing more, fellow-citizens—a wise and frugal Government, which shall restrain men from injuring one another; shall leave them otherwise free to regulate their own pursuits of industry and improvement; and shall not take from the mouth of labor the bread it has earned. This is the sum of good government, and this is necessary to close the circle of our felicities.[4]

Government was to be a watchman, a policeman protecting every person's rights against violation by others. That would safeguard every individual's life and liberty and leave the individual free to pursue his or her happiness. Government, it was doubtless assumed, should also several safety, health, and morals. Government itself, of course, should let people alone; inter alia, it should not tax them more than was essential.†

For the founders' generation the social contract was not a myth or a hypothetical construct; it was a real compact. The parties to the contract—the people—sought to assure that it would be carried out by building in safeguards: the separation and balance of powers of government to prevent corruption and abuse of authority,[5] and periodic elections to review the performance of the people's agents and maintain the consent of the governed. In some respects, perhaps, this contract, like contracts generally, could be enforced in court, if the courts were independent of the political branches. The people could also revise their contract to change their government, replace their representatives, reconsider the authority they delegated. Ultimately, the people—not any few individuals—could terminate the contract and reconstitute themselves in a new political society by a new compact.‡

---

*Thomas Paine distinguished "that class of natural rights which man retains after entering into society, and those which he throws into the common stock as a member of society" because he cannot execute them himself (*The Rights of Man*, pp. 88–90).

†For Jefferson, I believe, it was not the business of the government to provide the people with the benefits of what the twentieth century was to call the "welfare state"; government was to leave the individual free to pursue his livelihood himself.

‡The individual, presumably, could leave society (if his obligations were paid) and seek admission to another society, or live outside society.

Like Locke's, Jefferson's political principles derived from and depended on individual consent. Societies are properly formed, and governments properly created, only by consent of the participants, and they owe their legitimacy and authority to that consent. Consent derives its effectiveness, its justificatory power, from the fact that all men are born equally free and autonomous, competent and responsible moral agents; they can therefore consent and make binding contracts. Responding voluntarily to perceived needs, men agree to form societies and consent to government and law, persuaded that the benefits of society are worth its costs and its risks. But the people do not, cannot, alienate their fundamental responsibility as moral agents, the right to govern themselves. They do not, perhaps cannot, delegate all their moral authority, give up all their autonomy or freedom, but only as much as is necessary for the limited purposes of government.

For Jefferson, I deduce, there were moral rights and obligations between men before there were political societies and governments. Because there was a moral community there could be a political community. In the state of nature before polities, in burgeoning communities, individuals enjoyed a moral right to security for their lives and persons, for their autonomy and freedom to pursue happiness, and all individuals had a corresponding moral obligation to respect the moral rights of their neighbors. Moral principles governed how property could be acquired and it was immoral for one person to take, invade, or injure another's property.* By the social contract, individuals make their previous moral obligations to respect each other's moral rights into political-contractual obligations as well. They create a government to secure their moral rights against their neighbors, perhaps also to help them carry out their moral obligations to respect their neighbors' rights. Society enforces the original moral rights and obligations between neighbors by developing laws and institutions—laws of tort, property, contract, a police system to prevent or undo violations, courts and procedures to determine rights, a system of criminal justice to safeguard them. The social contract gives the individual rights—valid claims on his or her society—to have the benefit of such laws, such police protection, and such legal remedies.

Of course, the same rights—life, liberty, property, pursuit of happiness—are to be secured also, perhaps *a fortiori,* against those individuals who are designated officials of government. Implicitly, however, individuals forming political society and delegating to representatives and officials authority to govern consent to invasions by government that would be morally unacceptable if committed by private persons, or if committed by officials in respects to which consent was not given. It is immoral, a violation of Y's moral right to live, for X to kill Y; it is not deemed immoral when X is an official executioner carrying out a valid capital sentence after Y is duly convicted of murder. It is immoral for X to deprive Y of liberty by imprisoning him, but not if X is the official jailer and Y

---

* I do not address here the morality of slavery. For Jefferson, one must assume, slavery could not be morally justified, even if slaves were "lawfully" acquired as property.

was duly sentenced to prison. It is immoral for X to take Y's property, but not if X is a sheriff or a tax collector acting pursuant to law. It is not immoral in principle when officials, pursuant to law enacted by the people's representatives acting within their delegated authority, exert other coercive authority with respect to ourselves or to others that would offend our moral principles if done by private persons; when government representatives conscript persons for national defense, tax to provide for the common welfare, or take property for public use (subject to compensation); or regulate the freedom of persons and the use of property generally, for valid public purposes; or exercise coercive authority to administer justice in order to secure private rights, to establish and maintain the common principles of the common law—tort, contract, property law—or to enforce civil rights acts. Of course, coercive authority of government is morally acceptable—whether I am their object or my neighbor is—only if it is within authority delegated, and is necessary, reasonable, and fairly administered.

Jefferson's (Locke's) political theory, I think, justified such coercive official action because, originally, the individual, as one of the people, consented to it when he or she consented to government. In most circumstances, authentic consent removes moral objections even to coercive private actions, and perhaps *a fortiori* to public acts that serve the common good. Therefore, insofar as an action of government is within the scope of the consent—within the agreed purposes of government—and does not violate any of the rights retained by the individual, it is politically justified, and violates no moral principles either. A coercive official act beyond the scope of delegated authority, or in violation of someone's retained rights, would violate his or her political rights and, as no better than private coercion to which he or she did not consent, is immoral as well.

The examples I have cited are of coercive actions that would violate our moral intuitions if committed between individuals, but that are acceptable when done in line of official duty because consented to in the social compact. Behind ancestral principles, however, must be other moral intuitions as well, principles other than the immorality of violating an individual's autonomy without his or her consent. For, surely, the objection, say, to a "rigged" trial or to a coerced confession is not merely that it was not authorized or consented to, but that it violates moral principles, that it constitutes immorality that cannot be cured even by consent. I think Jefferson's theory did not permit anyone to sell himself into slavery, or alienate other inalienable rights and freedoms. There are independent principles of justice and morality reflected in the constitutional dispositions designed to assure that innocent men and women shall not be convicted of crime, or that even guilty men shall not suffer cruel and unusual punishment; there are similar principles behind the prohibitions on ex post facto laws, on bills of attainder, perhaps on double jeopardy.

JEFFERSONIAN PRINCIPLES AND
CONSTITUTIONAL JURISPRUDENCE

I have attempted to distill the political theory of the constitutional fathers, and the moral assumptions that seem to underlie their idea of rights. Though we think of the Constitution as Madisonian (and in important respects Hamiltonian), our idea of rights is Jeffersonian: The idea of rights articulated in the Declaration of Independence is reflected in constitutional text. But the jurisprudence we have spun out of that text has lagged behind and diverged from Jeffersonian principles. In the growth of that jurisprudence, text and canonical exegesis have dominated, but theory has been at best assumed, often neglected or abandoned. The reasons for the divergence of doctrine from theory are complex. I cite two: We became committed to constitutional text and to the judicial remedy for monitoring it; and, as regards rights, the text was—is—deficient.

It is not necessary to repeat what we owe to John Marshall. In establishing judicial review he helped make the courts what they are today, the final arbiters of what the Constitution means, and the rock and the redeemer of our rights. But Marshall achieved his success by establishing the Constitution as law, the thing of courts and lawyers. His justification for judicial review was that the Constitution was written law, and the courts had the unique responsibility and talent to expound law.[6] Since Marshall, the courts, concerned to establish judicial supremacy, and mindful of their political weakness and the delicacy of their function, grounded their authority in the constitutional text ordained by the people and sought to reassure those who feared "government by judiciary" by promising to cling to that text. The text became all: what was written is the effective Constitution. The Justices continued to proclaim that "it is a *constitution* we are expounding,"[7] but they felt constrained to look only into the text; what was not there was excluded.* And among the elements missing from the Constitution was its theory. And so, the Supreme Court said in 1850:

> . . . [W]e have not felt ourselves at liberty to indulge in general remarks on the theory of our government. That is a subject which belongs to a convention for the formation of a constitution; and, in a limited view, to the law-making power. Theories depend so much on the qualities of the human mind, and these are so diversified by education and habit as to constitute an unsafe rule for judicial action. Our prosperity, individually and nationally, depends upon a close adherence to the settled rules of law, and especially to the great fundamental law of the Union.[8]

Dogma and method that had developed perhaps to help justify judicial review shaped constitutional history for political purposes as well—when Congress and

---

* In time, the ascendancy of philosophical positivism in the nineteenth century also tended to impel judges to treat the Constitution as positive law and to eschew external sources that had the smell of natural law. See, for example, cases cited in note 19.

the President determined their own authority and responsibility, or when the people considered their social compact. We were condemned to be textualists, "interpretivists"; other parts of our hagiography—notably the Declaration of Independence—were excluded from the jurisprudential canon; ancestral theory might sneak in, but only occasionally, and in the guise of construction of the constitutional text.*

Since our constitutional jurisprudence is limited to and by the text, it is shaped by the fact that, by Jeffersonian standards, the text is deficient, one might say "congenitally defective." As written, the Constitution was not designed for the purposes it has come to serve. It was supposed to support a small, supplemental, superstructure of government, imposed on powerful, self-sufficient state governments subject essentially to their own constitutions; it has become, without significant amendment in respects here relevant, the constitution of a powerful national government largely subordinating state governments and itself governing the people. The United States Constitution was designed for minimal government for a small population and a pre-industrial economy; it now supports the complex government of a nuclear superpower, urban, highly industrial, and a welfare state. Among the weaknesses of the Constitution for its aggrandized function, I suggest, are respects in which it does not conform to essential principles of Jefferson's constitutionalism: a constitution as social compact, retained rights, government for agreed-upon purposes.

THE CONSTITUTION AS SOCIAL COMPACT

The founding generation, I think, saw the Constitution as their social compact. The United States Constitution declares itself to be a social compact: Such, I believe, is the purpose and purport of the preamble, in which "[W]e the people ... ordain and establish this Constitution." But was it an authentic social compact? And is it our social compact?

"We the people" who ordained the Constitution were not all the inhabitants. It has been estimated that "the people" who voted for the delegates to the state

---

*Through Marshall, too, the courts came to judicial review as part of their daily business of deciding cases and controversies. See *Marbury v. Madison*, n. 6. Unlike twentieth century counterparts in Western Europe, the Supreme Court is not a constitutional court with unique powers and wielding unique remedies. It decides constitutional issues while acting as a court of law in the British tradition. It has therefore limited itself by an entire code of reasons for not deciding issues; and its quiver contains only the traditional remedies of English common law and equity courts, subject to inherent as well as self-imposed limitations. For example, the courts will enjoin officials not to give effect to an act of Congress that violates the Constitution; they do not command Congress to adopt a different law or to appropriate money to carry out a constitutional obligation, even if such an obligation could be found in the Constitution.

Despite their commitment to the text, the courts felt obligated to conclude that the Constitution is not complete in that it does not include all the powers of the United States inherent in its nationhood and international sovereignty, such as powers over foreign affairs and immigration. See *U.S. v Curtiss-Wright Export Corp.*, 299 U.S. 304 (1936).

conventions that ratified the Constitution constituted some 5 percent of the inhabitants.* "We the people" did not include slaves, for they were property, not persons, not part of the political society being established; in some states even free blacks could not vote. The people did not include women.† The people included only property owners, those (I quote from the Virginia Bill of Rights) "having sufficient evidence of permanent common interest with, and attachment to, the community." Was a constitution so ordained a proper social contract?

More troubling, is the Constitution of the framing generation properly our constitution, is their social compact our social compact? It is difficult to justify that conclusion by Jefferson's principles. The people of 1789 may have deemed their values eternal and their rights timeless, valid for their children's children as for themselves. But in principle, surely, the autonomy and sovereignty of the people of two hundred years ago did not include the right to impose their values on their descendants; their moral principles are not necessarily ours; their consent does not justify coercive authority over us.‡ Later generations might decide that their ancestors improperly alienated rights that were unalienable; or, to the contrary, they might decide it wise to delegate to their government new kinds of authority for new purposes, and retain less autonomy for themselves. We are as autonomous as they were, equally endowed with unalienable rights. Their principles would warrant us in writing our own social contract and substituting our own terms with each other and with government, terms that would reflect our views of the proper purposes of government and that would retain the rights and liberties that we consider inalienable or that we do not wish to alienate.

Thomas Jefferson indeed may have sensed that difficulty when he suggested that a constitution expires automatically after nineteen years.[9] But nineteen years after 1789, President Thomas Jefferson did not act as though the Constitution had expired; rather, he felt bound by his oath to preserve, protect and defend it, and to take care that it be faithfully executed. Perhaps Jefferson would have said that the consent of every new generation may be presumed, and the original contract remains valid and effective, unless the people reconstituted themselves in a new polity by a new compact. But is that consent authentic, is our acquiescence in the original social compact properly presumed? Do the people today prescribe to the same terms, wish to retain the same rights, accept the same purposes of government, share eighteenth-century moral principles and intuitions—except in so far as we mobilize ourselves to reconstitute our society anew, or succeed in amending the ancestral compact by the difficult procedure imposed on us by the founders?

Perhaps it was this difficulty that early caused neglect of the character of the

---

* In half the states almost half the delegates voted against ratification, and in some states the authenticity of the successful vote might not pass scrutiny. See generally R. Schuyler, *The Constitution of the United States* (New York: Macmillon, 1923), ch. 4, esp. p. 138.

† In theory, perhaps, some of them were represented by family males.

‡ Thomas Paine rejected Burke's suggestion that the people were bound by agreements made by their ancestors, whether with king or with parliament: "The vanity and presumption of government beyond the grave, is the most ridiculous and insolent of all tyrannies" (*The Rights of Man*, pp. 63–64).

Constitution as social compact, and led instead to a jurisprudence that treated the Constitution as positive law, even if positive law of a higher order. Like other positive law, it controls unless superseded by later law of equal authority properly adopted, and what is in the Constitution can be superseded only by new constitutional provision ordained according to the prescribed process of amendment. At the same time, however, some abiding commitment to the Constitution as social compact among the people of every generation may have shaped some of that constitutional jurisprudence. Some have suggested that the people of every generation do indeed acquiesce in the original compact, but they tacitly update that continuing, self-renewing social contract; every generation, therefore, has felt entitled to read some rights reserved and some delegations to government in the constitutional text as adjustable to time and context. It has been suggested also that the people have effectively delegated to the courts authority to calibrate, reinterpret and reshape the text to reflect the contemporary social compact, the original compact as the contemporary people have tacitly revised it. That, however, is not what the courts generally admit they are doing, or think they are doing. That view of our jurisprudence, moreover, would require the courts to find and articulate some way of determining what changes in the original social compact the people of the United States at a given time have tacitly adopted—what new purposes the people today assign to their government, what new authority is being delegated, what rights are now being subjected to that authority and which are being retained.*

There is a different set of difficulties with treating the United States Constitution as our contemporary social compact. For the Constitution was born without principal ingredients of a social compact, and age has not cured and has even aggravated those defects. A direct and immediate descendant of the Articles of Confederation, "a more perfect union" of the states, the Constitution was declared to be ordained by "We the people" as had been the constitutions of the several states, but the compact implied in that preambular phrase was largely rhetorical and symbolic. The small federal superstructure which the framers projected was not, and was not expected to become, a significant government with significant relations to the people, implicating their rights. The real social compact remained the state constitution, the polity that the people had contracted for was the state polity, the government instituted to secure their rights was the state government; the United States Constitution was only a small "codicil" to state social compacts.

Some four score and seven years later, after civil war, the Constitution was amended, and the country was on the way to being what it is today. The federal government became a real government, the dominant government, supervising —and soon in substantial measure superseding—the states in responsibility for the rights of the individual. But the Constitution was not changed to reflect that

---

* In our federal system, there is yet another difficulty. In ordaining the original Constitution, the people decided how much governmental authority was to be delegated to the new federal government, how much was being left to the states. Are the people in every generation tacitly deciding also a new redistribution of responsibility between states and federal government?

transformation. Although the Preamble permanently proclaims the Constitution to be the social compact of every succeeding generation, the body of the Constitution has remained essentially the compact of 1787 of the people of 1787 to create the government of 1787. Major, radical amendments followed as the peace treaty of the Civil War, but there was no attempt then, or since, to make the Constitution a complete compact for the complete government that the federal government has become. Never supplied were the elements essential to a Jeffersonian compact—those found in the ancestral state constitutions: articulation of and commitment to the theory of constitutional government, undertakings of the people to each other, reaffirmation of popular sovereignty, a statement of the purposes of government, a list of the rights the people retained and of the powers delegated, directions to and empowerment of government to do that for which Jefferson said government was instituted—"to secure these rights." Commitment to text discouraged any effort to supply those missing elements from outside the Constitution, perhaps by invoking the Declaration of Independence as the implicit theoretical foundation of the Constitution.

The consequences of these defects have troubled our polity since the beginning, surely since the United States government became *the* government of the United States. The limited conception of the government of the United States, and the limited conception of "We the people," have continued to maintain largely indirect elections for national office, and state control of qualifications for voting. Even the constitutional amendments addressed to suffrage did not take suffrage from state control, nor did they recognize the right of the people, all of the people, to vote.* Only some twenty-five years ago [10] did the Supreme Court, by constitutional constructions that are hardly obvious and that some consider dubious, put together a constitutional right for all to vote and to vote equally, and thus found in the Constitution authentic popular sovereignty and the consent of all the governed—which by Jeffersonian principles is the only basis for legitimate government.

For Jefferson, all men were created equal, therefore autonomous, therefore able to make contracts—including the social contract—and to create political society and government. It is incredible today, but the word "equality" was not in the original Constitution, nor in the Bill of Rights. We have not to this day filled that historic—and embarrassing—lacuna. Since the Fourteenth Amendment (1868), there is in the Constitution a requirement that states not deny the equal protection of the laws; on the face of the Constitution, there is still no commitment by "We the people of the United States" to equality, no contract with, no command to, the government of the United States that we shall all be

---

* A State cannot deny the right to vote on account of race (Amendment XV), or sex (Amendment XIX), or age (Amendment XXVI), but in principle those Amendments did not assure anyone a right to vote: they assured only that if the state gave the right to vote it could not deny it to anyone on account of race, gender, or age. Note that—on the face of the text—religious and other invidious discriminations remain not forbidden. Not until 1964 was the Constitution amended to remove a property requirement—the poll tax—as an obstacle to voting (Amendment XXIV). See essay 7.

equal in its eyes, nothing to prevent Congress, or the President, or the federal courts from discriminating on account of race, religion, or gender. It has taken some intellectually and historically dubious constitutional construction by the Supreme Court in the second half of the twentieth century to remedy that defect in fact.[11]

For Jefferson, I have suggested, the social compact was a contract among all persons constituting the people, and between each person and the people, to respect each other's rights and to create institutions to secure those rights; the compact also includes the conditions that govern the government to assure that it respects our rights. But only the last part of that compact is in the United States Constitution and in constitutional law: Only that aspect of the social compact that imposes conditions on government is constitutional law; one member of the people cannot enforce the compact against another individual, or against the people. As law, notably, the Fourteenth and Fifteenth Amendments protect only against "state action," against violation by government, not against private invasion of rights; and the power that the amendments gave Congress to secure rights is limited by the same conception. Then, having hung that doctrine on a literal reading of the Fourteenth Amendment—"no State shall" * —we have read the state action requirement also into the Bill of Rights, although in largest part the text does not compel it, and might have been read to include protection of rights against violation by individuals, in accordance with a Jeffersonian compact. A complete Jeffersonian constitution would have included an agreement among the people to respect each other's rights, including their equality; an agreement that the government to be created would respect those rights, including equality; an agreement that not only authorizes but requires government to protect every person from actions by his or her neighbor as well as from official actions that deny individual rights, including equality.

Ironically, despite our commitment to text, our jurisprudence has excluded even the small amount of political theory that is in our text, in the Preamble. John Marshall invoked the Preamble in a leading case,[12] but the Preamble has not been law,[13] and nothing has been permitted to hang on it. One might suggest that, as the Preamble sets forth the basis of our polity, it is relevant for the interpretation of the text as amended, including the Bill of Rights. Since the Preamble affirms the character of the Constitution as a social compact, the Constitution might have been read as though the compact were spelled out, as though it included what it was intended to contain, what would have been included had it been foreseen that we were establishing a national political society with a real national political government. It might be instructive to

---

* The words chosen reflect perhaps the immediate concerns of the authors of those Amendments to prevent official political subjugation of blacks; it is not obvious that they intended to continue to deny constitutional protection against private violation of rights. Only the—perhaps fortuitous—absence of a reference to the state in the Thirteenth Amendment gave warrant to reading in it direct constitutional protection of one person against enslavement by another. That fortunate omission later created an opportunity for a jurisprudence that freedom from slavery implies protection against private discrimination on account of race as a badge of slavery.

speculate as to what our constitutional law would have been if the Constitution had incorporated the Declaration of Independence, if only by reference.* Or, if it had included, from John Adams's Massachusetts Constitution of 1780:

> The body politic is . . . a social compact, by which the whole people covenants with each citizen, and each citizen with the whole people, that all shall be governed by certain laws for the common good.
>
> Each individual of the society has a right to be protected by it in the enjoyment of his life, liberty and property according to standing laws.
>
> Every subject . . . ought to find a certain remedy, by having recourse to the laws, for all injuries or wrongs which he may receive in his person, property, or character. He ought to obtain right and justice freely, and without being obliged to purchase it.[14]

With such text, might the courts have proceeded to articulate the terms of the compact between citizens, and between the citizen and the people, and given them constitutional effect and remedy? Might they have enforced the obligation of society to provide laws and remedies, even perhaps by mandamus to the legislature? Might the courts—when the federal government effectively became supreme to the states in respect of the individual's relation to society—have upheld civil rights acts without regard to interstate commerce, without limitation to state action? If so, can all or some of that be read as implied in the social compact implied in the Preamble?

RETAINED RIGHTS

We have done better by Jefferson in respect of retained rights. The original Constitution contained little reference to rights. The federal government being designed as only marginally a government, it was not seen as implicating rights, or having any significant concern with them. Proposals at the constitutional Convention to include a bill of rights did not carry. From an abundance of caution—and prescience—the Bill of Rights became a condition of ratification and was added by constitutional amendment.

Except in that it omits any reference to equality, the Bill of Rights is Jeffersonian, reflecting the principles of the Declaration.[15] The Bill of Rights does not grant rights; it only recognizes and guarantees them. For example, Congress shall make no law abridging "the freedom" of speech, press, assembly, and "[t]he right of the people to be secure"—these are not grants of rights, they refer to and incorporate pre-existing rights. Because rights do not derive from the Constitution, the framers of the Bill of Rights were not impelled to enumerate them all. They enumerated, I believe, the rights they were most concerned to protect

---

*Compare the reference to the French Declaration of the Rights of Man and of the Citizen in the recent constitutions of France, and the consequences for French constitutional jurisprudence. See essay 10.

in light of their recent history, corresponding to those contemplated by Jefferson and enumerated in early state constitutions.* They include the freedoms specified in the First Amendment, protection for property, and the inherent rights to privacy and personal freedom subject to the legitimate needs of government in the criminal process. Basic civil rights went without saying. The Ninth Amendment—affirming that there are other rights retained by the people—was, I believe, not merely a residual clause from abundance of caution; it represented and articulated the basic principle that the individual has rights before and without the Constitution, only some of which it seemed desirable to mention in the Constitution.[16] The Ninth Amendment, therefore, would seem to provide a firm basis in constitutional text for identifying other rights, by determining what rights the people had originally, naturally, then subtracting what they delegated to government. Identifying a right as retained within the purport of the Ninth Amendment would be legitimate constitutional construction, not a daring usurpation.

In fact, we have not used the Ninth Amendment. Constitutional jurisprudence built instead on express rights provisions and to that extent, at least, text (or textualism) triumphed over theory. The explanation, I believe, lies in our history. Before the Civil War, rights hardly figured in constitutional jurisprudence, since the federal government impinged on individuals only minimally; rights of individuals in respect of the states were not governed by the federal Constitution (and the federal social compact), and the Bill of Rights, including the Ninth Amendment, did not apply to the states.[17] The Civil War amendments, notably the Fourteenth, subjected individual rights vis-à-vis the states to federal scrutiny but as an ad hoc addition. Those Amendments were not integrated into the Bill of Rights and subsumed under its Jeffersonian theory including the Ninth Amendment; the jurisprudence of the Civil War amendments was based wholly on interpretation of their text. Slowly, the Fourteenth Amendment, and its due process clause in particular, became the "rights compact" in relation to the states. Later, much later, when rights became significant in respect of the federal government, the jurisprudence that was developed for purposes of the Fourteenth Amendment and the states came to control federal rights as well, and due process in the Fifth Amendment became a textual basis for additional retained rights against the federal government. The Ninth Amendment remained unused.

But the triumph of text over theory, and the demise of the Ninth Amendment, have not been complete. In the development of due process jurisprudence, theory and moral intuitions have echoed strongly and continue to do so: the due process clause became the receptacle of that theory, "the Ninth Amendment" of the states (and secondarily, derivatively, of the federal government). In that development, theory has struggled continuously with text. Powerful voices have feared the uncertain, theological, "natural rights" overtones that the due process clause came to reflect, especially after that clause was abused by the judiciary.

---

* Even the state constitutions did not purport to include a complete catalogue of rights.

Felix Frankfurter thundered that the due process clause must go.[18] Justice Hugo Black did as much as any man to make it go, to empty it of substantive content, to limit constitutional rights to the few substantive rights expressly included in the Bill of Rights, to keep the courts from putting other substantive rights back.[19] But the textualists have not succeeded. Commitment to inherent, retained rights—Jeffersonian theory and moral intuitions brought up to date—came back into the Constitution, even for Justices Black and Douglas, through extravagant—or imaginative—readings of constitutional text.[20]

And so, though the due process clause has provided a constitutional text and the appearance of applying that text, it has been filled from outside the Constitution, and its jurisprudence in fact continues to reflect much of Jeffersonian theory. That theory gave some warrant to treating the word "liberty" in the due process clause as the vessel containing the individual's original autonomy and providing it constitutional protection.[21] Jeffersonian theory more than text makes that clause available to vindicate the social compact by compelling government to justify every invasion of individual autonomy and freedom; it implies the right of the people to insist that our representatives govern rationally and for the public good.[22] It protects all of a person's retained autonomy—"the right of the citizen to be free in the enjoyment of all of his faculties"; "to contract, to engage in any of the common occupations of life, to acquire useful knowledge, to marry, establish a home and bring up children, to worship God according to the dictates of his own conscience, and generally to enjoy those privileges long recognized at common law as essential to the orderly pursuit of happiness by free men."[23] It implies the right to travel and the freedom to have an abortion.[24] It makes it less of a distortion to find in the term "liberty" in that same clause when applied to the federal government the right to equal protection of the laws. Chief Justice Warren's statement that "it would be unthinkable that the same Constitution would impose a lesser duty [of equal protection] on the Federal Government" than on the states[25] may be historically, textually, and contextually ludicrous, but equality in society, equality before the law, is—like liberty—a retained right and inherent in the social compact.*

One might also find in the underlying theory of antecedent rights support for the heightened sensitivity which under contemporary jurisprudence demands compelling public interest to justify invasion of important rights. It is not implausible that the people's consent to official invasion of life, liberty, property, to interference with pursuit of happiness, is not to be inferred as readily, or construed as extensively, when important rights are in issue (see essay 7).

The due process clause, however, has hardly become a full equivalent of the Ninth Amendment and of Jeffersonian theory. Although substantive due process seems here to stay, continuing unease over its legitimacy, and uncertainty as to its content, have meant slow and uncertain identification and development of unenumerated rights. Even rights that for the founding generation, I believe,

---

* Equality, Rousseau said, protects liberty. See Rousseau, *supra*, book I, chs. 6–8; also book II, ch. 4.

were obvious and primordial—the right to marry and found a family, the right of parents to determine the moral education of their children, the presumption of innocence, or the freedom to travel—were not confirmed in our constitutional jurisprudence until our own day.[26] And because of reliance on text instead of underlying principle, "life, liberty, or property" became the sum of rights—not the pursuit of happiness, not other retained rights difficult to squeeze out of, or into, that text. It was not fully accepted that liberty meant autonomy until the abortion cases and the new privacy. Rights expressed in those particular constitutional articulations, reflecting and focusing on concerns immediate to the framers of the amendments and their times, have lent themselves to narrow construction—as when the Supreme Court held that honor and reputation are neither "property" nor "liberty" and therefore do not enjoy constitutional protection under the due process clauses.[27] Or that corporal punishment in the schools, even if cruel and unusual, is not punishment for crime and therefore not within the meaning of the Eighth Amendment.[28] In those cases Jefferson might have asked rather whether the objects of either of those official invasions was an aspect of autonomy (liberty) or was inherent in the right to pursue happiness, and whether either was given to government to invade for a proper purpose of government.*

We have been loyal—some would say too loyal—to Jefferson's retained rights in one less happy respect. The concept of retained rights implied rights that came with the individual from presociety ("the state of nature") into society. That suggested essentially rights of autonomy and liberty, perhaps also equality; it did not readily suggest rights based on needs of community and mutual responsibility. For Jefferson and his time, the "welfare state," I think, was not within the social contract.† There was no right to welfare assistance in the state of nature; it was not, then, a right that it was the purpose of government to secure (and for which the people consented to be taxed).[29] And our constitutional jurisprudence has adhered to that conception. As a matter of constitutional law, at least, there is no right to be free from want, no obligation on society to secure such freedom. So the Supreme Court has told us in *Dandridge v. Williams* about welfare payments; in *San Antonio v. Rodriguez* about education; in other cases about housing and work.[30]

---

* One can only speculate as to whether Jefferson would have included the freedom to engage in homosexual practices within the unalienable right to pursue happiness. Perhaps he would have agreed that the people had delegated to government the right to enforce "morals" as they conceived of them.

† The Constitution was ordained, as the Preamble tells us, to establish justice and to promote the general welfare, and Congress is authorized (Article I, section 8) to tax and spend for the general welfare, but those phrases in their original intent, I believe, were not used to incorporate conceptions such as those of the twentieth century nurtured in a welfare state. For the framers, justice and the general welfare would be the result of the kind of government to be established, a government committed to accepted, limited purposes. On the other hand, Thomas Paine, I note, considered the provision of such benefits to be an entirely appropriate purpose of government. See *The Rights of Man*, pp. 265–70. There is evidence, however, that in fact localities followed earlier English practice of assuming some responsibility for the poor, and the obligation to provide or promote education found its way early into state constitutions.

PURPOSES OF GOVERNMENT

"To secure these rights, Governments are instituted among men." For Jefferson, surely, governments are obligated to secure individual rights. Perhaps, indeed, one can interpret Jefferson as suggesting that to secure individual rights is the sole purpose of government, and authority to use coercive action is delegated to government only to the extent necessary to secure individual rights. More likely, however, the people may consent to delegate authority to government for public purposes not designed directly to secure individual rights, such as the security of society or other societal values.

The purposes of government have not received much attention in constitutional jurisprudence. The Preamble to the Constitution articulates the purposes of the Constitution but, when ordained, they were the purposes not of government but of Union: it was the "more perfect union" being created that would "establish justice, insure domestic tranquility, provide for the common defence, promote the general welfare and secure the blessings of liberty."* Government generally was largely left to the states and the purposes of government were articulated in the constitutions of the states.

The failure of the Constitution to inscribe the purposes of government has shaped, perhaps distorted, our rights jurisprudence. Since rights were not in the original Constitution, were not seen as any concern of the new central government or even as relevant to its limited role, the federal government was not mandated to do what Jeffersonian governments are instituted to do—"to secure these rights"; indeed, Congress was not even empowered or authorized to do so. When the Bill of Rights was added, nothing was done to modify the purposes of government accordingly. Promoting, protecting, ensuring rights, as by civil rights acts, was not made the business of the federal government. Constitutional support for legislation to protect rights against invasion by the states after the Civil War had to be built into the Fourteenth Amendment (and that support was found to be insufficient for some of what Congress sought to do).[31] There were no other civil rights acts for almost a hundred years, and constitutional support for laws beyond what the Fourteenth Amendment provided had to be pieced together in substantial part from text and principles designed for other purposes, notably the Commerce Clause. From various powers of Congress, then, we have built substantial authority to act to secure rights. But to this day, nothing in the Constitution requires Congress to enact such legislation. Congress is perhaps empowered but it is not required to secure life, liberty, property or my pursuit of happiness against interference by officials or by my neighbor.†

*The powers given to Congress were essentially union-related, e.g., the power to regulate interstate commerce, to establish a uniform naturalization law, to declare war. The President was given the power to make treaties.

†Congressional attempts to strengthen the right to vote by extending it to eighteen-year-olds were held beyond the power of Congress and required constitutional amendment. And Congress, it was held, could not secure rights against private invasions. See *Oregon v. Mitchell*, 400 U.S. 112; *Civil Rights Cases*, 109 U.S. 3 (1883).

The purposes of state government were not part of our national constitutional jurisprudence. The United States Constitution has imposed numerous limitations on the states, but it has not been held to require a state to act affirmatively to live up to its Jeffersonian purpose of safeguarding individual rights. In general, our constitutional jurisprudence does not recognize an affirmative obligation on the state, supported by judicial remedy, to provide police protection, pass laws, create institutions, appropriate money or do whatever else is necessary "to secure these rights."[32]

Jefferson's view of the purposes of government, I have suggested, may have had limiting implications as well. If government is instituted only to secure rights, arguably its coercive authority is not to be used for other purposes. If the purpose of legislation must be "rights-related," the Supreme Court's decision in the abortion cases, for example, can be seen as protecting a woman's inherent retained autonomy where the state could not show an authentic rights purpose, a countervailing right of a living person (the fetus not being accepted as a "person" having rights). Similarly, if government may act only to secure rights, may it use coercive authority to protect us from ourselves, say by forbidding smoking, by requiring motorcyclists to wear helmets, by preventing suicide? Is it securing rights when it forbids other "victimless" acts—where the participants are consenting adults? Or does Jefferson's principle imply a "harm principle"—government may act only to secure another's rights from harm?* These and similar issues continue to trouble our constitutional law, but Jeffersonian theory has not been explored in resolving them.

For Jefferson, I have said, the poor had no *right* to be free from want. A different question is whether the founding generation, in their social compact, saw relieving want—providing food, housing, health care, education—as proper purposes of government. In their tradition, I think, feeding the needy was charity. Even for those who saw it as a moral duty to give charity, it was an "imperfect," indeterminate obligation; no person was morally obliged to give charity to any particular other person.† If the implication of that moral stance is that it is therefore not within the social contract for government to tax one individual for the purpose of saving another's life or for meeting his or her other basis needs, we have come a long way from that moral view and that social contract.‡ Public spending to feed the starving, or even for lesser needs, for

---

*This was expressly provided in the French Declaration of the Rights of Man and of the Citizen, proclaimed in 1789 when Jefferson was in Paris (Arts. 4 and 5). The requirement of a rights-related purpose may have implications for theories of punishment. A state may punish those who have violated the rights of others so as to prevent them from doing so again, to rehabilitate them, or to deter them and others. But is the state acting to secure anyone's rights when the purpose of punishment is wholly retributive?

†The Anglo-American moral (and legal) tradition has not imposed a general obligation even to save life, and society has not punished or applied other sanctions against one who fails to do so. One has no obligation to save a drowning man, even if one can do so without any undue risk or at no undue cost; there is no obligation, *a fortiori,* to shelter, cure, educate. The Good Samaritan is a volunteer; Anglo-American law imposes no legal obligation to be a Good Samaritan. See also Introduction and essay 3.

‡The Supreme Court has refused to address the moral question (raised in the guise of

health care and education, has long been upheld as within the legislative power of the states, and within the taxing-spending power of Congress. Have we simply construed constitutional language (the spending power) without the social contract in mind, finding in it purposes of government to which there has in fact been no consent? Or have we recognized that our social compact is not as limited as Jefferson's perhaps was, that under the contemporary social compact the accepted purposes of government are larger than they were in the eighteenth century because our moral intuitions have developed?

At the least, if social welfare is charity, we have long ago accepted that giving such charity is "for the general welfare," that the social contract authorizes government to give such charity, and that the people have agreed to be taxed for that purpose. Today it is plausible even to suggest that welfare needs are not charity but a matter of individual entitlement and corresponding obligation. If the obligation falls not on any one of us, it is the obligation of all of us together, and the social contract includes as a purpose of government the carrying out of the moral obligations of the people, of the society as a whole. If so, welfare spending is not merely constitutionally permissible, but is a constitutional obligation of government.* It is a different question how such a communal obligation, and possible remedies for fulfilling it, fit within our constitutional jurisprudence; whether it is a federal or state responsibility, whether and how courts should enforce the obligation. But the purposes of government are the concern of those who govern, and of the citizen. Whether or not the courts find a constitutional right and a judicial remedy, the people, for half a century, have recognized that the needy are entitled, have a moral right, a claim upon the community for necessary assistance to meet their basic needs, and that there is now consent to be taxed to carry out that indeterminate, communal obligation. Our social compact today, I believe, accepts a broader purpose for government, including the promotion of "the general welfare," conceived as larger than the sum of particular rights narrowly conceived.†

---

invoking the due process clause), saying that taxpayers have no standing to know. See *Frothingham v. Mellon,* 262 U.S. 447 (1923).

* Doubtless influenced by the international human rights idea, the draft Constitution voted by the citizens of the District of Columbia for their proposed new state would establish at least some social welfare as a responsibility of the state. Provisions in existing state constitutions have been interpreted as requiring the state to provide some welfare benefits. See, e.g., *Tucker v. Toya,* 43 N.Y.2d 1 (1977).

† Attention to the purposes of government might have given a different focus to *Lochner* (*Lochner v. New York,* 198 U.S. 45 (1905), and spared us thirty years of that misguided doctrine. The State of New York had enacted a statute forbidding bakers to work more than ten hours a day or sixty hours a week. The United States Supreme Court held that the legislature violated a baker's freedom of contract and therefore deprived him of liberty without due process of law. But the Court did not ask whether that invasion of liberty—regulation to protect an individual against the pressures of poverty on his liberty, and the consequences of such not-so-free contracts in a competitive economy—was within the purposes of government that the people accepted in their social compact and in respect of which they had consented to incidental invasions of their autonomy. Instead, without consideration, the Court apparently assumed the contrary—that economic laissez-faire was a fundamental principle of the social compact, and that economic regulation was not a legitimate purpose of government—a view

A focus on the purposes of government might also help rationalize our jurisprudence of rights in relation to public interests. Government may invade "preferred freedoms," or distinguish on the basis of suspect classifications in respect of fundamental rights, only where the state interest is "compelling," but we have not developed a calculus of "compelling interests" and such a calculus might well be related to the purposes of government under the social compact.[33]

The purposes of government, and the rights sacrificed to them, determine also the rights retained, and a theory of the purposes of government may cast light also on rights that cannot be invaded regardless of purpose. Both public purpose and retained rights may be informed by the moral assumptions of the social compact. What rights were retained, what hard core of individual autonomy, privacy, integrity, dignity, cannot be invaded regardless of public purpose?*

JEFFERSONIAN THEORY AND CONSTITUTIONAL REMEDIES

The political theory of American constitutionalism sees the Constitution as social compact. I know of no other theory better to explain, or justify, or legitimate treating the Constitution today as higher law, limiting democracy and representative government.

The Constitution as social compact requires a contemporary compact by the people today. It is not satisfied by ancient wisdom, no matter how worship-worthy the ancestors or how wise their prescriptions. American constitutionalism does not accept the social compact of two hundred years ago unless the people today reaffirm and adopt that compact as their own. In fact, as we know, there has been no constitutional convention since the first one, and nothing that could indisputably be deemed a constitutive expression by the people that could substitute for such a convention.† It may be that the people of each succeeding generation have not had confidence in their ability to reconstitute themselves anew more wisely. Perhaps they would rather leave well enough alone; perhaps they have not thought about it or wished to be bothered. Perhaps, then, we may accept even unconsidered acquiescence as tacit reaffirmation of the original compact.

Yet the Constitution we have is less than adequate as the expression of our contemporary social compact. The Constitution does not contain even all that the founders believed to be essential in a social compact, the principles proclaimed in the Declaration of Independence and ordained in early state constitu-

---

for which there was no support in the original social compacts, state or federal, or any basis in any updated social compact tacitly adopted by the people in 1905 (when *Lochner* was decided).

*Was there consent—is consent effective—for government to resort to torture, whatever the purpose or interest? Is it permissible to sacrifice some for all for any purpose—as in war? If so, must it be by lottery or pursuant to some other "neutral principle" of selection?

†For Jefferson, then or now, a constitutive expression is not to be confused with what legislators enacted in the past or even what they enact today.

tions. The Constitution does not contain what, I believe, the people today would consider also essential to their social compact—a commitment by government not only to respect individual rights but to secure and promote them, and a clearer, longer list of retained rights including rights to freedom from fear and to freedom from want.

The failure of the founders to include all of their social compact in the constitutional text that they have bequeathed to us has resulted in a constitutional jurisprudence that does not measure up to the underlying principles of constitutional government and does not support the continuing legitimacy of the Constitution as a social compact. I do not fault the founders:* It might have been impossible to put into the Constitution even what a decade earlier had been readily, enthusiastically, written into state constitutions. Surely, any inkling that what was being created in Philadelphia in 1787 was a real government, with direct relations to the people, would have caused the Constitution to be rejected by the many who were jealous for the autonomy of their state polities.

I do not fault the courts: judicial review might not have survived if the courts did not root themselves, stick to, or at least purport to stick to, the ancient sanctified text, and to the traditional judicial context and remedies. Having moored themselves to text and the interpretive process, perhaps—in general— their principal readings of the Bill of Rights and the Fourteenth Amendment were not only necessary but proper and desirable, the moral imperative of fidelity to the laws of interpretation and of judicial process.

Perhaps, too, the courts would not have done better with their difficult task if they became entangled in political theory and morality, ours or that of our ancestors. What *is* in our contemporary social compact, what *are* the rights we now wish to retain, what *are* the purposes of government we now accept and for which we now delegate authority? Perhaps, then, the social compact had better be left to rhetoric or to political theory rather than to constitutional law. Perhaps, retained rights are too open-ended a mandate for a judiciary, especially now that we are a democracy and courts now sit in judgment on more authentic representatives of a whole people.

Jefferson's theory of compact, consent, retained rights, and the purposes of government, and its moral assumptions and underpinnings, may not, then, provide answers to all our jurisprudential uncertainties. They are nevertheless, I believe, useful, relevant and legitimate stuff for the development of that jurisprudence. If the courts are firmly committed to applying only the written Constitution, that Constitution includes the Ninth Amendment, and the due process clauses that have become surrogate for it; and Jeffersonian theory, brought up to date, is legitimate and relevant to the interpretation of those clauses and of rights generally.† If it is too late for the courts to begin to find constitutional protection

---

*In a famous compliment Gladstone saw the Constitution as "the most wonderful work ever struck off at a given time by the brain and purpose of man." The Constitution has proved to be a marvelous achievement and has served incredibly well, though it was not the realization of an ideal plan, but, what Charles and Mary Beard called a "mosaic of their second choices." See essay 7, n. 2.

†The new right of privacy, for instance, can be authentically supported as a zone of retained

and constitutional remedies for private violations of rights, the social compact helps provide a firmer basis for Congressional legislation against such private invasion of rights.*

The theory of rights, and its primacy in the social compact, are relevant also to our conception of the institutions to whose care our rights are entrusted. Jefferson and his fellow constitution-makers counted most on separation of powers, checks and balances, and federalism to maintain the compact and preserve rights; and although the influence of these political arrangements is inevitably ambiguous, undramatic and difficult to prove, there is little reason to doubt that they remain a bulwark against tyranny.† The evidence is clear that our ancestors contemplated also some role for the courts; in any event, judicial review is now established as the principal remedy for monitoring the constitutional compact. For Marshall judicial review was (or was made to appear) a distasteful function, inevitable because incidental to a court's obligation to decide a case; for us, although that function continues to be wrapped in the general judicial power of deciding cases or controversies, judicial review is now intrinsic to our idea of rights and essential to its realization, our hallmark and pride and a source of envy around the world.

For me, that means that all efforts to limit the role of courts in ensuring respect for rights go counter to our rights theory and are violative of our deepest values. This includes threats by Congress to curtail or hamper the jurisdiction of the courts in rights cases; our idea of rights requires rather enhancing judicial competence, wisdom, independence—and the responsibility of Congress, the President, the Senate, is to assure and protect that judicial role. Also unfortunate have been cyclical dispositions by the courts themselves to limit their role in adjudication of rights. I do not suggest that one can, or should, readily convert our courts into "constitutional courts," free of limitations of case or controversy and of some of the prudential reasons the Supreme Court has developed for not hearing cases; but in rights cases they are to be resisted and limited.‡

I do not except from my concern for the judicial remedy the recurrent debates about the legitimacy of judicial review in a democratic society. In those debates one misses close attention to our constitutional theory. To the framers, the fact that judicial review was undemocratic was not critical, indeed hardly relevant: the founders were republicans not democrats. Surely then, but even now, major-

---

autonomy not submitted to governmental control, surely not to public purposes that are not rights-related.

*Attention to social compact might have given the courts a more receptive perspective on the legitimacy of Congressional efforts to regulate campaign spending, to prevent what is in effect a property requirement for holding office never contemplated by our ancestors—as we had finally eliminated their property requirement for voting.

†The lesson of Watergate is one dramatic proof.

‡In particular, there is little justification or excuse for the "political question doctrine" as a reason not to decide a rights issue. See Henkin, "Is There a 'Political Question' Doctrine?" 85 *Yale L. J.* 597 (1976). In rights cases that doctrine effectively denies a remedy, a basic element of the idea of rights. In general, also, the rights idea so depends on the judiciary as to require less concern with the niceties of old equity practice, deriving from a tradition that did not count on the judiciary to vindicate rights against government, and to warrant greater imagination in the use of remedies by state as by federal courts, under state and federal constitutions.

ity rule is not the all of our constitutionalism; individual freedoms antecede, and are the condition of, popular government. Judicial independence, judicial review, judicial supremacy, have prevailed *because* they are nondemocratic, even antidemocratic.* Judicial review is functionally justified today because it is necessary to vindicate the rights retained against majority government, which now, as two hundred years ago, are a cornerstone, I dare say *the* cornerstone, of our constitutionalism. If that role, inevitably, gives the courts supremacy and finality—infallibility†—which is subject to abuse, one might ask whether it is worth the price. But whether it is or not, it is an authentic, homegrown response to the needs of our conception of rights.

Indeed, from the perspective of Jeffersonian principle, the debate about the democratic character of judicial review misconceives the character of the American commitment to constitutionalism and popular sovereignty. As was clear in the beginning, "the people" appear in our political theory at two different times in two distinct roles. In 1787 the people ordained the Constitution, making the social compact: they constituted the government, fixed its purposes, defined its authority, determined what rights they retained. Later, continuously, the people have governed through their chosen representatives, under the Constitution. The people as "governors," then, were to be limited by what the people as "constitutors" had concluded in the social compact. The people as governors act through the legislature and executive; the courts have become the surrogates for the people as constitutors. Contemporary invocations of democracy to decry judicial review turn Jeffersonian principles on their head. They exalt the people as governors over—and to the exclusion of—the people as constitutors. In effect, they embrace democracy and reject constitutionalism.

For Jeffersonians, the authentic issue today is not the democratic character of judicial review; it is, rather, the more profoundly revolutionary one—the continuing legitimacy of the Constitution. Is the constitutional text the expression of the will of the people today in their fundamental and superior role as constitutors? Jeffersonian principles warrant the courts in sticking to the text only to the extent that it is found to be the contemporary social contract. It is a constitution the courts are expounding, but it is *our* constitution they are expounding. The question is not whether the courts may deviate from the ancestral text, but perhaps whether they *must* do so, in favor of what the people wish to have in their social compact today, reflecting their conceptions of the purposes of

---

*The "nondemocratic" character of the judiciary is commonly exaggerated and misconceived. Appointed by the President with the consent of the Senate, the federal judiciary is no less democratic than the executive branch, including the heads of executive departments, the administrative agencies, and their millions of employees. In the framers' conception, the President himself was not to be elected by the people. The "democratic" argument against judicial review applies particularly to the courts' power to invalidate legislation enacted by elected representatives, but judicial review of legislation was probably seen as a form of checks and balances, like the presidential veto, which is also in the hands of one who—originally, surely—was not elected by the people.

†"We are not final because we are infallible, but we are infallible only because we are final." Justice Jackson, concurring, in *Brown v. Allen,* 344 U.S. 443, 540 (1953).

government, of delegated authority, of retained rights. If that is too radical, too daring a question for courts to entertain, if for practical-political reasons they must assume the continued legitimacy of the Constitution as the contemporary social compact until the people as constitutors tell them otherwise, theory suggests that courts might reach for the tacit revisions in the dispositions and underlying moral assumptions of "We the people" as best as they can be determined, at least where lacunae and ambiguities in the text permit, perhaps by way of the due process clauses as they have come to be.

Recourse to the theory of rights should also caution us against total and exclusive preoccupation with and reliance on the judicial remedy. As it has become, the judicial remedy against governmental violation of rights is strong and effective, but it is a limited remedy. It is limited by the judicial commitment to a defective constitutional text. It is limited by the nature of the judicial process, by political-institutional considerations, and a prudential jurisprudence developed by the courts for not hearing cases.[34] It is limited because courts are not legislatures and cannot supply the kind of support for rights that requires legislation. But legislative support for rights in the United States has also suffered from neglect of the theory of our rights. Because rights were not an original responsibility of Congress under the Constitution, the courts may have felt compelled to construe narrowly federal responsibility and Congressional authority added by amendment.* But if the Constitution is what the courts say it is for their purposes, the constitutional text, I have suggested, is not the whole of our social compact for other purposes of government. The inadequacy of text does not vitiate or impair obligations under the underlying social contract, neither the responsibilities of government nor individual obligations as parties to the compact and as constituents of the people. If the powers of Congress were once deemed limited by the text, the obligations of Congress within their powers are not so limited; and, in fact, we know that Congressional power has proved to be sufficient when it chose to act. If courts cannot lightly invoke our uncertain contemporary social compact to frustrate democratic decision, the political branches can readily invoke it to support decisions that reflect that compact. If the courts cannot determine the terms of that contemporary social contract, Congress and the state legislatures can make such determinations for their purposes. It is for political society, for government, for the people to whom government is accountable, to assure the obligations of that compact, obligations of action as well as inaction. Government—and citizens—must indeed refrain from violating rights, must respect autonomy, freedoms, immunities. But government must also act affirmatively to "secure," to ensure, individual rights. Government—federal and state—must pass laws, create institutions, appropriate funds, to enable each of us to exercise his or her part in self-government and to make it effective; to secure life, liberty and the pursuit of happiness for all equally, against private violations as well as against corrupt officials, as by civil rights legislation; to

---

* Particularly the Fourteenth Amendment in the wake of the Civil War. See *Civil Rights Cases,* 109 U.S. 3 (1883).

carry out the communal obligations to assure life and basic needs for all, so all can maintain liberty and a minimum of equal dignity, and pursue happiness.

Fidelity to Jefferson would also require that Congress and state legislatures read rights back into legislative purposes and responsibilities. It makes a difference whether government is intent on securing individual rights, or on some general welfare of some larger entity, the state or the nation; it makes a difference whether we focus on democracy or on individual rights. Both are part of our social compact, but we begin with rights; democracy, too, is subject to rights; its purpose is to promote rights. At all times, state governments, with or without federal compulsion or prodding, have their own responsibility to secure rights under their state compacts. Recalling that state constitutions were the authentic embodiments of the political and moral principles of the founding generation, one can properly look to the states, which can more easily update their constitutions, more fully articulate rights, provide more powerful remedies.

At the least, I am persuaded, some conceptualization of constitutional jurisprudence will make it more coherent—even if we call much of it interpretation of the due process clause. And greater articulation would render it more acceptable. It may enlighten philosophers as well as budgeteers as to what are our authentic values, which are the proper choices when hard choices are to be made. It would, I think, give Jefferson his due, bring our Constitution back to its roots in the Declaration of Independence, justifying our living by and celebrating our two-hundred-year-old Constitution.

7

Constitutional Rights—
Two Hundred Years Later

THE United States is commonly acknowledged to be a country in which individual rights—human rights—are effectively safeguarded against abuse by government, and the United States Constitution is commonly exalted as the instrument of that protection. Yet one who reads the Constitution, which is being celebrated this year (surely the foreign reader), might be hard put to find the source and the basis of that reputation.

In this essay I suggest, in brief compass, how the Constitution became the instrument of rights we know today. I venture an explanation of the "defective" condition of the constitutional text; describe the constitutional idea of rights and its jurisprudential consequences; trace the development of its content and of the institutions that give it effect; and appraise their strengths and deficiencies to the contemporary eye.

RIGHTS AND THE ORIGINS OF
THE CONSTITUTION

The instrument that was signed in Philadelphia in September 1787 contained no reference to the idea of rights, and mentions hardly any of the human rights

From *The United States Constitution: The First Two Hundred Years*, R. C. Simmons, ed., Manchester; Manchester University Press, in association with the Fulbright Commission, London (1989).

recognized and valued today. A bill of rights was added by amendment in 1791 but it suffered glaring deficiencies. Additional amendments during the intervening centuries added some guarantees for rights, but on its face the Constitution today still has serious inadequacies by contemporary human rights standards. Neither the Philadelphia text nor the amendments appear to provide for institutions and procedures designed particularly to ensure respect for individual rights, and even the acute reader is not likely to perceive whether and how such respect is ensured.

I have offered one explanation for inadequacies in the constitutional text as it relates to rights, part of a larger observation about the "genetic defects" of the Constitution due to its origins, purpose and design.[1]

In 1776, independence from Great Britain brought two related but different developments, statehood and union. With independence, the thirteen colonies became thirteen states, created in the spirit of and pursuant to the political theory articulated in the Declaration of Independence. Each state had a constitution, including—indeed, in some cases beginning with—a bill of rights.

The states might have remained thirteen independent states, but from the beginning they saw themselves as constituting "the American nation" and they contemplated political union of some kind.* The first attempt at union, represented by the Articles of Confederation, proved less than satisfactory. Therefore, delegates came to Philadelphia in 1787 to amend the Articles so as to improve the Union. Instead of amending the Articles, they produced the Constitution of the United States, replacing the confederation of states with a single federal state by erecting a national government above the state governments.

In Philadelphia, in 1787, at what came to be called the Constitutional Convention, the focus was not on principles of government and the relation of the individual to society, but on the needs and uses of union. The dispositions of the new Constitution addressed problems of union, not of governance generally. The new union was to have a "government," but it was not to be a complete government, or even the principal government on the American continent, but a small, partial, supplementary segment of government. The new federal government was to have power to address problems of union, of interstate and foreign relations; internal governance, and the relation of government to the individual, were to remain the province of the states. The new Constitution did not replace, subsume, or modify the state constitutions and the state governments; only the *links between* states were transformed into a small superstructure of government over, and above, the state governments, "to form a more perfect union" (Preamble, U.S. Constitution).

And so, one may say, the state constitutions descended from the Declaration and its principles of self-government, whereas the United States Constitution descended from the Articles and its concerns with union. American principles of government, American constitutionalism, were alive and well-formed before confederation, and they remained largely unaffected by it. In principle, and

---

* On the same day in June 1776 on which a committee was appointed to draft a declaration of independence, another committee was appointed to draft articles of union.

perhaps in fact, constitutional government would have remained alive and well had the new-born states abandoned the effort to confederate and gone thirteen separate ways; had they become two or three confederacies (instead of one); or had confederation survived and succeeded under the Articles, and the Constitution never been born.

This brief genealogical excursion may explain why, unlike the Declaration of Independence and the state constitutions, the United States Constitution articulates no political theory and contains little political rhetoric. All the political theory in the Constitution is that implied in the fact of a written constitution, and in the words "We the people . . . ordain this Constitution." All the rhetoric is in a few borrowed, undefined references to "Justice" and the "Blessings of Liberty." Powers were allocated to different, more-or-less separate, branches of the new government, but there is no articulation and justification of the philosophy of separation-of-powers.* Even federalism, which was, of course, original, is not articulated or justified in principle, and owed less to Locke and Montesquieu than to the small experience of our ancestors, to their fears and needs, and to their political compromises.[2] There was no bill of rights—of course: individual rights were not implicated in the issues of union that were the concern of the new superstructure of government.

The Bill of Rights was added by constitutional amendment, as had been promised in order to achieve ratification, but those Amendments did not include a theory of government, or even a theory of rights.† And it was hardly a complete bill: it guaranteed a few rights the colonists had enjoyed as Englishmen and that they wished to secure against the new government; it guaranteed a few rights the colonists had not had under English rule but that they now wished to secure. The amendments did not include many basic personal and civil rights; even its principal preoccupation, the guarantee of fair criminal process, was incomplete and some of the provisions included are ambiguous.

Two hundred years later, the same United States Constitution serves what has become a real government, for many purposes *the* real government in the country, enjoying large, dominant, supreme power. But the Constitution has not been replaced, enlarged, or even significantly amended for that new role. Some of the genetic defects were corrected by later amendments; most of them were not. In the course of history, additional rights were recognized, some rights were extended—and some narrowed—by construction and interpretation. A theory of rights was not developed, and theory has remained largely irrelevant to constitutional jurisprudence.

---

* As there is in the early Virginia and Massachusetts constitutions.

† Even with the Bill of Rights the United States Constitution lacked much of what we identify with American constitutionalism. It took nationalizing influences in American life, legitimized by nationalistic interpretations of the Constitution; it took the Civil War, and the constitutional amendments that constituted the peace treaty ending it; it took another American contribution—the Supreme Court—to establish the United States Government, the United States Constitution, and especially American constitutional rights, as we know them today.

NATURAL RIGHTS AND CONSTITUTIONAL RIGHTS

Those who framed the United States Constitution were committed to the idea of rights as expressed in the Declaration of Independence of 1776 and in early state constitutions.* All men—human beings, female as well as male—are equally endowed by their Creator with certain unalienable rights, among them life, liberty, and the pursuit of happiness. Human beings come together in society and institute government to secure those rights. Government derives its legitimacy from the sovereignty of the people and maintains legitimacy by the consent of the governed. The legitimacy of a government and the conditions under which it governs are best confirmed by a written constitution, a social contract ordained and established by the people. The people delegate to the government the authority it needs for the purpose of governing, but the people —and every individual—retain rights that government must respect. The idea of rights implies limitations on government, even on the people's representatives. The rights retained include a right to continuing self–government—to be governed by representatives chosen by popular suffrage and accountable through periodic elections. The constitution can be terminated or replaced by the people, but it, and the rights it protects, cannot be suspended by the government.

That idea of rights was expressed and given effect in the constitutions of the states established in 1776 and thereafter. Each constitution derived its authority from the people of the particular state. Each state constitution reflected the idea of rights and committed the state government to respect those rights. The United States Constitution, as drafted in 1787, did not include a bill of rights.† The dominant view at the Constitutional Convention was that a bill of rights was not necessary. The new federal government to be created pursuant to the Constitution would not have powers that might impinge on individual rights. Individuals would continue to have their principal relations to the state in which they resided, and their endowed rights would be protected by the state constitution and by state institutions. Some of the framers also thought, apparently, that bills of rights were not necessary or desirable generally: individual rights would be safeguarded by the institutions and the arrangements that the Constitution established.[3]

The arguments against including a bill of rights proved not to be persuasive and, as a condition of ratifying the Constitution, strong sentiment demanded a promise that a bill of rights would be added. A series of constitutional amendments, which came to be known as the Bill of Rights, was adopted in 1791. Those amendments do not express, but clearly reflect, the idea of rights ex-

---

*For a fuller exposition of the idea of rights as exemplified in the Declaration of Independence, see essay 6.

† It forbids bills of attainder and ex post facto laws (Article I, section 9), and guarantees jury trial in the federal courts (Article III, section 2), but does not refer to any of the prominent freedoms most valued then or now.

pressed in the Declaration of Independence. The Bill of Rights did not grant rights; it took them as granted. "Congress shall make no law abridging *the* [pre-existing] *freedom*" of religion, speech, press, assembly. *"The* [pre-existing] *right* of the people to be secure" against unreasonable searches and seizures shall not be violated. The Ninth Amendment made clear that rights anteceded and were independent of the Constitution: "The enumeration in the Constitution of certain rights shall not be construed to deny or disparage others retained by the people."

In principle, then, an individual's rights do not derive from the Constitution, do not depend on their enumeration in the Constitution, and are not limited to those enumerated there. But two hundred years have brought the conception of "constitutional rights"—rights rooted in and guaranteed by the Constitution— with attendant consequences. Rights are constitutional in the sense that the Constitution and the Bill of Rights confirm the idea of rights and enumerate some of them. The people of the generation that ordained and established the Constitution exercised and confirmed *their* endowed rights as they instituted government to secure those rights. For those who were born or who came later, their rights anteceded the Constitution only in a theoretical sense: the Constitution already existed and it confirmed their antecedent rights.

Rights are constitutional also in the sense that the Constitution gave them new applications. Before the Constitution, there was no federal government and, of course, an individual's rights could not be claims upon such government. Under the Constitution, a federal government was established, and the Constitution and the Bill of Rights recognized and guaranteed the individual's endowed rights as limitations on the authority of that government. On the other hand, rights against one's neighbor, or—with minor exceptions—against state and local governments or officials, remained outside the purview of the United States Constitution.

The constitutional character of rights was confirmed when the courts became the principal guardians of individual rights. The jurisdiction of the federal courts is limited, for our purposes, to cases and controversies "arising under this Constitution." (U.S. Constitution, Article III, section 2). The courts have seen their responsibility as that of safeguarding only rights referred to in the Constitution; the courts have been reluctant to enforce natural rights ("endowed by their Creator") not cited in the Constitution. They have been unwilling even to identify and give effect to the retained rights reserved by the Ninth Amendment. Even enumerated rights are protected by the courts only to the extent provided or contemplated by the Constitution, that is, against violation by the government ("state action"), not by private persons. However, the courts have found and protected (against state action) rights implied in a broad conception of "liberty" of which a person may not be deprived without "due process of law."

The "constitutionalization" of rights may have also brought some modification in the conception of rights as they relate to the public interest. Under Jefferson's principles, the people give up some of their antecedent rights to the government for the purposes for which it is instituted; all other rights are retained. Even rights that are subjected to the authority of government are sacrificed only to the extent necessary for legitimate governmental purposes. It is not clear whether for Jefferson any rights are retained "absolutely," whether any right is wholly excluded from invasion by governmental authority, even for legitimate public purposes. It has been suggested that, originally, some rights— such as the freedom of speech or the free exercise of religion—were narrowly defined and as so defined were absolute. Today, surely, rights under the Constitution are generally seen as not absolute.[4] Even the fundamental freedoms of speech, press, religion, and assembly guaranteed by the First Amendment might be sacrificed to compelling public interests.* Some balancing of individual right and public interest is also clearly implied insofar as life, liberty, or property is subject to be taken by "due" process of law, as search and seizure is permitted if it is not "unreasonable," or punishment if it is not "cruel and unusual."

RIGHTS GUARANTEED BY THE CONSTITUTION

The Bill of Rights guarantees the freedoms of speech, press, religion and assembly (Amendment I), and the security of the person and his home, papers and effects against unreasonable search and seizure (Amendment IV). The federal government may not deprive a person of life, liberty or property without due process of law, or take a person's property for public use without just compensation (Amendment V). A person accused of crime by federal authorities is guaranteed a speedy public trial by jury, with counsel. The accused enjoys a privilege against self-incrimination, and a right to be confronted with witnesses against him and to have compulsory process for obtaining witnesses in his favor (Amendments V–VI). The accused may not be put in jeopardy twice for the same offense (Amendment V). Excessive bail may not be required, and a convicted person may not be subjected to excessive fines or to cruel and unusual punishment (Amendment VIII).

The Bill of Rights had notorious lacunae. It did not abolish slavery or guarantee freedom from slavery or from involuntary servitude in the future. It did not forbid the federal government to practice racial or other invidious discrimination: the commitment to equality, prominent in the Declaration of Independence, was not in the Constitution of 1787 and was not in the Bill of Rights. The Bill of Rights did not guarantee the right fundamental to the Jeffersonian conception, the right to vote.† There is not even a constitutional right, surely not an enforceable right, to have government secure the individual's life, liberty, or pursuit of happiness,[5] the purposes for which, Jefferson said,

---

* See the discussion later in this chapter.

† Under the Constitution, suffrage was originally accorded only for the purpose of electing members of the House of Representatives. Even that right was restricted to persons who enjoyed the right to vote for the most numerous branch of the legislature of the state in which they resided (Article I, section 2).

government is instituted: a person cannot make a constitutional claim that he has not been provided adequate police protection, or security against an external enemy.*

Even the safeguards against arbitrary detention and police abuse, and the guarantees of fair criminal process, were insufficient. The Constitution provides that the privilege of the writ of habeas corpus may not be suspended except in limited circumstances,† but the uses of the writ are not otherwise guaranteed, and the grounds that permit detention are not indicated in the Constitution. The Bill of Rights does not declare the presumption of innocence or require that a jury determine guilt beyond a reasonable doubt. The Fourth Amendment forbids unreasonable search and seizure but does not declare the consequences of such illegal police activity. The Fifth Amendment provides that a person shall not be compelled to be a witness against himself, and the Eighth Amendment bars cruel and unusual punishment, but nothing in those amendments (or elsewhere in the Constitution) prohibits torture or other inhuman treatment by the police other than as punishment or for the purpose of inducing a confession. An accused enjoys the right to have the assistance of counsel for his defense, but it is not clear that the framers contemplated that counsel must be provided to those who cannot provide their own.

With minor exceptions,‡ the original Constitution did not protect against violations of rights by the states; the Bill of Rights, too, when adopted, applied only to the federal government.[6] And Congress had no authority to provide protection against state infringement of individual rights by legislation. State constitutions and state laws protected rights against infringement by state officials, but those rights were not governed by the United States Constitution, and were not enforced by federal law or monitored by the federal courts.

Constitutional protection for individual rights was increased in major respects following the Civil War. The "peace treaty" of that war took the form of three constitutional amendments. The Thirteenth Amendment outlawed slavery. The Fourteenth Amendment established the right to United States citizenship, and provided that no state shall abridge the privileges and immunities of such citizenship, or deprive any person of life, liberty, or property without due process of law, or deny any person the equal protection of the laws. By the Fifteenth Amendment the right to vote cannot be denied on account of race. The principal provisions of the Fourteenth Amendment provide national protection for specified rights against their violation by the states: the federal courts could monitor

---

* By today's standards the Bill of Rights was deficient in that it safeguarded only "negative" rights—"freedom from, freedom to"—the rights of man as they existed "in the state of nature," before government. There was no right to social or economic benefits—no guarantee of a person's basic human needs, no right to education, to social security, to health care.

† Under the United States Constitution, only the privilege of the writ of habeas corpus can be suspended, and only in case of rebellion or invasion, and—it is accepted—only by Congress (Article I, section 9).

‡ "No State shall . . . pass any Bill of Attainder, *ex post facto* Law, or Law impairing the obligation of Contracts." Article I, section 10. "The Citizens of each State shall be entitled to all Privileges and Immunities of Citizens in the several States." Article IV, section 2.

state compliance with those provisions; Congress was given power to enact laws to enforce them.

During more than a hundred years since that time, there have been no further amendments to extend constitutional safeguards for individual rights, except as regards suffrage. Three amendments (in 1920, 1960, and 1971) forbid denying the right to vote on account of sex or age (for persons over 18) or for failure to pay a tax. For the rest, the Constitution reads today in respect of rights as it did in 1870. And since the principal clauses of the Fourteenth Amendment apply only to the states, as regards the federal government—except for the slavery and the voting amendments, and the clause defining citizenship in the Fourteenth Amendment—the constitutional text has not been changed since the Bill of Rights was adopted in the eighteenth century.

And yet, constitutional rights in the United States have been transformed, and might be unrecognizable to those who framed the Bill of Rights, even to those who framed the Civil War amendments. The development of rights reflects transformations in the life and character of the United States, and the influence of ideas, both indigenous and foreign. A major influence for the development of rights, and an impetus to other forces promoting rights, has been the growth of the role of the courts in interpreting, sometimes reinterpreting, constitutional text. Under judicial aegis, individual rights in the United States have developed directly and indirectly, gradually as well as in quantum leaps, but little of that judicial support for rights and little of the growth of rights occurred before the middle of the twentieth century.

CONSTITUTIONAL RIGHTS BEFORE THE SECOND WORLD WAR

Constitutional rights before the Civil War were not a significant constitutional preoccupation, and the federal courts gave them little support. Toward the end of the eighteenth century, Congress enacted the Alien and Sedition Laws, which were challenged both as being beyond the powers delegated to Congress and as violating rights under the First Amendment, but those laws were short-lived and the Supreme Court did not consider their validity.[7] Those laws apart, Congress exercised little legislative power during that period, and few federal laws impinged on the individual. Of the few constitutional provisions that guaranteed rights against violation by the states, only the clause forbidding impairment of the obligation of contracts was frequently invoked, and commonly by corporations rather than by individuals.[8] For the principal outrage to rights— slavery—the Constitution provided neither remedy nor right. The Constitution maintained slavery; it even required fugitive slaves to be returned.* Indeed, in *Dred Scott,*[9] the Supreme Court, invoking the Fifth Amendment, held that an

---

* See Article IV, section 2. The Constitution also precluded any legislation before 1808 to end the slave trade. See Article I, section 9.

act of Congress that liberated a slave if he had been brought to a "free state" deprived the owner of his property without due process of law.*

A leap in constitutional rights followed the Civil War. The Civil War amendments were a second Bill of Rights, some would say a second Constitution. Those amendments abolished slavery and established basic rights; in their effect, the amendments nationalized individual rights, subjecting the actions of the states—of the Northern victors as of the vanquished South—to federal constitutional limitations, to scrutiny by the federal judiciary, and to protection by act of Congress.

The Civil War amendments, however, did not do all that some desired. They did not clearly incorporate the Bill of Rights and make it applicable to the states. They did not guarantee other civil rights against invasion by the states, or require the states to provide political or economic and social benefits.† The amendments did not apply to the federal government so as to supply some of the deficiencies of the Bill of Rights. Even what the amendments promised, moreover, was less than fully realized. Narrow interpretations reduced their safeguards, as well as the powers of Congress to enforce them. The Supreme Court's construction of the Privileges and Immunities clause of the Fourteenth Amendment reduced that clause to very little.[10] As a result of other narrow constructions of that amendment, principal provisions of the Civil Rights Acts adopted between 1866 and 1875 were held invalid as beyond the powers of Congress.[11]

The end of Reconstruction in 1876 terminated Congressional concern with the rights of blacks, and emboldened states, particularly Southern states, to establish new patterns of violations of rights. During the next half century the Supreme Court invalidated a few blatant racial discriminations, but accepted many subtle ones.[12] In 1896, it held that racial segregation—"separate but equal"—did not deny the equal protection of the laws,[13] a principle that remained constitutional doctrine for more than half a century. What is more, neither Congress nor the courts took steps to assure that separate was in fact equal. Equality suffered, too, as the courts legitimated other traditional, "natural" inequalities, upholding, for example, the authority of the states to exclude women from the practice of law.[14] Efforts to promote what are now called economic and social rights by regulation of wages, hours, and labor relations were held to be beyond the powers of Congress, and forbidden to both federal and state govern-

---

*By today's lights, there were some positive developments during those years. Public education burgeoned and spread under the authority of the states, though these were not conceived as involving rights, surely not rights under the United States Constitution. Congress also developed early a broad conception of "the general welfare" for which it could spend federal funds (Article I, section 8); a century later that conception supported the emergence of the United States as a welfare state, affording what came to be considered by the international community as "economic and social rights." See essay 1.

†Strictly, the Fifteenth Amendment did not even guarantee the right to vote to Blacks. It forbade discrimination against Blacks on account of race. But neither Blacks nor whites had to be given the right to vote; Blacks, like whites, could be denied the right to vote on other grounds. For almost a hundred years, both whites and Blacks could be denied the right to vote if they did not meet property requirements, or failed to pay a poll tax, or were illiterate.

ments—because they were not within the proper purposes of government, because they constituted deprivations of property and infringements of liberty of contract.[15] During and after World War I, narrow readings of the Bill of Rights led the courts to accept stringent limitations on freedom of speech.[16]

CONSTITUTIONAL RIGHTS TODAY*

The rapid growth of human rights in the United States came with the New Deal (1933–1939), and accelerated after World War II. Perhaps under the influence of world events that transformed the United States in many respects, and of a new *Zeitgeist* including the international human rights movement, constitutional rights in the United States were radically modified both in gross and in detail.

Rights in the United States are large and complex, but the Constitution still has the same words with which the United States began, the Bill of Rights has not been formally amended, and even the Fourteenth Amendment seemed to promise only a little. It is easy today to overlook the limited conception of individual rights held by the framers—of 1787 as well as 1868—and the radical transformation in that conception in the latter half of this century.

Originally, the rights declared in the Bill of Rights were essentially political, protecting, it has been said, not the rights of man but the rights of gentlemen. The freedoms put in first place—speech, press, assembly—were seen primarily as political liberties with political purposes; it is open to question whether they sought to safeguard individual "self-expression," or even radical political heresy. Even the guarantee of the free exercise of religion may have reflected a desire to avoid religious hostility more than concern for individual conscience. The "right of the people to be secure . . . against unreasonable searches and seizures," the guarantee of "due process of law," the protection of property against confiscation, the catalogue of safeguards for those who might be accused of crime, were couched as rights of every person, but they seem to have reflected a desire to safeguard the established, respectable citizenry against various known forms of repression by tyrannical governments, rather than tenderness and respect for any individual, even the least worthy. The Civil War amendments, too, were probably not designed to realize radical advances in human rights generally, but only to abolish slavery (as some of the states and other countries had done earlier), establish the citizenship of the former slaves, and remove disabilities and other "badges" of slavery for black citizens.

Today, the conception of rights and the constitutional jurisprudence of rights ring very differently. By radical reinterpretation, the Supreme Court held that the Fourteenth Amendment had effectively incorporated, and rendered applicable to the states, the principal provisions of the Bill of Rights†—freedom of

* In this section I draw on my book *The Rights of Man Today* (1978), ch. 2.
† Incorporation also "homogenized" rights against the federal and state governments, ren-

speech, press, assembly, religion, the security of the home and the person, and virtually every safeguard for persons accused of crime.[17] Now, every state law impinging on important freedoms, and every state criminal trial, is subject to scrutiny by the federal courts. And Congress has the power to protect rights against violation and provide remedies for violations by state legislatures, by state or federal courts or officials.[18]

Even more radical, perhaps, was the expansion of eighteenth-century rights in conception and content. Without formal amendment, the Constitution has been read to protect new rights and old rights newly conceived. The Constitution has been opened to every man and woman, to the least and the worst of them. Constitutional protection has moved beyond political rights to civil and personal rights, rooted in conceptions of the essential dignity and worth of the individual. The Constitution safeguards not only political freedom but, in principle, also social, sexual, and other personal freedoms, and individual privacy, autonomy, idiosyncrasy. Notably:

- Freedom of speech and press now protects advocacy even of radical ideas or expressions that are deeply disturbing or offensive, as long as expressions do not incite to violence or other unlawful action; it protects not only political and religious expression but also economic speech and publication, e.g., labor picketing and commercial advertising, as well as "self-expression" even if it approaches "obscenity."[19] Speech is protected even when it is "symbolic," as in wearing an arm band to protest a war; one's money, too, may talk, without ready limits, as by contributions to political campaigns.[20] The press enjoys freedom far beyond its relevance to the political process. The freedom to publish is now associated with the reader's "right to know"; prior restraint on publication as by censorship, requirement of license, or by injunction is virtually excluded.* The right to publish and the right to know may outweigh also the right of an official or of another "public" person to be free from libel, or the privacy rights of even private persons.[21] Freedom of speech and press includes a right of access to a public forum.[22] It includes also the freedom *not* to speak or publish, to speak and publish anonymously, to be free of governmental inquiry into what one thinks and says.[23] Out of these rights and the right of assembly, the courts have made a right of association, of anonymous association, of nonassociation.[24]

- Freedom of religion means not only that there must be no state interference with, but also no burden on, the free exercise of religion. The prohibition

---

dering the rights essentially the same in every state as they were against the increasingly interventionist federal government. In a separate development the Court in effect held that the equal protection of the laws was required of the federal government as of the states (see text at n. 28 and essay 6 at n. 11).

* *The New York Times* could not be enjoined from publishing confidential official documents relating to the Vietnam War because the Government could not persuade the Supreme Court that there was a compelling need for such prior restraint on publication. See *New York Times v. United States,* 403 U.S. 713 (1971).

on establishing religion requires a wall of separation between church and state. Neither the federal nor the state governments may give financial aid to religious institutions or permit Bible reading or prayer in public schools. Government must not advance or inhibit religion or be excessively entangled with religion.[25]

- Freedom from unreasonable search and seizure applies—though perhaps differently—not only to the home but also to the office and the automobile; not only to physical but also to technological intrusion, e.g., wiretapping; not only to incursions by the police, but also to visits by health and fire inspectors.[26]

- Perhaps the greatest expansion has been in the rights of those accused of crime. The Bill of Rights—its principal provisions applicable also to the states—protects not only the respectable and innocent against the governmental oppressor; even criminals have rights to a fair trial (without improperly obtained evidence), to counsel (provided by the government if the defendant cannot provide his own), to freedom from self-incrimination and from comment on one's failure to testify.[27]

- The equal protection of the laws has also acquired new ramifications. By new interpretation of the due process clause of the Fifth Amendment, the Constitution now effectively requires of the federal government the same equal protection of the laws that the Fourteenth Amendment expressly commanded to the states.[28] All racial classifications—by state or federal government—are suspect, and invidious discrimination on account of race, "whether accomplished ingeniously or ingenuously," is readily rejected.[29] Official separation of the races, even "separate but equal," is outlawed.[30]

- There has been a fundamental and, I believe, irreversible transformation in the constitutional status of women. Discriminations against women on the basis of generalizations reflecting stereotyped and outdated sociological assumptions no longer seem "natural" and inevitable, and are invalid. And the new equality of the genders entitles males also to freedom from unwarranted discrimination.[31]

- The poor, too, have some rights to equal protection. A state that offers for pay benefits that only the state provides—a criminal appeal, a divorce—must make them available gratis to those who cannot pay.[32]

- Other once-axiomatic inequalities are no longer acceptable. The states cannot deny to aliens welfare benefits, public employment, or admission to the professions; they cannot maintain irrelevant distinctions between legitimate and illegitimate children.[33] Other once-excluded categories are now included: prisoners have rights, as do military personnel, mental patients, pupils in the schools; children have rights independently of and even against their parents.[34]

- In the Constitution now are new rights, for example a right to travel, abroad as well as interstate; a local residence requirement as a condition of enjoying rights or benefits is invalid because it burdens the right to travel.[35]

- In what can be seen as a reversion to the eighteenth-century principle of antecedent natural rights to individual autonomy and liberty, the courts have found an area of fundamental individual autonomy ("privacy"). Hence, the state may not forbid the use of contraceptives, or the resort to abortion in the first trimester of pregnancy, or indulging oneself with obscene materials in private.[36] Parents may send their children to private schools; they may even refuse to send their children to high school at all when to do so would offend their religious scruples.[37]

- Finally, the United States has become a democracy. The indirect election of the President through an electoral college remains in the Constitution (Article II, section 2; Amendment XII) but has been largely reduced to a formality, and the Presidency is now generally responsive to popular suffrage. The Constitution seemed to leave voting qualifications to the states, but later Amendments forbidding the denial of the vote on invidious grounds (race, sex, age, poverty) have supported voting rights legislation that has rendered suffrage virtually universal in fact. In effect, the Supreme Court has built a constitutional right to vote, and a right to a vote of equal weight, out of a few straws, including the right to the equal protection of the laws.[38]

The explosion of rights I have described confirms the essentially open character of the Constitution, and constitutional rights as the fruit of a continuing synthesis of immutable principle with contemporary values both homegrown and imported. Old assumptions are reexamined, stereotypes are penetrated, and rights are accepted today that were not conceived a few decades ago.*

Perhaps the inevitable consequence of expanding and proliferating rights was the clear emergence of the principle of "balancing" individual liberty and public interest to determine the limits of each. The courts do not now attend seriously to objections that economic and social regulation limits individual autonomy or liberty, but in principle all governmental action must justify itself as a means rationally linked to some public purpose.[39] Rights are not absolute, however, and virtually every right might, in some times and circumstances, give way to some other public good. Some individual rights and freedoms, however—speech, press, assembly, religion, old and new privacy, freedom from racial discrimination—are fundamental, preferred; invasions are suspect, will be sharply scrutinized, and will be sustained only for a compelling state interest.†

In the second half of the twentieth century, one constitutional blessing is noteworthy: the constitutional theory of the framers, the institutions they established, the availability of the judiciary to adapt and develop the general principles of the Constitution and to arbitrate political controversy—as well, no doubt, as great good fortune—have saved the United States from extraconstitutional government. There have been no emergency suspensions of the Constitution or of particular rights, such as have bedeviled constitutional government and human

---

*On the horizon may be rights undreamed of—a right to be born and a right to die, and rights for the dead and the unborn.

†The Supreme Court has not done well in justifying the weight it gives to particular rights and has done virtually nothing to explain the weights assigned to different public interests.

rights in other countries. The Constitution does not provide for its own suspension, and that has never been attempted, even in time of war. Habeas corpus was suspended during the Civil War and on two or three other occasions; other rights have been curtailed during war: the relocation of Americans of Japanese ancestry during World War II was an inglorious chapter, held by the courts at the time to be constitutionally permissible.[40] But there have not otherwise been mass detentions or other major derogations from rights.

I have been discussing constitutional rights—the rights Americans enjoy as higher law, regardless of the will of majorities and of their representatives and officials. But, by interpreting the constitutional powers of Congress broadly, the courts have unleashed and encouraged Congress to expand individual rights. The extension of federal power, notably the Commerce Power, has enabled Congress to legislate against private discriminations (e.g., on account of race) and other private infringements.[41] Expansive interpretations of the Civil War amendments have permitted sophisticated legislation to protect the right to vote and to safeguard the exercise of some other rights from official or private interference.[42] Imaginative lawyers and sympathetic courts have found that old civil rights acts give protections against invasions of newly conceived rights,* prohibiting, for example, private discrimination in the sale or rental of housing or in admission to private school.[43]

By contemporary human rights standards, perhaps the most significant legislative extension of rights has been that which, beginning some fifty years ago, brought economic and social "rights" to the inhabitants of the United States. These rights did not come easily. Except for public education provided by the states early, the welfare state began slowly. The United States has become a welfare state not by constitutional imperative or encouragement but, indeed, over strong constitutional resistance. Welfare programs had to overcome resistance to governmental intervention and "activism," resistance that flew the flag of individual autonomy and limited conceptions of government; resistance to various economic regulations, flying the flag of economic liberty; resistance to strong federal government, flying the flag of states' rights; resistance to massive governmental spending based on heavy progressive taxation, flying flags of property, liberty and equality; the Sixteenth Amendment was required to permit a federal progressive income tax, on which the welfare state depends.[44] Only after deep economic depression did traditional fear of government begin to give way to demands upon government—for intensive regulation of business and labor relations, for minimum wages and maximum hours, social security, expanding government employment and government work programs—with constitutional reinterpretations to make them acceptable.

A second world war, decades of technological, political, and social change, and ideas and examples from abroad proliferated welfare programs and magnified

---

*Congress has also created the "right to know" by freedom of information acts. It has extended the right of conscientious objection to military service. It has created rights to a more healthful environment. Federal example has encouraged emulation by the states, and some states have taken such rights further.

them manifold. Economic and social benefits have effectively established equal entitlement as regards minimum basic needs; they have even moved United States society a few steps from equal opportunity to somewhat less inequality in fact. But not being constitutional rights, economic and social entitlements are subject to political and budgetary restraints, sometimes also to recurrent ideological resistance. In the 1980s, the drive for lower taxes and higher defense expenditures, some ideological commitment to "market forces," and some resistance to the welfare state in principle, significantly weakened economic-social "rights" in the United States. But the United States remains a welfare state and welfare programs are likely to increase again.

The 1980s have also seen some regression in constitutional rights. Since the scope and content of rights are ultimately decided by the Supreme Court, they will fluctuate with changes in judicial interpretation. After the luxuriant growth I have described, the Supreme Court entered a period of consolidation and retrenchment, perhaps of reaction. In the 1980s there have been more restrained readings of the Constitution, greater reluctance to increase individual protection, a tendency to give greater scope and weight to public authority, particularly in the criminal process. There are suggestions of greater judicial toleration of state "accommodation" rather than "neutrality" in its relations to religion; the right of privacy has been held not to include the right of adults to engage in private homosexual activity.[45] Some fear that the case upholding the right of a woman to have an abortion may be restricted if not overruled. New fears—increasing crime, spreading AIDS—bring proposals that would threaten established constitutional guarantees, and some of these proposals may be upheld.[46] But whatever the years ahead bring in detail they are not likely to weaken the commitment to individual rights now more than two hundred years old.

The rights of man in the United States, it need hardly be said, are far from perfect. Past sins are grievous and notorious: genocide and lesser violations of the Indian; slavery, racial segregation, and other badges of slavery for blacks; other racial, ethnic, and religious discriminations, including relocations and concentrations of citizens of Japanese ancestry in time of war; Chinese exclusion and other racist immigration laws (see essay 8); postwar anti-Communist hunts, which also "chilled" political freedoms of others; and many more.

If these are for the largest part happily past, there are still racial discriminations and inequalities, at least de facto, and debatable acceptance of instances of private discrimination.[47] Valued freedoms are sometimes empty for those unable or afraid to exercise them, or who are denied access to media that will make them effective or competitive. There is poverty, unemployment (which falls particularly heavily on blacks and other minorities), inadequate housing and health care, even hunger, and there are wider economic inequities and inequalities. Immigration, exclusion, and deportation laws are built on outdated conceptions, such as the absolute right of Congress to exclude and deport.[48] Some object to balancing away rights in principle or to the balance struck in particular instances, say, the preference for the right to know over the right of privacy.[49] Some see violations of rights in laws against obscenity, in other limitations on newspapers and newspapermen, in regulation of other communications media; some have objected to constitutional tolerance of laws against group libel.[50] Some see retrogression in "affirmative action" discrimination in favor of the once-oppressed to the disadvantage of others.[51] Some see failures of rights in excessive toleration, in respecting freedom for those who abuse it, in too much "legalism" at the expense of order, in failing generally to provide freedom from fear. Even where principles are unexceptionable, there are ever-present instances where practice deviates from principle and is not readily remedied; at various times, in various places, there have been accusations and some evidence of "political justice"—denial of due process and equal protection to "leftists," to blacks, to "longhairs," to the deviant, or the stranger. Police abuses are too frequent and notorious, and new technology available to government threatens essential privacy.

But in all, I conclude human rights—civil-political as well as economic-social rights—are alive and reasonably well in the United States.

THE ENFORCEMENT OF RIGHTS:
CONGRESS AND THE COURTS

The framers of the Constitution, including those who appended the Bill of Rights, expected that tyranny and oppression would be avoided by preventing the concentration of political authority. Individual rights would be safeguarded by federalism—by dividing authority between the federal government and the states—and by separation of powers and checks and balances among the branches of the federal government. Secondarily, perhaps, the framers expected that Congress might have power to enact some laws against some abuses of rights, and that the courts would monitor governmental respect for rights in some measure and by some means.

It is difficult to determine to what extent the original expectations have in fact been realized, and how much United States constitutionalism has moved beyond all expectations. Federalism and the separation of powers, though transformed during two hundred years, doubtless continue to prevent the concentration of power and some of the abuses that concentrated power brings. But today, constitutional guarantees rather than institutional arrangements are perceived as the principal safeguards of rights, and the courts are seen as their primary guardians, with Congress in a supporting role. During the eighty years before the Civil War, Congress enacted little that could be characterized as civil rights legislation, perhaps because Congress did not seem to have the power to do so. In the wake of the Civil War, under new powers granted to Congress by the Civil War Amendments, Congressional civil rights acts loomed large, but they were largely nullified by the courts, and Congress did not enact significant civil rights legislation again for a hundred years, until the 1960s.

Today, civil rights laws are important safeguards against executive and police violations. But only the courts can protect against violations by Congress, and the courts monitor and enforce constitutional rights also—indeed principally—against violation by the states, including state legislatures, state executives, state courts. It is not incorrect to conclude that against the bureaucracy, whether state or federal, against state legislation, and to a lesser extent against acts of Congress, individual rights are safeguarded in the United States by an alert, independent judiciary, activated by individuals, public-interest groups and energetic legal professionals.

In enforcing constitutional rights, the courts have also determined their scope and content. In deciding that the Fourteenth Amendment incorporated most of the Bill of Rights, the Supreme Court gave the courts a major role in monitoring the state criminal process as well as state regulation of religion, expression and assembly. The courts read the due process clauses as including substantive as well as procedural limitations, and the rise and fall—and rise—of substantive due process have determined the ebb and flow of judicial enforcement. Periodically, judicial activism encouraged legislative activism, and new—as well as old—civil rights acts in turn gave the courts new opportunities to determine the limits of rights by (or in the guise of) statutory interpretation. Congress has rarely "corrected" judicial interpretation.[52]

Judicial supremacy is established in constitutional jurisprudence and is commonly seen as the hallmark of—and the linchpin of—United States constitutionalism. But to credit the courts with the radical growth of rights in the United States is too simple. Often the courts have merely acquiesced in and legitimated what political authority (both state and federal) had done. The influence of the courts, moreover, has not been constant and linear. During the course of United States history, courts have sometimes construed constitutional safeguards narrowly, reducing the scope of constitutional protection of rights or denying to state or federal legislatures the power to safeguard or promote rights. At different periods, courts have been more activist or more self-restrained, more liberal or more conservative, in their reading and application of the Constitution. But, after two hundred years, the principle of judicial review, and the central part of the courts in the protection of rights, are deeply entrenched. The United States has become a democracy with universal suffrage, but a democracy subject to individual rights; and the courts determine the scope and content of those rights and calibrate the balance betweeen representative government and individual rights.

In the United States, the judicial role in rights enforcement has often been, and in the 1980s is again, a focus of controversy. At the beginning of the twentieth century the Supreme Court earned condemnation for developing substantive due process and equating it with *laissez-faire,* for frustrating representative government and becoming a superlegislature. Retreat during the 1930s was followed after the Second World War by resurgent activism in support of political freedom, self-expression, separation of church and state, safeguards for those accused of crime, racial desegregation, a new zone of autonomy in personal matters such as the freedom of women to seek abortion. In the last decade of the second century under the Constitution, voices are again heard to challenge "government by judiciary," this time voices of a different ideology—the voices of "law and order," and "traditional" values.

The United States is sometimes described as a rights-ridden society. Surely, even as its democracy has improved, the rights of the individual have increased. The mix of democratic-republicanism and individualism are not universally commended or understood. But it remains, I think, an important if idiosyncratic expression by the United States of eighteenth-century ideas adapted to this country's place in the twentieth century. The United States regime of rights is envied and emulated, not always with success, as our idiosyncrasies flourish less well in less-hospitable cultures, in less-fortunate, less-stable societies.

The United States—with France—can lay claim to having launched the idea of rights and helped to give it political expression in national constitutions and in international instruments. The use of courts to monitor the tensions between individual autonomy and public good has been emulated in unlikely places: several European countries have established constitutional courts; France has something like it; the United Kingdom is seriously talking of a bill of rights to be given effect by the courts. International human rights courts and near-courts flourish. The eighteenth-century authors of the Declaration of Independence and the framers of the Constitution, and Thomas Paine, and even John Locke, might not recognize their offspring but they would not be uncomfortable at this two hundredth birthday celebration.

8

The Constitution as Compact and as Conscience: Individual Rights Abroad and at Our Gates

I HAVE chosen to leave the paths commonly trodden by students of the United States Constitution to address several small related subjects that have been largely neglected though they continue to trouble our constitutional jurisprudence. My subjects are:

1. the extent to which the United States Constitution recognizes and protects the rights of aliens in the United States.
2. the applicability of the Constitution to persons outside the United States; and
3. the Constitutional principles governing immigration to, and deportation from, the United States.

The rights of various categories of aliens, and the distinctions we retain between aliens and citizens, continue to raise constitutional issues. Even "undocumented" aliens recently have established new rights for themselves and their children, including the right to free public education.[1] The protections of the Constitution have been claimed by persons outside the United States who are not U.S. nationals—by victims of terrorism attributed to U.S. military forces in Central America, by women in Europe objecting to cruise missiles deployed near their homes, by a Polish refugee tried for hijacking in a United States court convened in Berlin.[2] The Constitution's relevance to immigration now arises in

From 27 *Wm. & Mary L. Rev.* 11 (1985)

federal courts throughout the United States—in Georgia, New York, and even Kansas.[3]

The three issues I shall address are very live. They are implicated daily when the United States takes certain measures, such as the Haitian Interdiction Program[4] to control immigration. Only recently the United States has been charged with discriminating among would-be immigrants present in the United States and with maintaining them in detention only because there is no place to send them.[5] Existing law still permits deporting resident aliens on grounds that could not be a constitutional basis for criminal conviction and punishment.[6]

These three issues have something else in common—the Constitution provides virtually no guidance for their resolution. The Constitution is silent concerning its applicability beyond the borders of the United States. Little is said in the Constitution concerning citizens, and nothing about aliens. As regards immigration, the courts admittedly have built a constitutional jurisprudence wholly on extraconstitutional foundations.[7]

I will suggest that, in the absence of textual guidance, our jurisprudence has looked to the theory of our Constitution as a social compact creating a community of righteousness with a government of conscience. I will also suggest that as to immigration and deportation, however, the existing constitutional doctrine violates that commitment to conscience.

My exploration looks back nearly a century to when the Supreme Court planted many of the seeds from which our constitutional law of individual rights has grown. In particular, I revisit three cases decided by the Court from 1886 to 1891, a scant five years. *Yick Wo v. Hopkins,* "a good old case," established constitutional principles of equality for aliens which still prevail. *In re Ross,* which addressed the Constitution's applicability outside the United States, was abandoned after a reign of nearly seventy years, though its spirit lingers on. *The Chinese Exclusion Case,* fountainhead of our constitutional law regarding immigration, is a "bad old case" crying for reexamination.[8]

CONSTITUTIONAL RIGHTS OF ALIENS IN THE UNITED STATES

The Constitution does not say whether it applies to citizens only or to aliens as well. The original Constitution refers to United States citizenship only as a qualification for the office of President and for service as a member of Congress, and refers to state citizenship only in the provision that requires that citizens of each state be entitled to the privileges and immunities of citizens in the several states.* The Constitution gave Congress the authority to establish a uniform rule of naturalization,† but the definition and the implications of citizenship (other

* Art. II, § 1, cl. 5; Art. I, § 2, cl. 2; Art, I. § 3, cl. 3; Art. IV, § 2, cl. 1.
† Art I, § 8, cl. 4.

than those specified) were uncertain even after Congress enacted the first natu-ralization law.[9]

The right to vote is perhaps the most significant implication of citizenship today, but no constitutional mandate limits that right to citizens. The original Constitution provided the right to vote only for members of the House of Representatives, and even this limited right was available only to individuals eligible to vote for the most numerous branch of their state legislature.* Whether all states originally limited voting to citizens is unclear.† The Virginia Bill of Rights, predating even the Declaration of Independence, provided for suffrage for "all men, having sufficient evidence of permanent common interest with, and attachment to the community."[10] On its face, such "attachment" does not neces-sarily imply citizenship.

Our concern here is with individual rights, and these, we know, the original Constitution scarcely addressed. The few provisions relating to individual rights —prohibitions of bills of attainder, ex post facto laws, and the impairment of contracts, and the jury requirement for federal criminal trials ‡—do not indicate whether they apply only to citizens or to everyone. The Bill of Rights, added by amendment in 1791, also does not specify whose rights it was designed to safeguard. The Fourth Amendment affirms "[t]he right of the people to be secure in their persons, houses, papers, and effects" and the Ninth Amendment refers to rights retained by "the people." Do these provisions protect only "the people" who ordained and established the Constitution, and therefore perhaps only those who were eligible to vote to ratify the Constitution? Are the "people" protected by the Fourth Amendment different from the "persons" to whom the Fifth Amendment provides the protection of a grand jury and the guarantees against double jeopardy, self-incrimination, and the deprivation of life, liberty, or property without due process of law? Furthermore, who enjoys the expressed freedoms of speech, religion, and assembly and the safeguards and immunities for those accused of crime?

Before the Civil War, none of these questions had attracted the attention of the Supreme Court. After the war, the Fourteenth Amendment established the criteria for United States citizenship and safeguarded the privileges and immun-ities of such citizenship against abridgment by the states. The amendment also provided, however, that no state "shall deprive any *person* of life, liberty, or property without due process of law; nor deny to any *person* within its jurisdic-tion the equal protection of the laws."

The Supreme Court considered the constitutional rights of aliens under the Fourteenth Amendment in 1886, in *Yick Wo v. Hopkins*.[11] Yick Wo, a resident alien of Chinese descent, had been convicted of violating a San Francisco ordi-nance regulating laundries. The evidence established that the ordinance had

---

*I. § 2, cl. 1. The Seventeenth Amendment, which provides for the direct election of senators, contains a similar provision.

†Today, however, states generally condition the right to vote on United States citizenship. E.g., Md. Const. Art. I. § 1: N.Y. Const. Art. II. § 1.

‡Art I. § 9, cl. 3: § 10. cl. 1; Art III. § 2, cl. 3.

been enforced in a manner that discriminated against persons of Chinese descent. The Court held that Yick Wo had been denied the equal protection of the laws.

The Supreme Court did not explore the nature of our polity in *Yick Wo*. The Court did not ask who ordained and established the Constitution or whom the framers intended to protect. The Court did not ask whether the Constitution as a whole applied to aliens; the Supreme Court addressed only the rights of resident aliens under the Fourteenth Amendment. Perhaps relying on the fact that one clause of the amendment spoke to privileges and immunities of citizens while the later clauses protected "persons," the Court stated simply and without any apparent difficulty, "The Fourteenth Amendment to the Constitution is not confined to the protection of citizens." After quoting the amendment, the Court added, "These provisions are universal in their application, to all persons within the territorial jurisdiction, without regard to any differences of race, of color, or of nationality; and the equal protection of the laws is a pledge of the protection of equal laws."[12]

Yick Wo remains the foundation of our jurisprudence concerning the rights of aliens in the United States. According to *Yick Wo,* the phrase "any person" in the Fourteenth Amendment's equal protection and due process clauses includes aliens. Later, the Supreme Court also held that an alien was a "person" for the purposes of the due process clause of the Fifth Amendment, which safeguards life, liberty, or property against deprivation by the federal government. According to subsequent Court decisions, aliens also are among the "people" entitled to the Fourth Amendment guarantee "to be secure in their persons, houses, papers, and effects, against unreasonable searches and seizures," the freedoms of the First Amendment, and the procedural safeguards and immunities provided in other amendments.[13]

Yick Wo confirmed that the Constitution, including the equal protection clause, protects aliens. Equal protection does permit reasonable classifications, however, and no doubt some distinctions between aliens and citizens are reasonable. Both the federal government and the states have distinguished between aliens and citizens for various purposes, but the question of which distinctions are reasonable and therefore constitutional continues to divide the Supreme Court. The Court has held that state discrimination against aliens creates suspect classifications that will be sharply scrutinized and will be upheld only if they serve a compelling state interest. The states, therefore, cannot deny welfare benefits, public employment, or admission to the professions to persons only because they are aliens.[14] Discrimination against aliens is not suspect, however, when the state deals with matters "firmly within a state's constitutional prerogatives" and excludes aliens from positions involving "discretionary decisionmaking, or execution of policy, which substantially affects members of the political community."[15]

Congressional distinctions between aliens and citizens apparently are ordinarily not suspect. The Supreme Court has never held that any congressional action discriminated against aliens in violation of the equal protection principles implied in the Fifth Amendment due process clause. Congressional authority to regulate aliens and to treat them less favorably than citizens has been justified by invoking considerations of national sovereignty, war and peace, and international relations generally.[16] The Court has sanctioned congressional actions linking the treatment of particular groups of aliens in the United States to the treatment of United States nationals by the aliens' countries of nationality.[17]

Yick Wo assured the constitutional rights of resident aliens in the United States against the states, and against the United States. Aliens physically in the United States other than as immigrants enjoy similar safeguards,[18] although they generally are subject to conditions upon entry, and many of the distinctions drawn between nonresident aliens and resident aliens or citizens are reasonable and do not deny equal protection of the laws. Whether the Constitution protects aliens outside the United States requires special consideration.

CONSTITUTIONAL RIGHTS OF ALIENS ABROAD

The Constitution does not state its geographic reach or, more specifically, whether it applies solely within the United States. The applicability of the Constitution outside the United States became an issue in the late nineteenth century in the case of *In re Ross*.[19] *Ross* involved a seaman charged with murdering a ship's officer aboard a United States vessel lying in a Japanese harbor. Pursuant to a treaty with Japan granting the United States authority to prescribe and enforce law for its nationals in Japan, and an act of Congress implementing this authority, Ross was tried before the United States Consul General. The Consul General convicted Ross and sentenced him to be hanged. Later, the President commuted his sentence to life-imprisonment. Ross brought a writ of habeas corpus in a United States district court claiming that his conviction was unconstitutional because he had not been indicted by a grand jury and had not been given a jury trial as required by the Sixth Amendment. The district court denied the writ and the Supreme Court affirmed unanimously. The Court said:

> By the Constitution a government is ordained and established "for the United States of America," and not for countries outside of their limits. The guarantees it affords against accusation of capital or infamous crimes, except by indictment or presentment by a grand jury, and for an impartial trial by a jury when thus accused, apply only to citizens and others within the United States, or who are brought there for trial for alleged offenses committed elsewhere, and not to residents or temporary sojourners abroad. . . . The Constitution can have no operation in another country.[20]

The Court concluded that constitutional safeguards were not available to Ross even though United States authorities had convicted and sentenced him to death, because Ross had committed his crime abroad and the United States had tried him abroad.

The Constitution, the Court noted, was "ordained and established 'for the United States of America.' " The conclusion that this meant "for the territory of the United States only" apparently was self-evident to the Court; it was neither proved nor discussed. It would have been more plausible for the Court to say that the Constitution was ordained for the political entity that it established and the institutions that it projected. *Ross* nevertheless remained a pillar of our constitutional jurisprudence until 1957.[21]

During those years the territorial reach of the Constitution became an issue in a different sense and context—the historic controversy as to whether the Constitution "followed the flag." As a result of the Spanish-American War, the United States had achieved its "manifest destiny" and had extended its rule to Puerto Rico, Hawaii, the Philippines, and elsewhere in the Pacific. In a series of *Insular Cases,*[22] the Court considered whether the inhabitants of these newly acquired possessions enjoyed the full protection of the Constitution. The Court, in widely split opinions, said "yes," "no," and "not quite." The answer depended on whether Congress had decided to "incorporate" the territory into the United States or merely to govern it while leaving it outside the Union as *a territory* of but not part of *the territory* of the United States. A congressionally incorporated territory was United States territory for all purposes, and the Constitution applied and governed official federal action there just as it did in the District of Columbia or New York. If Congress did not incorporate a territory, however, federal action affecting individuals there would be subject to considerations of fairness, but would not be governed by the specific provisions of the Constitution.[23]

The issue in *Ross* was not the issue in the *Insular Cases,* but the spirit of the earlier case pervaded the later ones. In *Ross,* the United States claimed no sovereignty over either the territory in which Ross murdered the officer, or the territory in which his trial took place. The United States applied its laws to Ross on the basis of his status as a seaman on a United States vessel, and the agreement between the United States and Japan. The Court refused to apply constitutional restraints because the United States had acted in a foreign country, not within the United States.

In the *Insular Cases,* on the other hand, the United States had imposed its laws upon, and conducted criminal trials in, territories over which it claimed sovereignty. The court held that congressionally incorporated territories became a part of the United States, therefore the federal government could not operate there free of constitutional limitations. Congress could, however, apparently determine that the rights guaranteed by the Constitution, including the freedoms of speech and religion, the right to privacy, security from unreasonable search and seizure, and the rights to counsel and a jury trial, were not appropriate for the inhabitants of a newly acquired territory. In that event, Congress could choose not to incorporate the territory and, in the spirit of *Ross,* the Constitution would not apply. Because the United States would continue to govern that territory, however, federal officials could not shed conscience completely. Officials governing under the authority of the United States had to be fair and decent.

The doctrine of *Ross* remained untested during the following decades. In time, the exercise of extraterritorial jurisdiction in foreign countries became unacceptable to those countries and to international mores, and it steadily disappeared.[24] During later wars, the United States did exercise jurisdiction over its armed forces in allied and occupied countries. In the special circumstances of war and occupation, however, those cases implicated only the Uniform Code of Military Justice and the laws of war, not the Constitution.[25]

The end of World War II brought the United States a new destiny, perhaps equally manifest; it became a superpower. For the first time, the United States occupied foreign countries and remained for decades.[26] Our government forged peacetime alliances, and acquired military bases in territories of friendly countries which were, and which remain, sovereign states. In both NATO and non-NATO countries, the United States jurisdiction over its armed forces has been governed by special regime, not by general constitutional principles. Pursuant to the North Atlantic Treaty and similar arrangements, the United States also has exercised jurisdiction over military dependents and over the civilian component of the defense establishment.[27]

A case involving one of these civilian citizens, *Reid v. Covert*,[28] signaled the death knell of *In re Ross* and heralded a new constitutional jurisprudence. As authorized by Congress, a military court tried and convicted the wife of a United States Air Force sergeant for the murder of her husband at an air base in England. The accused sought a writ of habeas corpus in federal district court, challenging her conviction because she was not given a jury trial as required by the Sixth Amendment. The district court issued the writ and the government appealed directly to the Supreme Court. The Supreme Court first rejected the claim on the ground that the constitutional provisions did not apply, but then granted a rehearing and reversed itself.

Justice Black, writing for four of the justices in the majority, declared:

At the beginning we reject the idea that when the United States acts against citizens abroad it can do so free of the Bill of Rights. The United States is entirely a creature of the Constitution. Its power and authority have no other source. It can only act in accordance with all the limitations imposed by the Constitution. When the Government reaches out to punish a citizen who is abroad, the shield which the Bill of Rights and other parts of the Constitution provide to protect his life and liberty should not be stripped away just because he happens to be in another land. . . .

The language of Art. III, § 2 manifests that constitutional protections for the individual were designed to restrict the United States Government when it acts outside of this country, as well as here at home. . . .

This Court and other federal courts have held or asserted that various constitutional limitations apply to the Government when it acts outside the continental United States. While it has been suggested that only those constitutional rights which are "fundamental" protect Americans abroad, we can find no warrant, in logic or otherwise, for picking and choosing among the remarkable collection of "Thou shall nots" which were explicitly fastened on all departments and agencies of the Federal Government by the Constitution and its Amendments.[29]

The Court dismissed the declaration in *Ross* that the Constitution had no operation in a foreign country. "At best," the Court said, "the *Ross* case should be left as a relic from a different era."[30]

Since *Reid,* no court has suggested that any constitutional provision is inapplicable because the challenged conduct occurred outside the United States.[31] For example, several circuit courts have subjected governmental actions on the high seas to constitutional limitations.[32] Recently, the United States Court of Appeals for the District of Columbia Circuit has held that a citizen's claim that his constitutional rights were violated when United States military authorities seized or authorized seizure of his property in Honduras without just compensation states a justiciable claim for relief.[33]

Reid does not tell us whether the Constitution applies abroad only to citizens or also to aliens. Although the Supreme Court stressed that *Reid* involved the constitutional rights of a United States citizen, the Court did not limit its holding or its reasoning to citizens. Wherever the United States acts, Justice Black said, it "can only act in accordance with all the limitations imposed by the Constitution." If constitutional limitations apply wherever the United States exercises authority, why not when governmental actions abroad affect aliens there? If constitutional provisions apply to both aliens and citizens at home, why not to both aliens and citizens abroad?

Although the Supreme Court has not addressed these questions since *Reid,* lower courts have recognized constitutional protections for aliens outside the United States in various contexts. For example, in *United States v. Toscanino,*[34] federal officials allegedly had kidnapped and tortured an alien in a foreign country and brought him to the United States for criminal proceedings. The United States Court of Appeals for the Second Circuit held that these acts violated the Constitution, and it invalidated the victim's subsequent trial in the United States. Courts have entertained objections by aliens aboard foreign flag vessels to unreasonable searches and seizures at sea.[35] A few years ago, a Polish national successfully claimed the right to a jury trial in a United States court specially convened in Berlin to try him for hijacking a plane to escape his country.[36] In the summer of 1984, the women of Greenham Common, Great Britain, urged a federal district court to rule that the deployment of United States cruise missiles near their homes violated the Fifth and Ninth Amendments.[37] In that case, the court refused to consider their claims because it concluded that they raised political, nonjusticiable questions, not because the plaintiffs, non-United States citizens in Great Britain, could not invoke the protections of the Constitution. Apparently, in the spirit of these cases, a foreign national held under United States authority abroad could seek release on habeas corpus in a United States court.

CONSTITUTIONAL RIGHTS AND IMMIGRATION

The Supreme Court has considered claims of constitutional safeguards by aliens outside the United States only in the context of immigration laws, most notably in *The Chinese Exclusion Case* of 1889.[38] Initially, immigration to the United States essentially was free of restrictions and, in fact, the United States actively encouraged immigration. Late in the nineteenth century, however, Congress began to limit immigration from some countries. In *The Chinese Exclusion Case,* a person of Chinese origin had been admitted to the United States lawfully, and had lived here for about twelve years. He left the United States with a valid document from immigration authorities authorizing his return. Later, the authorities denied him re-entry because an intervening act of Congress excluded him despite his prior residence and the promise that he could return.

The Constitution says nothing about immigration. The power to control immigration is not one of the enumerated powers of Congress. In an earlier case, the Supreme Court had held that control of immigration was within the congressional power to regulate commerce with foreign nations.[39] In *The Chinese Exclusion Case,* however, the Court substituted a radical innovation in constitutional jurisprudence. The Court concluded that, notwithstanding the principle of enumerated powers,* the United States has powers not mentioned in the Constitution—powers inherent in its national and international sovereignty. According to the Court, these powers include the rights of the sovereign to control its territory and safeguard its security. Congress can control immigration pursuant to this authority.†

The Court did not consider whether, or suggest why, these inherent powers differed from the enumerated powers of the federal government, which also are rooted in sovereignty. The Court could have held that the inherent powers, like the enumerated powers, were subject to constitutional limitations and safeguards despite their extraconstitutional origin.‡ *Yick Wo* might have supported the

---

*Art. I, § 1; Amendment X (any powers not delegated to the federal government are reserved to the states).

†The Court held that Congress could control immigration even in violation of a United States treaty.

‡Later, in nonimmigration cases, the Court said that the extraconstitutional powers inherent in sovereignty were subject to constitutional limitations: "Broad as the power of the National Government to regulate foreign affairs must necessarily be, it is not without limitation. The restrictions confining Congress in the exercise of any of the powers expressly delegated to it in the Constitution apply with equal vigor when that body seeks to regulate our relations with other nations." *Perez v. Brownell,* 356 U.S. 44, 58 (1958).

constitutional claims of a returning alien, but the Court apparently considered *Yick Wo* irrelevant, perhaps because Congress, not a state government, was involved. Perhaps the Court believed that aliens stopped at the border are physically outside the United States and therefore are not protected by the Constitution.[40]

The Chinese Exclusion Case remains the foundation of our constitutional jurisprudence concerning immigration. In subsequent court decisions and congressional acts, judges and legislators have interpreted the case as holding that immigration and immigration laws are not subject to constitutional restraints. Following this doctrine, Congress has been permitted not only to impose restraints on the number of immigrants and to choose among would-be immigrants according to reasonable criteria such as family ties or needed skills, but even to discriminate among potential immigrants on the basis of their national origin.* Congress thus may discriminate among potential immigrants, in effect, on the basis of race or religion without any judicial scrutiny, let alone strict scrutiny. Congress could exclude not only persons who had been convicted of a crime, suffered from a communicable disease, or posed a plausible danger to national security, but also persons who had engaged in radical political activities or had held radical political opinions that would be protected for persons already in the United States.[41] Congress could assert such grounds to exclude not only persons who had never been here, but also those who had lived here peacefully for many years and had left the country temporarily, as in *The Chinese Exclusion Case*.

In 1952, the Supreme Court held that immigration authorities could exclude a returning alien acting on undisclosed evidence without a hearing.[42] The Court also held that immigration authorities could detain an excludable alien indefinitely if no country would accept him. Even if an alien had been a long-term resident of the United States, the Court said, Congress could exclude him at will. Congress can exclude or deport an alien even for political activity that could not support a criminal conviction because it would constitute deprivation of liberty without due process of law.[43]

THE NEED FOR A NEW DOCTRINE

Individual rights have flourished in the United States since World War II, but they have not shaken the legacy of *The Chinese Exclusion Case*. Since *Ross* died, aliens abroad apparently receive the same protections against unconstitutional actions by United States officials as do citizens. Aliens abroad, however, and even those physically in the United States but not lawfully admitted, are not

---

* Such limitations have been reflected in successive Immigration Acts. They never have been challenged successfully because of the principle deemed to have been laid down in *The Chinese Exclusion Case* that the power of Congress with respect to immigration is plenary and not subject to constitutional restraint.

protected against the enforcement of unfair immigration laws because to date these laws have been beyond the reach of the Constitution. Even aliens lawfully resident in the United States, although they enjoy the rich heritage of *Yick Wo* and the same safeguards as citizens, under cases still in effect can be deported for little or no reason. As a result, failure to seek and obtain naturalization leaves an alien forever vulnerable to deportation.

Lower federal courts have extended this pernicious anomaly. They have construed *The Chinese Exclusion Case* as holding not only that aliens have no constitutional rights regarding admission, but also that they cannot challenge immigration procedures that discriminate without reason among persons of different races or nationalities, and that they cannot challenge decisions to intern them indefinitely even when the only reason for the internment is the lack of a country willing to accept them.[44] A federal district court recently rejected a challenge to the Haitian Interdiction Program, under which United States Coast Guard vessels not only prevent persons from coming to the United States to seek asylum, but also forcibly return them to the authorities of the country from which they fled.[45]

More than seventy years ago, in a case involving the deportation of an alleged prostitute who had lived in the United States for more than five years, Justice Holmes wrote: "The attempt to reopen the constitutional question must fail. It is thoroughly established that Congress has power to order the deportation of aliens whose presence in the country it deems hurtful."[46] Almost forty years later, Justice Frankfurter wrote: "If due process bars Congress from enactments that shock the sense of fair play—which is the essence of due process—one is entitled to ask whether it is not beyond the power of Congress to deport an alien who was duped into joining the Communist Party." Frankfurter continued:

[M]uch could be said for the view, were we writing on a clean slate, that the Due Process Clause qualifies the scope of political discretion heretofore recognized as belonging to Congress in regulating the entry and deportation of aliens. And since the intrinsic consequences of deportation are so close to punishment for crime, it might fairly be said also that the ex post facto clause, even though applicable only to punitive legislation, should be applied to deportation.

But the slate is not clean.[47]

Since Justice Frankfurter's statement, many other slates have been cleaned, including *Ross,* of the same vintage and spirit as *The Chinese Exclusion Case.* Individual rights have become our hallmark and our pride. Official racial discrimination has been uprooted in all other contexts. Congress itself has eliminated the racism of an immigration policy based on national origin.[48] Alien rights in the United States have flourished, and the Supreme Court has recognized alienage as a suspect classification requiring strict scrutiny when state action is involved. *The Chinese Exclusion Case*—its very name an embarrassment—should join the relics of a bygone, unproud era.[49]

The three cases I have explored, and their different legacies, became part of our constitutional jurisprudence. These doctrines, however, differ from most of the law the Supreme Court has promulgated. The Court did not seem to rely upon interpretation and construction of constitutional text. In *Yick Wo,* the Court arguably relied on the Fourteenth Amendment language protecting "persons," not merely citizens, and in *Ross* it purported to rely on the statement in the Preamble that the Constitution was ordained and established "for the United States of America." The other cases cite nothing in the Constitution. *Reid v. Covert,* rejecting *Ross,* rested on an assertion that the United States government "has no power except that granted by the Constitution." In *The Chinese Exclusion Case,* the Court insisted that its holding had no basis in the Constitution.

The inescapable conclusion is that despite some nod to language, this jurisprudence does not derive from particular constitutional provisions. Instead, it depends on the Constitution as a whole, its political theory, and its status and character in our polity. These bases cannot be found in the text of the Constitution. The Constitution itself gives few hints of the political philosophy of the framers, perhaps because the Constitution descended directly from the Articles of Confederation, not from the Declaration of Independence, and the framers were concerned with the issues of union, not the issues of governance and the relationship of the individual to society. The framers' political philosophy is more clearly reflected in our national birth certificate, the Declaration of Independence, and in the early state constitutions established pursuant to the Declaration.

The framers were committed to the social compact. Man is "endowed with . . . unalienable Rights," and "to secure these rights, Governments are instituted among Men." Jefferson's statement moved from the rights of men to the sovereignty of the people, but it did not define who "the people" were. Jefferson did not intimate what his theory implied for persons living in society who did not meet the indicia of membership in it, or for persons who remained outside society or lived in other societies. The Virginia Bill of Rights provides that "all men, having sufficient evidence of permanent common interest with, and attachment to the community, have the right of suffrage." None of the state constitutions, however, addressed whether the people could deny entry to the society and the compact when they instituted government or after government is instituted, or whether their elected representatives could deny entry later. These constitutions also did not address which reasons, if any, could justify such exclusions.

More importantly for our purposes, neither the Declaration of Independence nor the early state constitutions articulated the character of the social compact. The Declaration of Independence declared that "to secure these rights, Governments are instituted among Men." Was the Constitution only a compact establishing a government to secure the individual rights of the people creating it? Or, since they believed that all men, everywhere, "are endowed by their Creator with certain unalienable Rights," did the framers intend to create a government that would secure and respect the unalienable rights of all human beings, including those in their midst not party to the contract, and human beings in other societies upon whom their new government might impinge?

The constitutional history sketched above suggests that the Supreme Court has answered these questions inconsistently. *Yick Wo* supports the proposition that the compact was not only for the citizens who made it, but also for aliens in their midst. Later cases have shown that the compact applies not only to residents, but to all who become subject to the authority of the government.* *Reid* and its progeny abandoned the territorial view of the compact, affirming that individual rights must be respected wherever federal officials act. The lower courts, combining *Yick Wo* and *Reid*, have held that the compact undertakes to secure the rights of all who are, or who become, subject to the jurisdiction of the government, whether aliens or citizens, here or abroad.

The social compact, then, is not merely an arrangement for mutual protection; it is a compact to establish a "community of righteousness." It declares that a government instituted to secure rights must respect those rights. The United States must secure and respect not only the rights of the people who were party to the compact, but also of all others who come within its jurisdiction. If, in a world of states, the United States is not in a position to secure the rights of all individuals everywhere, it is always in a position to respect them. Our federal government must not invade the individual rights of any human being. The choice in the Bill of Rights of the word "person" rather than "citizen" was not fortuitous; nor was the absence of a geographical limitation. Both reflect a commitment to respect the individual rights of all human beings.

The compact recognizes the rights of all men and women everywhere and creates a government that must respect these rights. The United States may not deprive a person, whether a citizen or foreign national, of life, liberty, or property without due process of law. Our government may not take anyone's property without just compensation—citizen or alien, abroad or at home. I do not suggest that the Constitution "applies" throughout the world or that it gives "rights" to all human beings everywhere. The Constitution does not give rights, not even to us. Our rights, and the rights of people everywhere, do not derive from the Constitution; they antecede it. The effect of the Constitution, however, is to require the United States Government to respect these human rights, with which all men and women are endowed equally.[50]

This interpretation of our compact also should guide the application of our concept of equal protection. For those who live in the United States, alienage essentially ought to be irrelevant. The Supreme Court was right when it declared alienage a suspect classification. The states are entitled, though not required, to restrict the right to vote to citizens; the compact does not necessarily entitle states to deny resident aliens equal rights to be public school teachers or deputy probation officers.

Even more questionable are the remnants of the *Chinese Exclusion Case* reflected in our jurisprudence concerning congressional treatment of aliens. The Supreme Court never has invalidated any congressional act regulating aliens on

---

* Even *Ross* recognized the obligation of the government to respect the rights of noncitizens in the United States, and even of noncitizens residing abroad if the government brought them here.

constitutional grounds. Unlike state legislatures, Congress can exclude aliens from Civil Service employment and it even can deny welfare benefits, at least to some aliens.[51] Whatever the merits of particular regulations or distinctions, the attitude remains redolent of the *Chinese Exclusion Case*. Aliens, as a class, are here by sufferance, grace, and charity, according to this view. Their presence implicates national security, and their rights are subject to international barter.

Nothing in the compact excludes immigration issues from its concerns and principles. Doubtless, the compact and our society are not necessarily open to all comers at all times. The people, parties to the compact, may limit the numbers of new adherents and may exclude those who would endanger security or seriously disrupt order. The rhetoric of the *Chinese Exclusion Case,* however, identified any restriction on immigration with national security. Such rhetoric is empty. Discrimination because of race or religion bears little relation to security. Nor does national security require the detention of thousands of orderly, non-threatening aliens to encourage them to leave and to discourage others from coming. A people committed to equality and inalienable rights for all men and women should not permit its government to apply invidious criteria for admission. We should not allow our government, for example, to discriminate between Haitians and Cubans in immigration procedures, to detain aliens merely because they cannot be deported, or to interdict boats on the high seas and compel their passengers to return to the countries from which they fled. A compact of conscience should not exclude or deport permanent residents who have demonstrated "common interest with, and attachment to the community."[52]

The people of the United States ordained a compact that established a community of conscience and righteousness. The compact applies to everything done by the community and its officials, in the United States and elsewhere, affecting citizens and aliens alike, and concerning immigration no less than other matters. The rights our ancestors recognized as inherent and unalienable knew neither bounds nor state boundaries. Their polity should respect these rights without invidious inequalities, no arbitrary limitations on liberty, and no unnecessary interferences with those who risk all in the pursuit of some happiness.

PART THREE

Rights: Here and There

9

Rights: American and Human

AMERICAN rights need no introduction. As every schoolchild can recite, our rights are proclaimed in the Declaration of Independence and protected by the Constitution. Americans are aware of their rights, as if in their blood. We live our rights in our lives, daily.

Human rights, by contrast, are only come-lately to our common consciousness, but they are now spoken of easily in every language, in national politics and international diplomacy, in the learned jargon of professions and academic disciplines. Eschewing complex, controversial definitions, it is sufficient to say that human rights are those moral-political claims that, by contemporary consensus, every human being has—or is deemed to have, or should have—upon his or her society and government. These claims, these rights, are enumerated in international instruments—in the Universal Declaration of Human Rights, which has been accepted by virtually all governments, and in international agreements to which more and more nations are adhering at a steady rate.

American rights and international human rights are intimately related, yet they are different. I compare them in conception, in their character and status, and in content.

In addressing American rights I speak of American constitutional rights and American constitutionalism. I have summarized the sources and distilled the theory of these rights in the Declaration of Independence, and the early state constitutions. The content of our constitutional rights is to be found in amendments to the United States Constitution as construed and developed during two

From 79 *Colum. L. Rev.* 405 (1979).

hundred years of our constitutional history under the guidance of the Supreme Court of the United States.

American rights were born in the eighteenth century out of European ideas and antecedents. International human rights, born during the Second World War from revulsion at the horrors of Hitler, drew heavily on American constitutionalism (and on related constitutional developments in Europe and Latin America), but took also from a different ideology, from socialism and from other commitments to the welfare state. American constitutionalism developed in its own national climate and was nurtured and maintained by homegrown institutions. International human rights were developed by representatives of different nations, in a complex, unorganized political process; they are designed for diverse national societies, maintained by diverse national institutions, and monitored in uncertain, small ways by primitive international procedures in a loose international political system.

American rights were proclaimed by Americans in 1776 for themselves, but they were not claimed only for themselves. Declared by way of justifying independence from British rule—what we should today call "self-determination"— they reflect a political theory applicable to every human being, in relation to every political society, in every age.

I have set forth that theory more fully in essay 6. Briefly, for American constitutionalism, the individual had natural rights before the Constitution, before government was established. He or she gives up some rights to government for the limited purposes for which government was created, retaining the rest— substantial autonomy and immunities from governmental interference. The Constitution, then, does not grant rights; it safeguards the individual's preexisting retained rights.

Government was to be a policeman, leaving the individual free to pursue his happiness. The Constitution was ordained, as the Preamble tells us, to establish justice and to promote the general welfare, but those phrases should not be read with twentieth-century preconceptions nurtured in a "welfare state." For the framers, justice and the general welfare would be the result of the kind of government to be established, a government committed to the accepted, limited purposes. It was not the business of government to provide the people with "welfare-state" kind of welfare; government was to leave the individual free to pursue such welfare, his basic needs, himself.

Such was the theory of American government as it was conceived; and in constitutional principle, that is the theory of American government still. Compare, now, international human rights. International human rights are recognized as inherent, but it is not necessarily assumed that man is in principle autonomous, that rights antecede government. The international instruments nod to popular sovereignty, but there is no hint of social compact, or of continuing consent of the governed. Respect for retained rights is not a condition of government or a basis of its legitimacy; violation of rights does not warrant undoing government by revolution.

Like American rights, international human rights also, inevitably, implicate the purposes for which governments are created. But—unlike American rights originally—international rights surely do *not* reflect a commitment to government-for-limited-purposes-only. On the contrary, born after various socialisms were established and spreading, and after commitment to welfare economics and the welfare state was nearly universal, international human rights imply rather a conception of government as designed for many purposes and seasons. The rights deemed to be fundamental include not only freedoms that government must not invade, but also rights to the satisfaction of basic needs and to well-being that government must actively provide or guarantee. They imply a government that is activist, intervening, committed to economic-social planning for the society so as to satisfy economic-social rights of the individual.

That, in their theory, American rights antecede the Constitution and are above government, obviously gives them the highest status and significance. They do not derive from official grant; they are not enjoyed by official grace. They are fundamental rights of the individual, not merely restrictions on government. They cannot be taken away, or even suspended, without the people's consent; some of them may be "unalienable," so that the people could not give them away even if they wished to.

International human rights are less exalted in principle. Denominating them "rights" implies that individuals have a claim to them under some conception of natural law or some agreed-upon moral order, but international human rights have been declared by governments and depend on the continued willingness of governments to recognize and honor them. Rights based in international law or agreement, presumably, can be abolished or modified by new law or agreement, or can lose their vitality by erosive interpretations, or by desuetude.

The higher status of American rights, however, has had consequences that are not wholly favorable. First, if individual rights antecede the Constitution, they are not strictly constitutional rights. The Constitution, I have stressed, does not create, establish, or grant rights. But perhaps for that reason—because rights were not the responsibility, the preoccupation of the Constitution-makers—the Constitution does not deal with individual rights even in less-creative ways. The Constitution does not exalt, celebrate, or proclaim rights. In fact, the original Constitution virtually did not mention them. The Bill of Rights was added by a series of constitutional amendments, a postscript if not an afterthought, the price of getting the Constitution approved. With the Bill of Rights added, the Constitution explicitly declares our antecedent rights and provides that they shall be respected by government. But there was no thought of imbuing our Constitution with rights, of giving our rights constitutional stature and status. And no one thought to require, or even to authorize, the new federal government to secure and protect individual rights, or to nurture, promote or encourage their exercise and enjoyment.

And so, as we know, it is ordained that Congress shall make no law abridging the freedom of speech or of the press (Amendment I). But neither, apparently, was Congress to make law to promote or protect the freedom of speech or of the press, for no authority to do so was given to Congress by the Constitution.[1] Later, much later, general powers of Congress were interpreted as permitting such acts by Congress. Today, under its power to regulate commerce between states, for example, Congress can promote the freedom of speech or press in activities that are in, or that affect, interstate commerce—for example, in radio and television. Congress probably has authority also to spend money to promote the freedom of speech because it has power to spend money for the general welfare, and promoting such freedom is presumably for the general welfare. But Congress still cannot protect or enhance rights directly and completely; for example, although a complicated argument could be made and would probably prevail, it is not obvious that Congress could mandate the study of the Bill of Rights in the nation's schools. The very idea of legislating to protect rights, as by civil rights acts, was foreign to our original conceptions. It required radical constitutional amendment following the Civil War to make national civil rights legislation permissible, and thinkable, and that legislation was directed against state (not federal) violations.[2] After the first such program to implement the emancipation of the slaves, it was another hundred years before Congress embarked on another serious civil rights program.

A related consequence of our conception of rights as antecedent freedom is that the protection provided them by the Constitution is limited. The Constitution does not protect our autonomy and freedom against all invaders; it bars only their violation by government and its officials. Consequently, when, later, in the Civil War amendments, the constitution finally gave Congress authority to enforce respect for rights, that authority suffered similar limitations: it extended only to protecting rights against official state violation or where the state is otherwise involved. Congress was given no authority to protect rights against strictly private interference, and a string of Supreme Court cases later declared efforts to provide such protection unconstitutional. To this day, Congress can legislate against private invasions of autonomy or freedom only when they are badges of slavery, or when Congress can act under one of its general powers, for example where interstate commerce is affected.[3] And even the states, in whose constitutions rights loomed large, and which from the beginning might have promoted and protected rights against both official and private action without any constitutional hindrance, did not learn to shore up individual rights, or promote new kinds of rights, until our day.

Even what Congress *may* do, it is not constitutionally required to do; Congress is not *required* to do *anything* to protect or promote individual rights, or to make them effective, or more effective. Congress was not constitutionally required to exercise the power expressly granted it to implement the Civil War Amendments. The Civil Rights Acts, of which we are justly proud, were designed to support "negative rights," to help assure that individual freedoms or rights are not infringed; they do not involve society, or the law, in affirmatively promoting the enjoyment of freedom or rights. Congress need not appropriate money to make it possible for the poor to enjoy their rights effectively, and it may even use its spending power to discourage that enjoyment, for example by providing funds to finance childbirth but not abortion.[4] Congress is not required to add new twentieth-century kinds of welfare rights, or to assure that welfare benefits which it pays for are enjoyed equally.

International human rights have less-exalted status than American constitutional rights, and depend on uncertain national and international forces, but they aim further. While there is yet no authoritative interpretation of them, these rights are apparently independent, affirmative values, not merely limitations on government. In the International Covenant on Civil and Political Rights, states undertake not only to respect but also "to ensure" those rights, apparently against private as well as governmental interference.[5] A state is obligated to adopt such measures as may be necessary to give effect to these rights. For one example, the Covenant provides that the inherent right to life "shall be protected by law."[6] (The United States Constitution, on the other hand, requires only that government itself shall not deprive a person of life without due process of law.)

The exalted, extraconstitutional character of our rights may also be responsible for another handicap they suffer. The Constitution provides that individual rights are not to be abridged by government, but the framers did not deem it necessary and proper to say *how* our rights were to be secured against such violation, or what remedies should be provided to anyone whose rights had been violated.

The framers doubtless expected that our system of government—the separation of powers, an array of checks and balances, and the division of authority between federal and state governments—would, by preventing concentration of power, protect against invasions of rights. Periodically, the people could vote to replace their representatives with others who would do better by the people's rights. Between elections, individual officials could be impeached and removed from office for invasions of rights that resulted from treason, bribery, or other high crimes and misdemeanors. (Compare the case of Richard Nixon.) *In extremis,* there would presumably be another remedy, not articulated or even implied in the Constitution, but which our revolutionary ancestors could hardly deny: Because, as the Declaration of Independence told us, "to secure these rights" was the purpose for which government was instituted, the people had the right to "alter or abolish" their government whenever it "became destructive" of those rights.

Americans know—indeed the world knows—that American rights are protected by our courts. That too is not obvious from the Constitution. Since safeguards against invasion of rights, or remedies for their abridgement, did not appear to the framers appropriate for inclusion in the Constitution, it is perhaps not surprising that judicial review—going to court to vindicate our rights—also is not explicitly provided in the Constitution. Most scholars accept, however, that judicial review was contemplated by the framers, although without any clear view as to its scope and form. In any event, Chief Justice John Marshall, as we know, established judicial review at the beginning of the nineteenth century. It is interesting to speculate on what our constitutional history might have been had Marshall not dared, or had recanted (as apparently he later considered doing in order to escape the threat of impeachment by political opponents).[7] If the courts had not been available to protect our rights, would these rights have survived nibbling, or battering, by Congresses and Presidents, by state legislatures and governors and generations of lesser officials? Would the particular characteristics of our government—federalism, separation of powers and checks and balances—themselves have survived, and would they have prevented tyranny, as our ancestors expected? Would we have developed other institutions—human rights commissioners, ombudsmen or procurators-general—or other ways to protect our rights? Would we have done as well as Great Britain, our mother-in-law-and-in-rights, or would we have been less fortunate, like many peoples today, living under noble constitutions that are proclaimed, heralded, and often disregarded?

After 180 years the judicial remedy against governmental violation of our rights is strong and effective, honored by heady Congresses and powerful Presidents, by proud state legislatures and governors, and by the expanding federal and state bureaucracies. Judicial review is a powerful remedy. It is our hallmark and our pride, imitated by some countries, and envied in many others. It is, however, a limited remedy. It is limited in one, small sense because the courts act only when asked, and even in our sophisticated, knowledgeable society many do not ask. (If all asked, the courts would be overwhelmed.) Judicial review is limited by the nature of the judicial process, which does not, cannot, ferret out all violations—hence, for example, two continuing blots on our human rights condition, police abuse and prison conditions. Judicial review is limited in another small sense because courts have developed an entire jurisprudence of reasons for not deciding cases, even when asked, even though a violation of rights may have occurred, for example, when the particular plaintiff lacks standing, when the case is moot, or the issue is deemed "political," not justiciable.

Judicial review is limited also in a larger sense—because courts are not legislatures. They can refuse to give effect to unconstitutional acts, and they can often enjoin the application and enforcement of such acts.* But they cannot undo or repair past violations; they cannot, themselves, punish and thereby deter violations. They cannot otherwise make laws or appropriate money to ensure the enjoyment of rights.[8] For past violations there is no constitutional remedy. Courts, then, are necessary, but not in all ways sufficient, and in their strength, and in their insufficiency, the theory of our rights is implicated. Even activist and imaginative judges are not omnipotent in the face of constitutional language (or silence) and two hundred years of jurisprudence under the original conception. Few judges have been prepared to seek escape from conceptual moorings by abandoning the need for state action and protecting rights against private invasion. Few have been prepared to declare basic human needs—subsistence,

---

*From the Constitution, the Supreme Court has also inferred some particular remedies whereby the courts can give special effect to some rights and deter future violations. For example, the courts invalidate a criminal conviction if the trial was not fair, or did not satisfy other constitutional requirements; the courts exclude evidence obtained by unreasonable search and seizure.

education—to be fundamental rights even for the limited purpose of requiring a compelling state interest to justify spending less money for some children than for others.[9] Surely, except rarely and in the most special circumstances, courts have not thought to mandamus legislatures to pass laws and appropriate money to protect old rights or promote new ones.[10]

The courts cannot supply the kind of support for rights that requires legislation; and legislative support for rights in the United States, we have seen, has also suffered as a result of our theory of rights. There is no constitutional obligation upon Congress, or upon the states, to provide remedies, or to compensate victims for violations of their rights. A person improperly convicted of a crime, a person unlawfully detained, a person whose freedom of speech, or religion, has been abridged, often has no remedy at all, and if he has any it is only by legislative favor. The Civil War amendments to the Constitution *permit* Congress to provide remedies for some violations, and other clauses *permit* remedies for some others. But nothing in those Amendments, or elsewhere, obligates Congress to do so. Congress has in fact provided some remedies for some violations of individual rights[11]—making some violations a crime, authorizing money compensation to some victims and sometimes injunctions against future violations; and the courts have interpreted—some say misinterpreted— those provisions to expand the relief they offer.[12] State legislatures have also provided some remedies for some violations. But many violations of rights remain unrepaired and unremedied.

In contrast, the obligation of countries to "ensure" international human rights includes an obligation "to adopt such legislative or other measures as may be necessary to give effect to the rights."[13] A nation undertakes to ensure that any victim shall have an effective remedy for any violation. In one respect there is an express, additional requirement: "Anyone who has been the victim of unlawful arrest or detention shall have an enforceable right to compensation."[14]

And now to the rights themselves. There are large intrinsic similarities between American and human rights; there are important differences.

Americans were prominent among the architects and builders of international human rights, and American constitutionalism was a principal inspiration and model for them. In the result, most of the provisions of the Universal Declaration of Human Rights, and later of the International Covenant on Civil and Political Rights, are in their essence American constitutional rights projected around the world.

But there are differences—some small, some large, some uncertain. Some differences are due to differences in their histories, their sources, their methods of articulation. Because American rights do not derive from the Constitution, the framers were not impelled to enumerate them. American rights are still contained largely in delphic, eighteenth-century instruments, and much that is now part of American constitutional jurisprudence, found in those texts by exegesis and development in the intervening centuries, has to be distilled from a confusion of Supreme Court opinions. Some rights we assume to be obvious and primordial—such as the right to vote—were not confirmed in our constitutional jurisprudence until our own day.[15] International human rights were articulated recently, during a brief period, in writing. Inevitably, some differences developed in the course of translating American and kindred ideas to a universal screen, by diverse procedures, in a complex political process. American constitutional rights include, and are part of a comprehensive theory of, representative democracy; international human rights provide for universal and equal suffrage, but they were designed to be acceptable in political systems that differ from ours in important respects. Within the American as within the international system of rights there are conflicts of values, which may be resolved differently: for example, the International Covenant requires countries to prohibit propaganda for war, or advocating racial or religious hatred;[16] in the United States such a law would probably violate the freedom of speech or press. Some of our rights—for example, the right to a jury trial, or the prohibition on the establishment of religion—are peculiar to our own political climate and history, and do not commend themselves as universal necessity. Some American rights were adopted in essence, but not in detail, if only because our rights are not wholly clear in scope and definition even to us; and there is continuing disagreement, among Supreme Court Justices and among citizens, as to what our rights are or should be in particular respects.

Thus, international human rights include also rights that are not plain on the face of the Constitution, but that our courts have found to be constitutionally protected. Those who have not looked into our Constitution recently may have forgotten that some of our most precious and confirmed rights—for example, the presumption of innocence, freedom to travel, the right to marry and found a family, the right of parents to ensure the moral-religious education of their children, even the right to vote—are not visibly there; but they are explicit in the international instruments. On the other hand, protection for property, explicit in our Bill of Rights, was omitted from the international covenants, largely because of continuing controversy between developed and developing states as to whether a state that nationalizes alien properties must provide just compensation, but it is included in the Universal Declaration and it is commonly assumed that to own property and not to be arbitrarily deprived of it is a human right.[17]

Particular civil-political rights have wider scope in international human rights than under the Constitution. The International Covenant on Civil and Political Rights forbids torture and cruel, inhuman, or degrading treatment or punishment;[18] The Constitution forbids only "cruel and unusual punishment" upon conviction for crime (Amendment VIII). The constitutional provision is not applicable, then, we were taught by the Supreme Court, to corporal punishment in schools.[19] The Covenant bars capital punishment for pregnant women;[20] that was forbidden at common law, but might not be held to be barred by the Constitution.* Double jeopardy—being tried twice for the same offense—is

---

*The Covenant also prohibits capital punishment for an offense committed by a person under 18 years of age. In 1988 the United States Supreme Court invalidated a capital sentence

forbidden by both the Covenant and the Constitution, but 30 years ago five Justices of the Supreme Court held that the Constitution is not violated if a person is tried by both the federal government and by a state where the same act is both a state and a federal crime.[21] The Covenant requires separate confinement of persons accused of crime from those already convicted, and juvenile accused from adult accused;[22] the Constitution has not been held to require these. The Covenant provides that the "penitentiary system shall comprise treatment of prisoners, the essential aim of which shall be their reformation and social rehabilitation."[23] That has not been deemed a constitutional requirement, and in the United States today reformation and social rehabilitation seem to be dismissed as hopeless, unsophisticated, and outdated motivations. Criminal process apart, the International Covenant requires respect and protection for a person's honor and reputation; in the United States, the Supreme Court has told us, reputation is neither "liberty" nor "property" protected by the Constitution.[24] On the other hand, there is no international counterpart to the provision in our Bill of Rights denying to government authority to quarter troops in a private home in time of peace (Amendment III). The International Covenant has nothing comparable to our special constitutional safeguards in trials for treason (Article III, section 3).

I have mentioned small differences. On the face of the instruments at least, there is a major difference between the Constitution and international human rights documents in the emphasis on equality. While by our Declaration of Independence all men are created equal, while de Tocqueville and others have seen equality as a leading idea in American democracy, commitment to equality was missing from the original American Constitution and even from its Bill of Rights; difficult now to believe, the word "equality" is not to be found there.* Even later, after slavery ended and the Fourteenth Amendment gave us our "second Constitution," its commitment to equality is less than complete. Under that amendment "no *State* shall deny to any person the equal protection of the laws"; there is no such prohibition in the Constitution with respect to the federal government. That had to be inferred, much later, by historically and intellectually questionable constitutional interpretation, intoning "due process of law,"[25] the same clause that a hundred years earlier had been invoked to maintain Dred Scott in slavery. Today, as a result of these judicial readings, equal protection is probably required of the federal government quite as fully as of state governments, but our Constitution hardly rings with it. And the ordinary reader, at home and especially abroad, might find the absence of a provision forbidding the government of the United States to deny the equal protection of the laws, or to discriminate on account of race, or religion, or sex, an embarrassing lacuna.

The American conception of equality is limited. Both in constitutional prin-

---

for a crime committed by a person 15 years old, but in 1989 it upheld capital punishment for a crime committed by a person 16 years old. See note 39.

*Lord Acton noted that in Revolutionary France, "Liberty was the watchword of the middle-class, equality of the lower"; the United States today is one of a few middle-class peoples in a world of (economically) lower-class peoples.

ciple and in fact, the American commitment is to equal protection of the laws and equality of opportunity. For many, however, such equality is necessary but it is hardly sufficient. We know Anatole France's biting characterization of the majestic equality of the law which forbids rich and poor alike to beg, to steal, and to sleep under the bridge at night. More recently, our own poor and disadvantaged have questioned the adequacy, and reality, of such equality and have pressed the claim for less inequality-in-fact. But no such notions are in our constitutional jurisprudence. There is no constitutional obligation to distribute our great wealth more equitably. (Even the right to equalize a little, by taxing according to ability to pay, required the Sixteenth constitutional Amendment.) As a nation we are not even required to assure that equal amounts are spent for the education of each of our children, or to guarantee that welfare payments will be the same for every needy individual.[26] Since *Bakke*[27] we know that the Constitution permits some equalization by some kinds of "affirmative action" programs, but no one suggests that the Constitution requires such measures.

For international human rights equality is a principal theme. The major United Nations Covenants are permeated with the commitment to equality. Invidious discrimination on grounds of race, color, sex, language, religion, and other irrelevant characteristics are prohibited again and again, and even in time of public emergency.[28]

Different conceptions of equality may underlie the major difference between American and human rights. International human rights are as consistent with varieties of capitalism as with various socialisms, but the Universal Declaration and the Covenant on Economic, Social and Cultural Rights advance a few small, important steps toward an equality of enjoyment, in that all individuals are entitled to have the state ensure their basic human needs and other economic-social benefits.[29] That Covenant adds a galaxy of rights most of which are unknown to American constitutionalism—a right to food, clothing, housing, and education; a right to work, leisure, fair wages, decent working conditions, and social security; to physical and mental health, to protection for the family, and for mothers and children; a right to participate in cultural life. Although states adhering to the Covenant undertake to realize these rights only "progressively" and "to the maximum of available resources," the document uses language of right not merely of hope, language of undertaking and commitment by governments not merely of aspiration and goal. Some have asked whether it is meaningful to call these rights, since the undertakings are vague and long-term; they are unenforceable, if only because they require major governmental planning and program and are conditioned upon availability of resources. But in international law and rhetoric, they are legal rights, and in many societies, including our own, the language of rights is increasingly used and the sense of entitlement to such benefits is becoming pervasive.

The division between civil-political and economic-social rights, I note, is not sharp; a few of the rights in the Covenant on Economic, Social and Cultural Rights are constitutional rights as well. The right to join a trade union, for example, is protected in American constitutional law as an aspect of the freedom of association. The right to choose one's work is an aspect of constitutionally-protected liberty. If the government decides to make available economic-social benefits, invidious discrimination in providing them would be a denial of the equal protection of the laws. But, in the main, the rights in the Covenant on Economic, Social and Cultural Rights are not constitutional rights in the United States. Our rights theory supports rights deriving from, and vindicating, individual freedom and autonomy, not claims upon society to do for the individual what he needs but cannot provide himself. The Constitution tells government what not to do, not what it must do. The framers saw the purposes of government as being to police and safeguard, not to feed and clothe and house. Of the Four Freedoms Franklin Roosevelt proclaimed to the world, the Constitution guarantees three against abridgement by government—Freedom of Expression, Freedom of Religion, and Freedom from Fear. But there is no constitutional right to Freedom from Want.

Let there be no doubt. The United States is now a welfare state. Commitment to some minimum levels of individual welfare may not be of constitutional rank but it is deeply, ineradicably imbedded in our national life. Some will say that Americans have their basic human needs satisfied far better than do inhabitants of countries where these needs are labeled rights and whose governments have assumed international obligations to realize them. But we are not a welfare state by constitutional compulsion. Indeed, we became a welfare state in the face of powerful constitutional resistance: Federalism, and, ironically, notions of individual rights—economic liberty and freedom of contract—held the welfare state back for half a century. The United States is a welfare state by grace of Congress. But, as the Supreme Court has told us quite recently, there is no constitutional right to a minimum standard of "welfare" and subsistence, or of education. In constitutional principle Congress could, probably, abolish the welfare system at will, and the states could probably end public education. Surely the level of subsistence and the quality of education they provide are limited by political forces, not merely—as under the Covenant—by available economic resources. In the 1980s there was a strong move to cut welfare support in favor of huge arms programs and to permit major reductions in taxes. To the world, moreover, whatever the United States does in fact, it does not proclaim a national commitment in principle to meeting basic human needs. Americans are frequently reminded that our eighteenth-century philosophy, our kind of democracy, our national hagiography, show the United States committed to protecting property, but not to alleviating hunger, even of our own people.

There is another, different, happier, "lacuna" in the American Constitution, which Americans looking around the world today might note with pleasure and pride. It is a happy fruit of the ancestral political theory. In a constitution ordained by the sovereign people, constituting its social compact and its instructions to its official trustees and servants, there is no provision for suspending the Constitution or even the laws—and no provision for government other than by the people's representatives, that is, for government by decree. There is no provision for suspending any rights; only the privilege of the writ of habeas corpus can be suspended, and only by the people's representatives in Congress, only in cases of rebellion or invasion, only if the public safety requires it (Article I, section 9). Under the Covenant on Civil and Political Rights, a state may derogate from its obligations as regards many (not all) rights to the extent strictly required, in time of declared public emergency that threatens the life of the nation[30]—a condition which, alas, is frequently declared in many countries. Also, unlike some other, contemporary constitutions, the American Constitution does not mention the people's duties. Our ancestors knew they had duties—to God, to each other, and to their posterity—but these were not appropriate for a constitution. The Universal Declaration invokes the duties that an individual owes to his or her community, though it does not spell out what these duties are;[31] and it does not fairly imply—as some constitutions do[32]—that performing one's duties is a condition of enjoying one's rights.

I have compared American constitutional rights with international human rights, stressing—and thus exaggerating—the differences. The similarities are impressive, and the affinities are deep. And yet, it is not only of intellectual interest, but of considerable contemporary significance that the national commitments of the United States, as proclaimed in its Constitution, are below contemporary international standards, particularly in respect to equality and economic-social rights.

I would not urge that the United States Constitution be amended to correct what I have called its genetic defects (see essays 6 and 7). The Constitution is difficult to amend; surely, there has never been any disposition to amend it merely to illuminate it, so that all will see what is already there to the eye of a Supreme Court Justice. Nor do Americans feel the need to have the face of their Constitution "lifted," so as to modernize its statement to the world, as others have done with their national documents—if only because Americans see their Constitution as a living, work-a-day law, rather than as a manifesto.[33] In any event, an attempt to amend the Constitution to include an obligation on government to provide every person's basic human needs, or to improve the articulation of a commitment to equality, would surely, and quickly, drown in controversy.

But if Americans are not to express their contemporary national commitments through their Constitution, they might make their national statement, simply, by adhering to the principal international human rights covenants and conventions. Assuming international obligations to provide its citizens with basic human needs, and declaring them to be human rights, might even serve indirectly to elevate them in the constitutional conception.[34] Adherence would make explicit that the federal government must not deny the equal protection of the laws. It would express a national commitment to economic-social rights and dispel international misconceptions about where the United States stands on such rights. It would give Americans a few rights which the Supreme Court has not found in the Constitution. It would obligate Congress (or the states) to provide full remedies for violations of rights.

I have indicated the reasons why there is strong resistance to United States adherence to international human rights treaties, particularly in the United

States Senate, whose consent to ratification of the agreements is constitutionally required (see essay 5). In 1977 President Carter signed the International Covenants and two other major conventions and sent them to the Senate for its consent to ratification. But perhaps because he believed that many Senators are still "unreconstructed," perhaps because the executive branch itself is not wholly reconstructed, the President proposed that the United States enter major reservations, apparently designed to meet every possible kind of resistance.

One of the proposed reservations is probably necessary: the United States should not, of course, undertake any obligations that it could not carry out under the Constitution. For one instance—perhaps the only instance—the United States would probably have to enter a reservation or understanding to the article in the Covenant on Civil and Political Rights requiring states to prohibit "any propaganda for war," or "any advocacy of national, racial or religious hatred that constitutes incitement to discrimination, hostility or violence."[35] For the United States, such a prohibition would presumably violate the freedom of speech and of press, unless the prohibition were limited to circumstances where advocacy amounts to incitement to unlawful action.[36]

The other proposed reservations, however, are not necessary, and are deeply troubling. One of them would say, in effect, that courts in the United States will not apply any provision in the covenants until there has been legislation to implement them. That would invite new battles and delays in Congress, after the uphill struggle to obtain Senate consent in the first instance.[37] There is an unnecessary, ambiguous, confusing—and confused—statement leaving some implementation to the states, thus inviting further struggles in fifty state legislatures, and further confusion for the courts. Most disturbing is a series of reservations, understandings, and declarations, the thrust of which is that the United States will agree to do only what it already does; it will not undertake any obligation that would require any change in American law and practice. The purpose of these reservations is "to harmonize the treaties with existing provisions of domestic law."[38]

The notion that the United States would adhere to an international human rights agreement only insofar as it would require no change in the way it does things seems—to put it mildly—anomalous.* One would have thought that the principal purpose of undertaking obligations was to promise to do things one is not yet doing—in this instance, to improve one's ways, where necessary, to conform them to common international standards. And why would the United States wish these reservations? Why should it not supplement the constitutional rights of Americans in small, desirable respects, as it has supplemented them by national and state civil rights acts? Resisting and reserving every new commitment, however small, however desirable, will make the United States look ridiculous; how many times will it be noted that the United States is reserving the right to execute children and pregnant women?[39]

Some thirty years ago I wrote:

* Some have suggested that such a principle of reservation is invalid because it is incompatible with the object and purpose of the agreement.

Many will have deep sympathy for those who dream of old days thought good, or better; who yearn for decentralization even in foreign affairs and matters of international concern, for limitations on federal power, for increase in the importance of the States; who thrill to a wild, poignant, romantic wish to turn back all the clocks, to unlearn the learnings, until the atom is unsplit, weapons unforged, oceans unnarrowed, the Civil War unfought. The wish remains idle, and the effort to diminish power in this area for fear that it may not be used wisely is quixotic, if not suicidal. It is not the moment to attempt it when all ability, flexibility, wisdom are needed for cooperation for survival by a frightened race, on a diminishing earth, reaching for the moon.[40]

We have reached the moon, but the lesson is more urgent than ever; it is yet to be learned.

More than ten years have elapsed since President Carter signed the covenants and conventions. There has been no move in the Senate to consider them, no nudge of the Senate by the executive branch.

American constitutionalism can proudly claim an important part in the development of international human rights, and in their dissemination to every continent and corner. Europe has followed its constitutional lead; its ancestor in law and in rights, the United Kingdom, has seriously discussed the desirability of an effective Bill of Rights and judicial review.[41] An American kind of rights is now in 150 constitutions. Even the Communist states pay them at least the homage of lip-service, and consequently must pay them some heed in fact.

Universal acceptance of American ideas and American words is a compliment, but it brings the danger that others will seek to distort them to other meanings and other ends. Although rights are for living individual men and women, some would render them collective rather than individual, future rather than present, sacrificing individual rights and even basic needs today for economic development, for a larger gross national product, for a new international economic order tomorrow. Vigilance and participation is the price of maintaining an American kind of liberty.

The United States has done very well under its eighteenth-century Constitution, but it has also come a long way from its early years. The rights of gentlemen have now, finally, become the rights of man, of all men and women, and children; for Americans, too, freedom now means freedom from want as well as other freedoms. We arrived there by learning from others, from other peoples, other ideas. We still have some things to learn. We will learn better, I believe— and will teach and maintain our way more effectively—if we join the international human rights movement. As we are part of mankind, our constitutional rights are part of the human rights of all.

10

Rights: Here and There

I HAVE been moved to ask why the condition of human rights differs markedly between different societies in some, or many, respects. The answer, or answers, would doubtless require the combined explorations and wisdom of armies of anthropologists, sociologists, psychologists, political scientists, and others. My undertaking is a modest part, a constitutional lawyer's piece. I wish to examine different conceptions of rights and their consequences.

I hold it a truth that is self-evident, that, *inter* many *alia,* the condition of human rights responds in significant part to what I call a society's "rights system"—provisions in the constitution and in the laws declaring rights, and institutions for giving them effect. More or less purposefully, more or less knowingly, the constitution, laws, and institutions reflect a conception of rights. The theory of rights, I suggest, tells much about what a society believes, or believes it believes, and where human rights fit into its governing ideology, i.e., what it claims and what it aspires to in respect of rights. The conception of rights shapes laws and institutions and the rights which individuals enjoy in fact.

I speak of rights "here and there." "Here," the United States, "there," a few other places; inevitably, the United States in only some detail, other countries with even broader strokes. Principally I wish to compare the two leading perspectives on rights, the "liberal" and the "socialist," the individualist and the communal, and some variations on each as reflected in several contemporary

From 81 *Colum. L. Rev.* 1582 (1981).

societies. I do not purport to address the conception of rights in democratic theory or in socialist theory generally. I know of no authentic articulation of the theory of democracy. While socialist theory, on the other hand, is highly developed, its principal articulations antedate the birth of socialist states, and theory has not yet been comfortably accommodated to the realities of such states in the contemporary international system. I address, therefore, not democracy and socialism in theory, but the conception of rights in particular societies identified with liberal democracy or with socialism.

Americans know in an impressionistic way the difference in respect of individual rights between what we call the "Free World" and the Communist world, and we sense an unorderly variety of commitments to, or affecting, human rights in that spectrum called the "Third World." But is the Free World of one mind and one way in respect of rights? Is our conception of rights the same as that, say, of France, the other parent of the modern rights concept in the eighteenth century and a major influence on rights in different parts of the world today? What in fact are the significant differences in conceptions of rights between free world states and Communist states, and what are the consequences of these differences? Do third world rights systems reflect the same differences, and is being a Third World country itself relevant?

I have addressed rights in the United States (see essays 6 to 9). I summarize briefly, as groundwork for comparison:

Rights—human rights—in the United States are the product of a conception of preconstitutional moral rights, of constitutional guarantees, and of postconstitutional political and judicial implementation and enforcement.

The conception of rights in the United States is that proclaimed in the Declaration of Independence. Human beings are endowed by their creator with moral autonomy, liberty, and other rights. Exercising their inherent autonomy, the people, by social compact, establish a constitution and institute a government for agreed, limited purposes. Under the constitution, under constitutional government, the people retain sovereignty, and government is accountable to the people. Before any constitution, before government, human beings had natural, unalienable rights; after a constitution is established and government is instituted, individuals retain substantial autonomy, freedoms, and immunities from government.

The United States Constitution does not express the political theory that inspired it but that theory has continued to animate it and has shaped its growth. The Constitution is a social compact ordained and established by the people. The Constitution instituted a government reflecting principles—separation of powers, checks and balances, federalism—designed to prevent concentration of governmental power that might threaten individual rights.

The Constitution, as amended by the Bill of Rights, sets forth a number of the rights that government must respect—freedoms of religion, press, speech, assembly; the security of the person and of his home from unreasonable search and seizure; the protections of due process of law for life, liberty, and property; fair procedures in the criminal process and immunity from cruel and unusual punishment. By the Ninth Amendment, other rights not expressed are nonetheless retained. Later constitutional amendments abolished slavery, rendered United States citizenship indefeasible, guaranteed every person the equal protection of the laws, and prohibited the denial of suffrage on grounds of race, gender, age. The Ninth Amendment has been given no content, but the due process clauses of the Constitution were held to impose substantive limitations on the power of government. Government must justify any action affecting life, liberty or property as reasonably serving some proper public purpose. Liberty is broadly conceived to include essential autonomy.

The Constitution has grown in two hundred years, and its theory has shaped that growth. Slowly and at long last, popular sovereignty has come to mean representative government of virtually all the people. The republic has become a democracy. The theory of antecedent rights retained under the Constitution has inspired expanded readings of indefinite constitutional phrases, and rendered the Constitution open, living, growing. (Some suggest that every generation tacitly updates the social compact.) The living Constitution has helped bring rights to those who had had none, has expanded old rights and effectively brought new ones.

Constitutional rights in the United States, however, are limited by the original conception. They are rights that anteceded government and continue as freedoms and immunities from governmental interference; they do not include "economic and social rights."* The Constitution does not require government to provide social security or welfare assistance—food, shelter, health care, education—even for those who cannot provide these for themselves. The United States is a welfare state by grace of Congress and of the state legislatures, not by constitutional compulsion, and the adequacy of the welfare program is subject to political and budgetary restraints.

The Constitution guarantees individual rights but the means for enforcing that guarantee are not expressly provided. The fractionalizations of authority between the federal government and the states and among the branches of the federal government prevent the concentration of power and thereby invasions of individual rights. Congress has authority to implement and enforce rights protected by the Civil War (and later) Amendments, and it may use for human rights purposes its general powers, for example the power to regulate interstate commerce or to tax and spend for the general welfare. After the Civil War, and again in the 1960s, Congress enacted important civil rights legislation. But the Constitution does not require Congress to enact any such legislation and the laws Congress has enacted do not in fact prevent, deter, or punish all official violations, or compensate all victims of violations. The United States Constitution does not require either Congress or the state legislatures to enact and finance a welfare program.

The courts have become principal guardians of rights in the United States,

---

* Some economic and social rights such as the right to pursue work of one's own choosing and to join a trade union are protected under the United States Constitution as aspects of liberty and the right of association. See essay 9.

scrutinizing legislative and executive acts as well as those of the courts, in the light of constitutional limitations. The courts scrutinize strictly any invasions of political freedoms and of the zone of privacy, or the use of suspect classifications (such as race), and will invalidate such invasions or suspect classifications unless they serve a compelling public interest, as determined by the courts.

The power of the courts to safeguard rights is limited by constitutional restrictions, by the character of the judicial process, and by various self-imposed limitations. The courts will enforce only those rights expressed in the Constitution and—despite the Ninth Amendment—have been unwilling to identify and give effect to other rights retained by the people. They enforce rights only against "state action" and will invalidate private violations only when outlawed by Congress, to the extent that Congress has the power to outlaw such private violations. Courts can act only when requested by someone with standing in a ripe case or controversy. The courts can only address and remedy past violations; they can refuse to give effect to unconstitutional acts and enjoin future executive action; they cannot ordinarily mandate positive action by the legislature.

Other aspects of the American way with rights are probably shaped by our conception of rights. For example, for better as for worse, the accusatorial system of criminal justice responds to that conception. Criminal prosecution is an act of government against an individual—Commonwealth (or People) versus the accused—implicating his or her fundamental rights, which have to be safeguarded from the government. We protect individuals by providing them shields and weapons—a right to counsel, a presumption of innocence, rules of procedure and evidence. We do not seriously look to the representative of the people—the prosecution—to protect the rights of the accused. We insist on a judiciary independent of the rest of government, and in the criminal process we do not put courts on the side of "the people," the government; as in other contexts, we look to the courts to protect the individual against government. Since here the trial court is itself an instrument of the government's threat to the individual's liberty, we protect the individual against it too, by appellate review and collateral attack.

I have been writing of political and constitutional theory. There are also sociological factors and societal values that may rise to constitutional status or be equally compelling. In the United States, the theory of antecedent autonomy and the commitment to government for limited purposes have combined with both the high value placed on individual liberty and property, and the facts of geography, economics, demography, and sociology, to give freedom of enterprise and substantial laissez-faire a constitutional or near-constitutional character. A "puritan ethic," a high value on charity—the accepted domain of the church (for example, in caring for the poor, in education)—may also have discouraged burgeonings of the welfare state. Even when some societal responsibility for individual welfare was finally accepted, it was seen as secondary and supplementary. Especially in austere, conservative times, that responsibility is seen as only residual, only to help those who cannot help themselves, and only with respect to minimum necessities at poverty levels. The primary responsibility for individual welfare, for the pursuit of happiness and the achievement of security, was on the individual, supported by apolitical, voluntary, religious-social institutions, by private insurance schemes, or by fringe benefits of employment or of trade union membership.

Individual rights have been at the heart of the ideology of France, too.* The Declaration of the Rights of Man and of the Citizen of 1789 has reigned supreme, indeed alone, in French political hagiography. Like the American Declaration and American constitutions, the French Declaration declares pre-existing, inherent, natural rights.† Under that Declaration, too, rights are not a gift from society, but antecede it. Article 1 provides: "Men are born and remain free and equal in rights." Here, too, "the purpose of any political association is the preservation of the natural and imprescriptible rights of man." "A society in which rights are not secured, and powers are not separated, has no constitution at all." The rights of man are "liberty, property and resistance to oppression," a formula different from Jefferson's triad ("life, liberty and the pursuit of happiness"). The Declaration permits taking private property only for "evident public necessity" (Articles 2, 16, 17); the United States Bill of Rights permits it "for public use." But these differences do not necessarily have different implications or make different promises for individual rights in society. The axioms and assumptions are also similar to ours. The proclamation of equality implies the personhood of all individuals. The same underlying conception of justice is reflected, for instance, in an express declaration of the presumption of innocence, and in provisions against ex post facto law. In the French conception, too, the good society is the liberal society with freedom of thought and opinion, "even religious opinion" (it was the Age of Reason), and their unrestrained communication is "one of the most precious rights of man" (Art. 11).

In France, too, rights are part of a theory of government, and in France, too, that theory invokes social contract. But the conception of social contract and its consequence for rights are different. The American theory (usually traced to John Locke) insisted that by the social contract the individual retains autonomy and freedom as rights against society; respect for his rights by the people and its representatives is a condition of his entry into society and his submission to government. Under the French Declaration (apparently echoing Rousseau), the social contract creates "the nation," and the individual pools his hypothetical, antecedent autonomy in "the general will," withholding and retaining nothing.[1] The general will is expressed through law, and "all citizens have a right to concur in its formation."[2] ... The individual's inalienable rights are protected by the Nation, by the general will, through law. The Nation, through the law, will define the scope of individual rights in society, and will protect the individual against arbitrary action by government, i.e., by the executive. That the Nation through the general will, or the law itself, might violate the inalienable rights of an individual is inconceivable, an impossible conception.

The French Declaration, therefore, emphasizes and builds its rights on the

---

* Since writing this essay, I have developed the comparison between France and the United States more fully in a "bicentennial" essay, "Revolutions and Constitutions," 49 *La. L Rev.* 1023 (1989).

† Except where otherwise indicated, I rely on unofficial translations.

law and its authority. "What is not prohibited by the law may not be hindered; nor may anyone be compelled to do that which the law does not require." "No one may be accused, arrested, or imprisoned save in cases determined by law." "All who . . . execute, or cause to be executed, arbitrary orders must be punished, and every citizen summoned or apprehended by virtue of the law must obey immediately, and becomes culpable if he resists." "No man is to be interfered with because of his opinions . . . provided his manifestation of them does not disturb public order as established by law." "The free communication of thoughts and opinions is one of the most precious rights of man; every citizen may speak, write, and publish freely, except that he is responsible for the abuse of this liberty, in the cases determined by law."[3] On the other hand, in provisions redolent more of Montesquieu than of Rousseau, the French Declaration suggests that the law, too, is subject to limitations for the sake of individual rights. "The law has the right to prohibit only actions hurtful to society." "The law must impose only such penalties as are strictly and evidently necessary" (Arts. 5 and 8).

The political philosophy of the French Declaration, though not without its ambiguities, suggests a perspective on individual rights that differs from that of the United States in important respects. For the American founders the social contract was a reality as they formed their new, independent polities. As new polities, with new allegiances, in a new and isolated world, the differences between the rights of man and the rights of citizens were few and not stressed. In France the social contract was an ambiguous hypothesis. The Nation, and its polity, had ancient roots, even if revolution changed the form of government and the social structure. With reform by revolution, the concept, the status and the rights of *citoyen,* citizen, had to be established.

These differences between the two societies brought, or came with, others. In the United States, instructed perhaps by their recent difficulties with Great Britain, the framers saw rights as freedom from abuse by legislatures as much as (or more than) by the executive.* Later, Americans found protection against both political branches in an independent nonpolitical (or less political) judiciary. In France, the framers, reflecting a different history and a different revolution, saw dangers to individual rights particularly from the executive, and sought protection against executive abuse in representative bodies and in the law, even as, across the Channel, the British Parliament had become a bulwark for rights against the Crown. The people's representatives, and the law, could protect individual rights also against other powerful estates, institutions, and persons. Revolutionary France, moreover, breaking with *l'ancien régime,* rejected all its institutions including the judiciary which had supported the regime's dirty handiwork. In France, then, there was no tradition of judicial independence, of judicial defense against the executive and the police, as by writ of habeas corpus.

To compare the significance of the French Declaration for rights in France

---

*The very first provision in the Bill of Rights provides that *Congress* shall make no law abridging the major freedoms. United States Constitution Amendment I.

today with the American experience, one must take account also of stark differences in the histories of the two countries. The United States built a new society;
France sought to transform an old society over resistance of powerful, established
interests. Americans declared what they had; the French declared what they
desired. The United States incorporated its ancestral ideas into a national constitution and similar state constitutions, and they have essentially remained with us
until this day, threatened only once—by the Civil War—now long ago. France
has had Terror and Napoleon, alternating monarchies and republics, several
constitutions, extended wars and the vicissitudes of defeat in war in 1870 and
during the Second World War. The French Declaration, though followed by
other declarations and by constitutions, retained its special place, and remained
a brooding presence, its ideas never far or long from French consciousness. But
for a century and a half, until after the Second World War, the Declaration of
1789 had no status as law. During that century and a half, protection against
executive abuse remained a living concern, and institutions developed to guard
against it. They were not judicial institutions, for the judiciary never acquired
trust, prestige, and power even as a protector of rights. There was no move
towards giving courts the role of arbiter rather than participant in the criminal
process, and the presumption of innocence asserted in the Declaration carried no
implications to that end; there was no move towards a judicial writ of habeas
corpus or judicial search warrant.

Whether due to the influence of the Declaration or because it merely expressed what was in Rousseau and was congenial to the French spirit, the
supremacy of the law early became established as the ideal in the post-Revolu-
tionary tradition, even as the supremacy of Parliament was established in the
British constitutional system. The law, made by the nation's representatives,
could not violate the rights of individuals; rather, the law defined those rights
and protected them. Other institutions—for example, a powerful independent
press—were not as necessary. The press was free, and the law protected it and
even supported it.

The conception of rights and its history in France affected both their content
and their enjoyment in ways which many will see as more favorable than in the
United States. Since the Declaration was not law, and since in any event the
protection of individual rights was to be achieved by law, in France—unlike the
United States—"civil rights legislation" was normal and indeed a principal
function of the law. Rights were protected by legislation and had to be enumerated. The freedom to work, to engage in trade, was spelled out early, and
reiterated. The law could, should, did, protect rights not only against state
action, i.e., against the executive and the police, but also against invasion by
private persons and groups. While in the United States rights were seen as an
authentic continuation of antecedent individual autonomy, rights in France were
declared in the context of an established society (even if one in process of
transformation). They did not, then, see only the need to protect individual
autonomy against too much government; relying on the law to save them from
executive power and from powerful groups, they turned to the law also for other

needs and rights of a different conception. The Declaration of 1789 itself seemed to call for progressive taxation (Art. 13). Within a few years other declarations and constitutions (or draft constitutions) included other *"droits de créance"*— rights of affirmative obligation, not only of abstention. In 1791 and again in 1793, constitutions recognized the obligation of society to assure the livelihood of needy citizens by providing them either work or support for those incapable of working. Education was declared a necessity for all: society had to provide free public instruction for all citizens.[4]

In the nineteenth century, France continued to develop the obligations of the state, not merely its limits. France began to abolish slavery in the eighteenth century; in 1848, a new constitution declared the abolition of slavery and of press censorship, and the elimination of the death penalty for political crimes. But it also declared a series of affirmative obligations as duties for the state if not as rights for the individual. It added fraternity to equality and liberty. It committed the French Republic to assuring a more equitable distribution of the burdens and benefits of society, to improving the welfare of all, to raising every citizen to a higher level of morality, enlightenment, and well-being. It declared not only the freedom to work but a duty upon the state to prepare the individual for work and help him obtain it. It recognized, between the individual and society, other institutions—the family, various voluntary collective organizations. Increasingly, growing industrialization brought urban poverty and alienation; the working man and woman, his or her conditions of labor, and participation in determining one's social and economic welfare, were a continuing and growing concern and solicitude of the law. Man and his rights were not seen in philosophical abstraction: not the rights of man, but the rights and needs of real men and women—poor, old, sick, needy. France was a welfare state before the term was coined.

Unlike the United States, in its distant isolation, moreover, France was in the vortex of ideas and events in Europe. It contributed heavily to socialism and later felt the rumblings of the Russian Revolution. Unlike the United States, which has never known a meaningful socialist party, or even strong intellectual support for socialism, the ideas of socialism became part of French life and a continuing source of partisan and political issues as they never have in the United States.

After the Second World War, France had to reconstitute itself following defeat, occupation, liberation, victory. In the preparation of a post-war constitution, the ideas of 1789 and of socialism competed and merged, in quest of an "individualist socialism." The Declaration itself finally achieved the status of law, of constitutional law, being incorporated by reference in the preamble of the 1946 constitution and again in that of the 1958 constitution currently in effect. For the first time, rights were given status as constitutional law, so that the *Conseil d'Etat*—the highest administrative court—has been able to invoke the Declaration of 1789, when there was no relevant legislation, to invalidate administrative acts.[5] The preamble gave constitutional status also to the "fundamental principles recognized by the laws of the Republic" and proclaimed "the political, economic, and social principles most vital in our time."[6] There was explicit reference to rights of labor—the right (and duty) to work, the right to strike, collective bargaining, workers' voice in management—and welfare rights for the individual and his family—health care and free public education at all levels. These rights too, then, are constitutional law although the practical significance of giving such status to affirmative economic-social rights is yet uncertain. Rights reflecting intervening development were also added; for example, the equality of men and women is on the face of the constitution.[7] That France is a government of the people, by the people, for the people, has become constitutional principle.

The 1958 constitution also reaffirms the place of the law, as in the original theory of the 1789 Declaration: The law determines the rules concerning "civil rights and the fundamental guarantees granted to citizens for the exercise of public liberties."[8] Parliament, by law, defines and regulates rights and liberties, and the courts, ordinary and administrative, will give effect to what the law provides by means and remedies which the law has provided. The law also aids and supports rights both directly and indirectly. It protects them by criminal and tort law against violations. It also promotes their enjoyment. The emphasis on rights through law, as distinguished from rights as freedom from state control, has meant state involvements that are unknown in the United States. The press in France is free, but perhaps not as free by our conception: there are state involvements with it, including subventions and other forms of assistance, that we would not accept. The inquisitorial, as distinguished from our adversarial, criminal process, responding to other French traditions, may also reflect a conception of rights that involves the state in assuring their enjoyment. The separation of church and state, the product of France's history in the nineteenth century, reflects relationships closer to our own. But France has tuition grants for children in private school.[9]

The 1958 constitution, however, also gave France General de Gaulle's conception of a hybrid presidential-parliamentary system. One result was the provision giving the President power in national emergency to "take the measures required by the circumstances."[10] It is noteworthy (reflecting, no doubt, the different circumstances of the United States in 1787 and France in 1958) that France, historically committed to parliamentary supremacy, gave virtually unlimited emergency powers to the President. The United States, having no commitment to legislative supremacy, gives the single small emergency power in the Constitution—the power to suspend the privilege of the writ of habeas corpus—only to Congress.

Perhaps it required de Gaulle's radical breach in the French tradition of a parliament sole and supreme to bring to France also the radical notion that Parliament might itself be subject to constitutional restraints. It has not, however, brought judicial review to France. The courts have not risen appreciably. Their independence is declared in the constitution but it is the President who guarantees that independence. The constitution promised the courts a new role, the equivalent of the writ of habeas corpus, if the law so provides, but the law has not yet so provided. By 1958, however, the international human rights

movement and the universalization of human rights in national constitutions—
as well as the increasing appeal of the American experience with judicial review
—brought to France, too, the idea that individual rights require protection
against Parliament. But it came into the French constitution in its own special
form, not involving the courts, and maintaining the sacrosanctity of the law. In
the United States, law can be challenged only after it is enacted, only when it is
brought to bear on an individual to his detriment, only by the individual affected,
only in a court of law, before the ordinary judges, in an actual case or controversy. In France, the law still cannot be challenged, anywhere, by anybody. But
before it becomes law, and only before it becomes law, a bill of Parliament is
subject to review for constitutionality. A bill cannot be challenged by persons
whose rights would be violated by it; it can be challenged only by the President
of the Republic, the Prime Minister, the president of either of the two chambers
of Parliament, or, by later amendment, by sixty members of either house of
Parliament. A bill is challenged not in a general court, or in any court at all, but
in a constitutional council manned not by judges but by persons appointed to
this special task. If a provision of the proposed law is declared to be contrary to
the constitution, it cannot be enacted. Constitutional scrutiny in France, then, is
not a judicial function in the application of law; it is part of the legislative process,
available to participants in the process, including—principally—parliamentari-
ans of opposition parties. After a law is enacted, it—and all the law already on
the books in France—cannot be challenged by anyone, anywhere. Still, the
French constitution has achieved the status of higher law to prevent even the
Nation, "the general will," from enacting new inconsistent law.

France and the United States represent two strands in a single eighteenth-
century conception of rights. They have much in common, and some important
differences. In both, individual rights are part of a comprehensive theory of
government. It includes representative government, with separated branches. It
includes as well inherent individual rights, as ends in themselves, not merely as
instrumental to some overriding conception of the good society. Important rights
cannot be wholly sacrificed even for the general, public good. Rights include
liberty, equality, property, and substantial freedom of enterprise.

In the United States rights are essentially freedoms—including freedom from
the people's representatives in government, freedom even from the law if it is
excessive. In respect of freedom, it is the individual against the society, in
adversary relationship. One depoliticized public institution—the courts—has
become sufficiently independent of the rest of the government to serve as the
bulwark of the individual's rights. Other extragovernmental, antigovernmental
institutions help safeguard rights—e.g., the press. Other individual benefits,
including economic and social assistance, are not yet part of the conception of
rights, perhaps because we still hear ancestral voices declaiming the limited
purposes of government. The welfare system is underdeveloped—the product of
the political process, and subject to its limits and budgetary restraints. There is
tension between the aspiration to freedom, resisting governmental intervention,
and the aspiration to security and welfare, inviting more government.

In France, freedom is primarily not freedom from law but freedom through law. Its deepest commitment is to rights protected and nurtured by Parliament. The law and the institutions it has established protect the individual against the executive. The law also nurtures individual rights and helps realize them in fact. And it includes, as affirmative obligations of government, as individual rights, the economic and social benefits of the welfare state. Any ambivalence about government intervention seems muted.

The single page of the French Declaration, Lord Acton wrote, proved stronger than the armies of Napoleon. In our day, too, the influence of the French Declaration has been strong: on the Universal Declaration of Human Rights, on international covenants, and on the constitutions of many states in Latin America, Africa, and Asia. French influence has included its conception of rights as protected by law, including, therefore, in principle, comprehensive legislative programs to promote and ensure civil and political rights. France has also helped bring into the world's constitutional idiom economic and social rights inspired by socialism. But, of course, France has not been an influence for subjecting the parliament and the law to effective constitutional restraints. That rights can be suspended by the President in emergency has found response; alas, in many countries (unlike France), it has not remained a hypothetical power. Even in France and her political progeny, however, the American conception of rights as superior law, protected also against the parliament by independent, nonpolitical institutions, has captured imaginations.

A political ideology to which individual rights are basic is sometimes contrasted with socialism. Today, however, many countries that denominate themselves socialist—including the USSR and the People's Republic of China—have indicated a commitment to human rights. Many socialist states have adhered to international human rights covenants, implying, and frequently asserting, that their citizens enjoy the rights recognized in these instruments. The 1977 constitution of the USSR devotes some twenty articles to the rights of its citizens.[11]

There have been many socialisms, and some have combined socialist principles with deep attachment to individual rights. Not Marx's socialism.[12] In an industrialized bourgeois society, Marx thought, the worker is inherently and inevitably exploited and alienated and individual rights are an illusion and a deception.* Individualism, and its reflection in claims to individual rights, are obstacles to be overcome on the road to Communism. In the historically inevitable Communist society of the future, after the state has withered away, individualism will have been eliminated, and it will be meaningless to speak of individual rights. All members of the society will find themselves free and fulfilled in community.

Today socialist societies exist in socialist states, although perhaps, in theory and in principle, they may see themselves as on the road to a pure, stateless

---

* Marx did support rights for the proletariat, however, as a step toward socialism. In fact, Lenin later declared that the democratic republic is the shortest road to the dictatorship of the proletariat.

Communist society. Theories of socialism, even if called Marxist, have had to relate to actual socialist states in an international system that, whatever the inexorable laws of historical necessity may be, immediately reflects the iron laws of national interest and power, international politics and economics. As a result, contemporary socialist states, with socialist theory far behind, have had to respond to the rise and the appeal of the idea of human rights. In socialist states, we are told, the citizen enjoys rights. What is the conception of those rights?

In the Marxist-Leninist-USSR conception, man is not born free and cannot achieve freedom in society generally. Freedom, moreover, as commonly understood in the context of bourgeois societies, is an empty, deceptive aspiration. Under this view, other individualist assertions, indeed the very idea of individual "rights" as claims against the society, do not address the true aspirations and potentialities of man in society. Man can achieve true "freedom" only in community, in a socialist society. The dominant value or goal, perhaps the only "right" of the individual, then, is to live in a socialist society. In such a society, a person enjoys, meaningfully and fully, benefits, opportunities—call them freedoms, rights; however, these are not freedoms from or rights against the society, but rights and freedoms within it, as a member of society.

The socialist state is organized to maintain and protect the socialist society. It has not come about by a social contract of the people, but was created by leaders dedicated to achieving the dictatorship of the proletariat. Later, as in the USSR, as the 1977 constitution declared, "the aims of the dictatorship of the proletariat having been fulfilled, the Soviet State has become a state of the whole people." [13] Then, the people are sovereign and the sovereignty of the people is reflected in a representative government of "democratic centralism" in which every citizen has the right and the duty to participate. The Communist Party is the "leading and guiding force of Soviet society and the nucleus of its political system" (Art. 6).

In the socialist state the constitution is neither a contract among the people establishing the state nor a contract between the government and the people. It is not prescriptive, normative, but descriptive as well as programmatic. The Constitution is a proclamation, a manifesto, by the leaders to the people, describing the society that exists, its institutions and its values, as well as its aspirations and plans. It provides not a blueprint for a system of government to be, but a map of a government that is. It also sets forth the rights (and duties) of citizens, but rather than prescribe what must be, these declarations describe what is— i.e., not the limitations that government must observe but the rights and benefits that the government provides and those it promises. While it is declared that "[t]he Constitution of the USSR shall have supreme legal force," and all laws and other official acts shall be in conformity with it (Art. 173), the leaders of the people interpret what the constitution means and can also amend it formally when necessary. Of course, a descriptive, programmatic constitution also makes promises, creates expectations, influences official behavior. It will not serve its purposes if it is too far removed from the reality it purports to describe, if promises are not kept.

Rights that the individual enjoys in socialist society do not antecede the state.

They are not entitlements based on natural law, original autonomy, or social contract. They are not rights against the state. They are the rights and benefits conferred by the socialist state as aspects of life in a socialist society. They are "rights" in that every citizen earns and enjoys them. They cannot be "claimed" against the state or against the people as represented by the highest representative organs, for if the socialist state does not grant a right it does not exist. Rights can only be claimed against particular officials if bureaucratic mistake or inefficiency fails to provide them.

The rights granted by the state, and proclaimed in the constitution, are those that inhere in socialism. And they exist and are enjoyed only insofar as they are consistent with socialism. Enjoyment by citizens of any right or freedom, then, must not be to the detriment of socialism, of socialist society or the socialist state. Accordingly, Article 39 of the Soviet constitution provides:

> Citizens of the USSR enjoy in full the social, economic, political and personal rights and freedoms proclaimed and guaranteed by the Constitution of the USSR and by Soviet laws. The socialist system ensures enlargement of the rights and freedoms of citizens and continuous improvement of their living standards as social, economic, and cultural development programmes are fulfilled.
>
> Enjoyment by citizens of their rights and freedoms must not be to the detriment of the interests of society or the state, or infringe the rights of other citizens.

In this as in all else, there is, perhaps inevitably, some tendency to confuse the needs of socialism with the needs and interests of the socialist state, or of a particular socialist state at a particular time, as determined by particular leaders. The constitution of the USSR includes patriotic clauses no different from those that might appear in a nonsocialist constitution—e.g., a chapter on the Defense of the Socialist Motherland (Ch. 5). Individual rights, then, are subordinated to the security needs of the country and other national interests as determined by the leaders at the time.

That rights are granted only as instruments of socialism and only so far as conducive to socialism is reiterated in describing particular rights. For example, citizens are guaranteed freedom of speech "[i]n accordance with the interests of the people and in order to strengthen and develop the socialist system." Citizens have the right to associate "[i]n accordance with the aims of building communism." Moreover, since a socialist society depends on the cooperation of all the people, the citizen has duties to maintain the socialist society; and the enjoyment of rights depends on respect for duties. Article 59 provides: "Citizens' exercise of their rights and freedoms is inseparable from the performance of their duties and obligations." Or, in a crucial provision, "[c]itizens of the USSR have the right to work (that is, to guaranteed employment . . ." (Arts. 50, 51, 59, and 40). But that does not imply the right not to work. As the 1936 constitution made explicit, "He who does not work, neither shall he eat." [14] And, repeated in

1977: " 'From each according to his ability, to each according to his work.' "
Also: "Socially useful work and its results determine a person's status in society."

Socialism confers primarily the right to live in a socialist society, with the socialist economic system as its principal characteristic. The Soviet constitution therefore sets out that system, including public ownership of the means of production and minimal private enterprise and property. In keeping with the economic and social concerns of a socialist society, the right (and duty) to work is paramount, set forth as part of the basic system. Later in the constitution, a chapter declares the equality of citizens' rights—equality before the law, equality of men and women, equality of citizens of different races and nationalities (Ch. 6). In the catalogue of rights, therefore, economic and social rights come first— the rights to work, rest and leisure, health protection, old age maintenance, housing, education; also the right to enjoy cultural benefits in accordance with the aim of building communism. Then, a list of political and civil rights: freedom of speech, press, assembly, and the right to associate "in public organisations that promote their political activity and initiative"; freedom of conscience, that is, the right to profess or not to profess any religion; the inviolability of the person and the home; and the privacy of the citizen, his correspondence and communication. There is no provision, however, that the citizen enjoys freedom from involuntary servitude, from torture or cruel, inhuman, or degrading treatment or punishment, or from arbitrary arrest, detention, or exile.

The rights that the citizen enjoys in the socialist state are not theoretical, abstract freedoms; they are benefits that the state affirmatively provides and makes sure the citizen enjoys in fact. For example, the first paragraph of Article 50 provides: "In accordance with the interests of the people and in order to strengthen and develop the socialist system, citizens of the USSR are guaranteed freedom of speech, of the press, and of assembly, meetings, street processions and demonstration." But a second paragraph adds: "Exercise of these political freedoms is ensured by putting public buildings, streets and squares at the disposal of the working people and their organisations, by broad dissemination of information, and by the opportunity to use the press, television, and radio." Other rights proclaimed are also accompanied by a statement as to what the state does to enable the citizen to enjoy that right.

A crucial element in socialism, and a basic right of the citizen, is "socialist legality." Many rights are declared to be protected by law: "The privacy of citizens . . . is protected by law"; "No one may, without lawful grounds, enter a home against the will of those residing in it"; "Hearings *in camera* are only allowed in cases provided for by law. . . ."; "Judges . . . are independent and subject only to the law." (Arts. 56, 55, 157, and 155). The principle of socialist legality implies that officials, bureaucrats, and police cannot act by private fiat. We have seen that in France the law is limited in principle by a priori conceptions of justice and fairness; in the USSR the law must conform to the needs of socialism and the socialist state.

In the socialist society, then, the overriding value is not autonomy, individuality, liberty, equality, property, security, or any other individual value. It is socialism. It is the socialist society that contributes to the dignity, well-being, happiness, self-fulfillment of all individuals. The individual realizes himself in the collectivity. Living under socialism assures the individual his basic human needs, with dignity, and in freedom from exploitation and alienation. It assures equality, equal access to economic benefits, and equal protection of the laws. Deviations from equality are based only on contribution to socialism: " 'to each according to his work' "; "[s]ocially useful work . . . determine[s] a person's status in society." [15]

Within, and subject to, socialism, the individual enjoys freedom. But it is not freedom from socialism, but within socialism, indeed freedom as a means and an opportunity to maintain and protect socialism. Thus, liberty means the opportunity to participate in socialism. Freedom of choice is allowed so far as is consistent with socialism, for example, the choice of career if it is conducive to the best interests of society. But freedom, apparently, does not encompass those freedoms that are deemed not to be consistent with socialism, for example, the freedom to choose one's residence or to leave one's country and to return.*

In the Western conception we have seen that rights reflect assumed principles of justice, fairness, and the liberal state. In the Soviet Union, though, the good society is not the liberal state but the socialist state. Nor does Soviet socialism accept any independent concepts of justice as a priori limitations on socialism. In principle, it rejects "justice" like other natural law as the new mythology of the bourgeoisie (as religion was the old mythology).† In the socialist state, socialism is justice. What is required by socialism, what contributes to socialism or serves the interests of the socialist state, is just, fair, desirable.

I have suggested the conception of rights in the contemporary socialist states. But such states have been developing their conceptions of rights as they go along, and adapting them to contemporary circumstances and needs. They are not compelled to adhere strictly to Marx, or even to Lenin or Stalin. They can modify their conception to meet the needs not only of socialism or the socialist state, but also, for example, of socialist Russia. And those include the exigencies of life in a country with its own presocialist history and traditions in a world that responds to nonsocialist ideas—among them human rights. Hence, I believe, the many references to individual rights in the USSR constitution. Hence, too, apparent regard for nonsocialist conceptions of justice. The USSR, for example, proclaims socialist legality and equal treatment for those similarly situated. In the USSR, too, there are procedures patently designed to render it likely that, ordinarily, the innocent will not be convicted. Is that only because unequal justice, or convicting the innocent, is irrational, unscientific, and does not ordinarily serve socialism or the socialist state? Is it, perhaps, that respect for nonsocialist principles of justice and fairness also serves socialism, if only in that violation of those principles is in fact offensive to the citizen at home and brings discredit to socialism abroad? Or is there, in fact not yet caught up with by theory, an acceptance of common, "natural" concepts of "fairness," "justice"?

The socialist theory of rights is reflected in the institutions that give them

---

*Compare Universal Declaration of Human Rights, Art. 13(2): "Everyone has the right to leave any country, including his own, and to return to his country."

† Under socialist theory the only natural law is the law of historical necessity.

effect, but Socialist Russia built upon older Russian institutions and today it is not always obvious what is socialist and what is Russian. Since rights are whatever the socialist state provides, there can be no violation of rights by the state, and therefore no institutions to deal with such violations. Individual officials, however, can make mistakes or be inefficient or occasionally even malevolent, and here the socialist state provides for rectification. The 1977 constitution provides that "[c]itizens have the right to lodge a complaint against the actions of officials, state bodies and public bodies."[16] In a tacit compliment to Western institutions, the 1977 constitution also provides that actions by officials that infringe "the rights of citizens, may be appealed against in a court in the manner prescribed by law."* The Procurator-General, who is charged with assuring that officials comply with Soviet law, can demand compliance also with the rights declared and promised by the constitution. Against abuse by the Procurator, who is also the chief prosecutor, there is—in principle—appeal to the Supreme Soviet, the representatives of the people, to which he is accountable. (Arts. 164 and 108). In the 1980s a fresh wind that began to blow with Gorbachev's glasnost also promised some improvements in the condition of human rights, and may lead to modifications in socialist theory of human rights.

For our purposes there is not much different to say about the People's Republic of China, at least as it has been. China has been committed to Marxist-Leninist-Maoist thought, to the same theory of the state and the individual. There are differences among the succesive Chinese constitutions, and between the three Chinese constitutions and those of the Soviet Union, but the variations reflect no fundamental Sino-Soviet difference in system of government or conception of rights, only a desire to make a modified ideological declaration to the people or to the world.†

China's constitution, too, is descriptive, programmatic not prescriptive, manifesto rather than social compact. Benefits and privileges are denominated rights and granted so far as conducive to, or at least consistent with, the needs of socialism as the authorities perceive them. In principle, there is no conception of justice independent of socialism. Equality, liberty, and what we would call a fair trial are desirable when they are consistent with and conducive to socialism. In China, too, the needs of socialism have been identified with those of the Chinese state—even of particular leaders—as determined by them. China did seek to do without traditional institutions for the administration of justice, and now has felt obliged to reestablish a formal legal system. But there is yet no sign that a legal system will modify the basic conceptions.

In China, too, one may ask, how much is Communism, how much is China? Are there in Chinese traditions elements relevant to the conception and condi-

---

* See note 16. The manner was not prescribed by law for ten years, until 1987; under the law then enacted, there is some judicial review of some orders of the bureaucracy.

† For example, a statement in the 1954 constitution that people's courts administer justice independently and subject only to law was abandoned in 1975, when the courts were made expressly responsible and accountable to political authority. Although perhaps a more accurate description, it does not appear that any change was effected. See Xianfa (Constitution) of 1954, Art. 78 (P.R.C.), and Xianfa (Constitution) of 1975, Art. 25 (P.R.C.).

tion of human rights? The Chinese tradition had it that men (including governors) were good; there was no need for external limitations, surely not for means to enforce them. Socialism apart, then, a constitution in China might not be higher law, but only a statement to the world and to the people, designed to legitimize authority, to reassure and to mobilize the people.

Traditional China, too, did not emphasize the individual and individual rights. The contours of individuality, of the individual's proper domain and where it met another's, were not clearly marked. One's individuality, one's rights moreover, were not to be flaunted or asserted. The ideal was harmony and the individual's place and role were to conform to that harmony. There was a belief that at bottom the interests of all individuals harmonized rather than conflicted, and that institutions should reflect and seek that commonality of interests. That is different, but perhaps not too different, from the relation of individual to community in the socialist conception.

If theorists of socialism insist there is no "justice" independent of socialism, Chinese theorists of Chinese socialism seem to insist that of course a socialist society has to be just. The effort to dispense with a legal system and rely on informal, communal mediation and accommodation may have responded to Chinese traditions as much as to socialism. The decision to restore a legal system, and the legal system being restored, may also prove Chinese as much as socialist. Even before Communism, for a particular example, the Chinese would not have accepted the Western protestation that it is better to have ten guilty men go free than have one innocent man convicted. They believed that no single guilty person should go free and no single innocent convicted. They believed that truth could be and should be ascertained, and they had confidence in methods to do so. They desired confession as the best evidence. They considered the criminal law as a moral-educational exercise, and confession as purgative, educative. International human rights in China wear a *Chinese* socialist face.

In the socialist state, the dominant value is not individualism and individual rights, but the fulfillment of all human beings in a socialist community. Individual rights are not an intrinsic, independent good. There is no individual right that can defeat the public welfare. The principal individual right is to live in socialist society. Socialism provides the individual with particular rights, the reward of fulfilling his obligations to the socialist society. These include economic and social rights implied in the socialist system, and civil and political rights conducive to socialism, to enable the citizen to participate in socialism. There are no rights against society or freedoms from government, but rather rights and freedoms within socialist society. There is no tension between less government and more government; socialist government represents the people and is integral to socialist society.*

To compare often means to contrast. It might be instructive also to stress

---

* It remains to be seen how much change the Gorbachev era will bring to human rights in socialist theory and USSR practice. There is some reason for hope. In May 1989, events in China, too, raised hopes that new winds might bring some new respect for human rights; the dashing of these hopes for the present has not eliminated the prospects for change in the not distant future.

similarities, convergences. It is significant, surely, that socialist states like liberal states now subscribe to a common affirmation of individual freedoms. It is significant, surely, that liberal states like socialist states now recognize affirmative claims upon government to contribute to the welfare of the individual. There are similarities in detail deriving from common roots in a common cultural tradition that has shaped laws and institutions. The reader will have noted similarities in particular between the conceptions of rights in France and in the USSR. And, indeed, they have both been part of European history, and there has been particularly strong reciprocal influence between the two countries. In both France and the USSR the law is supreme, infallible. But in France, it is because the general will, the people represented in Parliament through a democratic political process, is infallible; the people will not infringe on the rights of the individual. In the USSR law is infallible not because the people are infallible but because socialism and its leadership are infallible. In France there is some socialism, but it is individualist socialism, with freedom. In the USSR it is at best some freedom, as much as socialism and an infallible oligarchy believe consistent with socialism and the needs of the particular socialist state.

The "Third World" was conceived, and named, to pronounce a pox on both older superpower worlds in international affairs. On the international stage, on which it is now prominent, the Third World has frequently and unanimously proclaimed commitment to human rights. The 100 and more national societies that comprise it have contemporary constitutions expressing commitment to human rights. But the Third World does not have a common tradition, a common political ideology, or a common conception of rights. Their constitutions have borrowed variously—from Great Britain or France, from the United States, from the USSR, from international instruments such as the Universal Declaration of Human Rights and the European Convention on Human Rights. In borrowing text, terms ("liberty," "equality," "socialism"), institutions, procedures, however, they have not necessarily taken also conceptions and philosophical perspectives.

There is, then, no single Third World conception of human rights, or even several Third World conceptions. Third World societies, however, have things in common that may add up to a perspective on human rights. All are new or newly constituted states. All are building new institutions. All are societies in transition. All are committed to economic, social, and political development.

Many new states were the product of revolution and some have suffered revolutions in their short lives. Revolutions are inherently disrespectful of human rights. Successful revolutions are sometimes in a hurry, and individual rights are an obstacle. Revolutionary regimes sometimes impose an ideology to which human rights are subservient. Thus, some revolutionary constitutions recognize rights only "within the limits of public interest and the principles of the Revolution" or "which comply with the revolutionary, national and progressive trend."[17]

Many Third World states are societies in flux. Unstable societies breed *coups d'etat* which do not readily give way to democratic institutions. Constitutionalism and constitutional succession become the exception. Opposition becomes treason. Oligarchic government in unstable societies sometimes seeks to impose a mood morally equivalent to that of war in which individual concerns and rights are not prominent. Sometimes there is also terrorism and counterterrorism and a state of more-or-less actual war. Then, national security is commonly and lightly invoked, and is readily identified with the security of a particular regime. Emergency is a continuing phenomenon, leading to derogations and deviations from the rule of law, to government by decree, to unlawful prolonged detentions. At such times, neither rules nor institutions limiting government apply. Surely, instability, emergency, and concern for national security do not encourage judicial independence; moreover, what a constitution permits—suspension of rights and other emergency measures—not even an independent judiciary can prevent.

New or transformed societies generally imply new institutions. Even if modeled after those of other nations, institutions will grow slowly and differently in local soil and climate. Institutions that will stand up to dominant political authority—for example, judicial review—are particularly difficult to establish. Independence of judges can be readily proclaimed, but independence in fact has to be assured, traditions of independence have to be developed, the idea of judicial supremacy has to be taught—to the judges themselves, to the governors, to the people. In the United States, for example, despite supportive common law traditions, judicial supremacy was not built in a day.* In newer countries, where the independence of courts is still hardening, judicial supremacy will thus come late, if at all, although the United States is a powerful and persuasive example.

All Third World countries are committed to development. Development takes many forms and many different roads are claimed to lead to it (see Epilogue). But all of them imply activist, interventionist government and, with the increase of state power, the need for a bill of rights becomes even greater. The drive to build a new society and raise its standard of living supports emphasis on economic and social rights as soon as possible,"to the maximum of . . . available resources."[18] Such emphasis provides reasons for cutting corners on representative government and individual participation, and for resisting claims of individual autonomy and privacy as restraints on regimentation. A right to development itself comes to be asserted as a human right, entitling it to compete at least equally with other, more individuated, rights. Some governments will stress that

---

* Although hailed as the father of judicial supremacy, John Marshall did not "take on" the most powerful political forces, but built judicial authority principally by prescient betting on the winning political side—the nation as against the states. Moreover, Marshall did not take on the political power to protect individual rights. The courts did not begin to do that until after the Civil War, indeed much later, after their power had been established. See Henkin, "Constitutional Fathers—Constitutional Sons," 60 *Minn. L. Rev.* 1113, 1140–42 (1976). It may be argued that the United States courts have *never* confronted important national abuses of rights. See *Korematsu v. United States,* 323 U.S. 214 (1944). See essay 7.

without development there can be no freedom, but for them that means that freedom must wait, and for some, that somehow government by decree—the elimination of opposition, prolonged detention, even torture—will build factories and increase gross national product. As many crimes have been committed in the name of development as Madame Roland said had been committed in the name of liberty.

What Third World states generally have in common helps give a particular flavor to human rights conceptions borrowed from the other worlds. Western human rights attitudes become here less "pure" Locke, Rousseau, or John Marshall; socialism less Marx-Lenin. Newness and the drive for development breed pragmatism and improvisation, and borrowed conceptions of rights are shaped by particular culture, history, geography, leadership, and fortune.

Consider two countries in Black Africa. Nigeria and Tanzania, at opposite ends of the continent, were both British colonies. Both are tribal patchquilts within borders rationalized only by the accidents of colonial rule. In differing degrees both are traditional societies rooted in the village and only overlaid by urbanization. In both, the imported, Western, statist, urban-individualist conception of rights meets a tradition of communality and authority. But human rights are not a foreign substance. In important respects the tribal village tradition may be more conducive and congenial to both values and practices on human rights than the contemporary "statism" that has come to them. Traditional Africa has known the legitimacy of government and the limitations it implies; the obligations of rulers, not too far from the rights of the ruled; due process of law, equal justice, equity, fairness, freedom of speech and the right to participate; freedom of residence and of movement; the right to life, to survival and subsistence; property and the right to work; forms of communal responsibility and social security; the rights of family, of women and children; privacy; human dignity.

In the 1980s, for many purposes, including human rights, Nigeria and Tanzania are two different societies. Nigeria is an eclectic variation on Western themes. Under British rule, Nigeria had developed some institutions in the British style, including a judiciary and an active bar. Nigeria obtained her independence easily, peacefully. In moving Nigeria to independence, Great Britain—itself without a written constitution or an active bill of rights—pressed for a constitution, including a bill of rights, if only to reassure tribal minorities and to protect remaining white settlers. The British-sponsored constitution was in the British tradition, with British-style institutions, including its courts, but it was also distinctly federalist and included a written bill of rights.

The history of Nigeria has been troubled. Tribal conflict led to civil war, followed by military rule. In time the military left, *mirabile dictu,* voluntarily and peacefully. Through all the troubled years the bill of rights remained, unquestioned in principle. In 1979, Nigeria adopted a new, homegrown constitution modeled closely after that of the United States but drafted by individuals reared in the British heritage. The constitution established a federal system, a president and a legislature, checks and balances. All institutions were busily engaged in learning their functions and roles.

The conception of rights in Nigeria was like those of the United States and Europe, its details modeled after the European Convention on Human Rights.[19] In addition to the basic political-civil rights, there was the rule of law—a legal system, hospitable to legal representation, impartial courts. But many rights bowed to the needs of defense, public safety, public order. And there was a provision for taking such measures derogating from life and liberty as are "reasonably justifiable" in an emergency declared by the President.[20] As in the United States, the courts were available for judicial review and for other protections of rights (but special courts were designated for final appeal in all Muslim cases). Unlike the United States, there was also a constitutional provision that the legislature shall provide for "financial assistance to any indigent citizen of Nigeria where his rights have been infringed, or with a view to enabling him to engage the services of a legal practitioner to prosecute his claim."[21] but the infrastructure is not yet there. A person in the city who was sophisticated, aware, and who could get to and pay a lawyer (who commanded high fees in a booming profession in a booming oil economy) could expect substantial justice and vindication of his rights. But the legislature had not yet provided meaningful legal services; and there was no Legal Aid Society, no Civil Liberties Union, no Legal Defense Fund to make judicial protection meaningful and effective for many. And the rights were rights of freedom, and not rights to less inequality. The courts could not, the legislature did not, do much for freedom from want in the richest country in Black Africa.*

As of the end of the 1980s, Tanzania is a variation on the socialist theme. The history of Tanzania is still largely the story of Julius Nyerere† and its conception of rights is his conception. He led and persuaded his new country to a distinctive socialism. But it is not conceptually pure socialism as regards rights. In principle, and generally in fact, for Nyerere, what socialism does not reasonably require to be regulated is free. There can be no freedom without development, but without freedom there can be no development.

In other respects, too, the perspective on rights in Tanzania requires assertions, favorable or unfavorable, to be qualified by "buts." Tanzania has universal suffrage. But it is a one-party state, the President's party, TANU. The Tanzanian constitution has no bill of rights, Nyerere having rejected it as unsocialist and as giving too much power to the courts. But there is a multimember ombudsman, the Permanent Commission of Inquiry. The Commission, reporting and responsible to the President, investigates complaints against the bureaucracy and the police, but cannot trouble the government or the party. There is,

---

* The 1979 constitution and the government it established did not last, and in 1984 military rule returned to Nigeria. It has not claimed legitimacy and there is promise of early return to constitutional government. Even military rule has not been starkly repressive and there is reason to hope that Nigeria will resume its way toward respect for human rights.

† Nyerere gave up the presidency in 1985 but has remained a significant presence, and what I say here remains generally valid.

however, an impartial judiciary and the rule of law, not of socialist legality, not law wholly at the service of socialism and the socialist state. In the index to one of the principal books on Tanzania there is no entry under liberty, or freedom, or autonomy, or individual.[22] But the Arusha Declaration of 1967, the manifesto of TANU, declares its principal aims and objects to include: "To safeguard the inherent dignity of the individual in accordance with the Universal Declaration of Human Rights."[23] And the TANU creed declares, in addition to the principles of socialism and its economic rights, that every individual has a right to dignity and respect; to freedom of expression, of movement, of religious belief, and of association; a right to receive from society protection of his life and of property held according to law. In Tanzania the press can be ordered to stop publishing "if the President is of the opinion that it is in the public interest or in the interests of peace and good order";[24] but the press publishes. The President can order detained anyone "acting in a manner prejudicial to peace and good order,"[25] and such orders shall not be questioned in any court. But apparently there are, and have been, only few in prolonged detention.

Nyerere had confidence in his ability and that of his party to govern wisely. For more than twenty years the government continued to be under the control of a benign leader. The Parliament continued to respond to his inspiration. There was no private sector, no alternative to the government or to the party. The villages were slowly being integrated and socialized. In the country at large there was a spirit of modesty, austerity—and some apathy—and a sense of equity, equality in the distribution of the national pie. But there was little pie. One might ask: Is there a clear conception of rights in Tanzanian socialism, and where are the institutions to maintain it? If today Tanzania presents a kind of socialism with a human face, it is Nyerere's face. As everyone in Tanzania asks: after Nyerere, what? *

CONCLUSION

The conceptions of rights are different, here and there. Rights as intrinsic to the definition of the good; or, other visions of the good—fulfillment, happiness, divine or natural order, the laws of society and historical necessity. Rights as ends in themselves; or, as means to other ends. Rights as inherent, or a matter of entitlement, preserved by social constitutional compact; rights as justice, as an independent, hard-core value, inviolable even for the sake of other social goods. Or, rights as grants by, aspects of, subject to, an overriding ideology, e.g., socialism. Rights as "freedom from," aspiring to increased individual autonomy and less government; or, rights as "having more"—more security, more benefits —through more law and more government. Different conceptions breed differ-

* Three years after Nyerere left the presidency, the question remains.

ent institutions: less government and less efficient government, as a matter of principle, with separation, and courts and ombudsmen and procurators to monitor limitations; or, more government to meet more needs, more efficient government, limited—at best—only by ultimate responsibility to the people.

The different, divergent approaches to rights are not equally likely to lead to respect for rights, or for different particular rights. Can they support a consensus such as that reflected in the Universal Declaration? The Declaration eschews philosophy. It does not call for confessions of faith in human rights, surely not in any particular version of the idea. It calls for recognition of and respect for particular rights, in fact. The two principal approaches to rights do not preclude such respect for *all* the rights articulated, if not from principle and conviction, then for other reasons, internal or external. The United States, "naturally" respectful generally of civil and political rights, can do what the consensus demands in economic and social matters. France can refine its standards and strengthen its institutions. The USSR (and China) can find in socialism, spin off from socialism, or adapt socialism sufficiently to include the authentic respect for civil and political rights called for by the Declaration. Nigeria can develop its new system with special concern to make protection for rights accessible and meaningful, and its wealth distributed so that it reaches everyone. Tanzania can find that its socialism leaves more room for freedom than theory suggests, and for institutions that will ensure respect for rights even when there is no benign leader.

In a pervious world, with modern communication, international and transnational influences have effected some homogenization of doctrine in the spirit of the Universal Declaration, rising above differences in conception. That doctrine may imply at least a consensus that government may be unlimited in purpose but limited in means, and should be monitored as to means by institutions—like the courts—removed a way from government. One can bridge the integrity of the individual and the good of the community, the ideology of rights and the ideology of socialism. What is difficult to bridge with any conception of rights is the identification of ideology with the state, right or wrong; paranoid preoccupation with "national security"; not a rule of law, even of socialist legality, but the existence of two systems, the constitutional system for every day, and a secret network of decrees and orders for some days for some people, rendering the constitutional system largely inoperative. One cannot bridge—I quote from the French Declaration of 1789—"ignorance, neglect, and contempt of the rights of man," still "the sole causes of public misfortune and the corruption of governments."[26]

Human rights may not be a single idea; it may even be the sum of pairs of ideas in tension. It includes freedom as well as security, welfare as well as justice, therefore more government as well as less government. But there is some common ground: the interests of individual men and women are the touchstone of legitimate government. That means that tyranny is abnormal, that oppression, repression need to hide, and lie, and apologize; it means also that the claim to freedom from want is as authentic as the other freedoms.

Two hundred years ago Thomas Paine wrote George Washington: "I have not the least doubt of the final and complete success of the French Revolution."[27] Two hundred years later its success and that of the Declaration of the Rights of Man and of the Citizen are not yet final or complete. To us, the success of the Declaration, devoutly to be wished, is necessary but not wholly sufficient. We, in a more doubting age, less given to looking for final and complete successes, can have some confidence for some success for the Universal Declaration of Human Rights.*

*This essay was first published in 1981 and human rights have not remained unaffected in the interim, here or there. I have noted intervening changes with some promise for human rights in the Soviet Union and perhaps in China. There have been human rights changes, some benign, some terrible, in many of the diverse countries constituting the third world—in Africa (including Nigeria and Tanzania), in Cambodia, the Philippines and the Republic of Korea, in Argentina and Central America. In its principal broad strokes, this essay, I think, remains essentially valid.

Epilogue: Human Rights and Competing Ideas

T O Americans, the idea of individual rights seems axiomatic, a "truth," "self-evident," Jefferson said. In fact, we know, the idea is modern and its wide acceptance only contemporary, since the Second World War. And though it is now, it appears, a universal "truth," universally self-evident, there are competing truths, and the idea of rights continues to arouse objection and resistance.*

Resistance to the idea of rights does not necessarily challenge the principal values enshrined in rights instruments. No one, no ideology surely, claims to favor arbitrary killing, or torture, or slavery, convicting the innocent or other forms of injustice, letting people starve or remain illiterate, or even lightly and carelessly invading privacy or denying freedom of speech or religion. What is sometimes resisted is the *idea* of rights, and its essential characteristics—the concentration on the individual and the exaltation of individual freedom and autonomy; the insistence that individuals have claims—by entitlement, as of right—upon their society; that society must mobilize itself to ensure these rights; that individuals can enforce their rights by judicial or other remedies; above all,

---

* I refer to alternatives or resistance to the idea of rights; I do not address here the sorry condition of human rights in various countries, the work of evil, corrupt, cruel, or blind men. To some extent, violations of rights may reflect resistance to the idea of rights or to some elements of it, but that is not always the case. In the United States, of whose record on rights Americans are justly proud, there are violations of human rights every day, as the courts continue to find; indeed, one might say, there are more formal, confirmed, recorded findings of violations here than anywhere else in the world. But that record is evidence not of rejection of the idea of rights but rather of commitment to it.

that the individual's rights might frustrate the will of those in authority, and "trump" the public good as determined by them.

It should not be surprising that there is resistance to the idea of rights. For thousands of years there have been conceptions of the good, of the good life and the good society, without the idea of rights. There are today important ideologies, rooted in ancient traditions, that long antedate the idea of rights and have not been adapted to assimilate or make room for rights. Most modern utopias (and not only the anarchic ones) have been based on the community not the individual, not on rights but on responsibilities. Indeed, for all of us in all societies, important relationships—love, family, friendship, neighborliness, community—have no need or even place for the idea of rights.

The bill of particulars against the idea of rights is long and weighty. From the perspective of some conceptions of the good society or the good life, the rights idea is selfish and promotes egoism. It is atomistic, disharmonious, confrontational, often litigious (as life in the United States shows daily). It is antisocial, permitting and encouraging the individual to set up selfish interests as he or she sees them against the common interest commonly determined. The idea of rights challenges democracy, negating popular sovereignty and frustrating the will of the majority. In principle as well as in detail, it may exalt individual autonomy over communality, egoism over *gemeinschaft,* freedom over order, adversariness over harmony. The idea of rights, it is argued, is inefficient, tending to weaken society and render it ungovernable. Exalting rights deemphasizes and breeds neglect of duties. It imposes an artificial and narrow view of the public good—of national security, emergency, public order, public morals —and takes critical decisions from those chosen to govern and the only ones capable of governing. In many societies and circumstances, the idea of rights helps immunize egotistic property interests and extravagant claims to autonomy and liberty, thereby entrenching reaction and preventing revolutionary social change.

Such objections, and others, have come from diverse ideas and ideologies. Some are variations on utilitarianism that claim to aim at maximizing total happiness and pursuing the good of society (or of some smaller collectivity) as a whole, but conflate human beings and do not take seriously the individual individually.* Prominent sources of objection today include unlikely bedfellows, those who look back and those who look ahead, religious and other traditional

---

* Utilitarianism is commonly epitomized in formulae such as "the greatest good of the greatest number," or "the greatest total happiness." Neither formula attends to the happiness of the individual, and either goal could be achieved by total sacrifice of many individuals. The human rights idea concentrates on the individual, believes that every individual counts equally, and limits the extent to which the individual can be sacrificed to the good of the majority, for maximizing happiness, or for the common good.

The rights idea is sometimes challenged also by "communitarians" who insist that the individual is inevitably "situated" in a community, and see the emphasis on rights as divisive. Proponents of the rights idea agree that the individual does not exist in isolation but claim that respect for individual rights contributes to community and is essential especially as communities grow.

cultures as well as some forms of contemporary socialism and prophets of modernization and development.

RELIGION AND OTHER TRADITIONAL IDEOLOGIES

Perhaps it is necessary, especially in the United States, to justify citing religion as an alternative ideology, as a source of resistance to rights. Most Americans see themselves committed to both rights and religion; they see freedom of religion as a basic right, and concern for that freedom as a main source of the idea of rights and of commitment to it. Americans (and Western Europeans and some others), moreover, generally live in essentially secular societies, and in the United States the Constitution insists on disestablishment of religion and stark separation of church and state. Our political ideology—including the idea of rights—seems largely distinct from, independent of, even unrelated or irrelevant to religion or religious ideology. Even the large majority of individuals in the United States who are described or who describe themselves as religious, do not seem to find in religion an all-embracing *Weltanschauung* that includes a complete political and moral ideology (that might not include rights). Or, perhaps, most Americans do not take religion seriously; perhaps they compartmentalize it, giving God only a little, and leaving very much for Caesar.

As a result, in the West, religion (and religions) generally appear to address rights only as the beneficiary of the freedom of religion; even when, occasionally, organized religious influence is exerted in the name of morality against some freedom—for example, against women's claim of a right to have an abortion, or against freedom to publish and read blasphemous, sacrilegious or obscene materials—the objections themselves may be couched in terms of competing rights. In other parts of the world, however, religion sometimes appears in opposition to individual rights, whether in parts of Islam where fundamentalism reigns (e.g., Iran), or in countries where Christian churches have supported authoritarian repression, as at times in parts of Latin America, in South Africa, in Poland. Relations to political authority apart, major religions everywhere (including those prevalent in secular Western societies) have claimed to be complete ideologies, and the relation of religion, of religious thought, of the theology or doctrine of different religions, to the contemporary human rights idea, is itself an ideological question.

Religion is not a single or simple idea, and its relation to the idea of rights is neither single nor simple. The major religions can fairly claim ancestry to values central to human rights: right and wrong, good and evil; justice and injustice; legality and illegality; the essential equality of men; the equal protection of the laws. But the major religions have ancient roots and their theology and ideology were largely formed before the idea of rights was conceived. To ancient Judaism, Christianity, Islam—I think, too, to the older Eastern religions and to other traditional cultures—the idea of rights, surely of rights against society, was unknown. The Bible, for example, knew not rights but duties, and duties were to God; when by God's law one's duties to God related to one's neighbor, the neighbor was only what we would call a third-party-beneficiary. (Even love—"Thou shalt love thy neighbor as thyself"—was a command, a duty; my neighbor had no "right" to be loved and surely no remedy for my failure to love, except perhaps to complain to God.) Of course, ancient languages did not have a word for rights, and even our later English word suggests its derivation from what is "right," from a theory of good, of justice, without connotations of individual entitlement. The idea of human rights, moreover, is a political idea, addressing man's relation to political society, and ancient religions and other traditional cultures did not have a modern kind of political society to which an individual might have modern-style relationships, and upon which he or she might make claims.

The idea of rights reflects principles of interpersonal morality; the major religions reflected principles of interpersonal morality without an idea of rights. Justice was a divine command enforced by God and sometimes by his surrogates on earth. For some injustices the victim had remedies, on earth as well as in some heaven. The same principles of morality and justice applied between individual and authority—for example, the king—both governed equally by God's law. Witness the prophet's rebuke to David for taking Uriah's wife, to Ahab for murdering Naboth for his vineyard.* But claims against authority were limited, the victim's remedies for denial of such claims were not on earth, which markedly reduced the likelihood that he would enjoy the earthly benefits divinely ordained for him.

Traditional values, moreover, were not those identified with the modern rights idea: The traditional ideal was not individual autonomy,† freedom, privacy—but conformity to God's will and to divine law. Early, and for thousands of years later, emphasis in religious thought was not upon the individual, but upon the community—the tribe, the people of Israel, the Church, Christendom, Islam—on God's will or the cosmic order. In the European medieval and feudal order, and in non-Christian societies in other parts of the world, the individual lived in a chain of hierarchical relations. The ideal was not individual freedom and autonomy, but conformity, compliance, cooperation, harmony, order. The guiding principle was not equality but concern for the hierarchies of the social order. Therefore, not contract, with its foundation in individual will and consent, but status, including responsibility to those lower in a hierarchical order as well as obligations to those higher up. Also, from a modern perspective, religions often achieved order at the cost of inequalities, of limitations on liberty, of suppressed individuality and of individual and social underdevelopment (and even spiritual underdevelopment), sometimes in association with ritual that included elements of cruelty.

*2 Samuel 11–12; 1 Kings 21.
†Doing what was right in one's own eyes was anarchy, depravity. Compare Judges 17:6, 21:24.

Individual rights, constitutional rights, human rights, rights against political authority, were a later and radical idea. It came after Protestantism—combining with economic and social forces—brought a stronger sense of the individual, emphasized not only the nature of the cosmos but man's nature, and began to see man as autonomous, private, and equal to other men, rather than as a social atom in hierarchical relations to others in society. The idea of rights came after the Reformation sundered the single Christian church and helped breach the identity of church and state, after balance of political-military power led to the secular state and to the modern state system. Dissenters began to claim rights for individuals (and for their churches) against the established church and against the political authority aligned with it. In such circumstances, religion— those dissenting religions at least—were no longer content to rely on authority's sense of duty, a duty of tolerance, charity or love, and to see man as merely its beneficiary; rather, religion began to see man's needs—his religious needs, and then other needs—as matters of right, of entitlement under higher law.

In new and diverse political-societal contexts, religious thought has had to address the idea of rights, as part of a general development of a theory of God, man and society. Now religion itself—and every particular religion—has had to develop attitudes toward modern society and modern political authority, if only in self-defense: many religions are somewhere the established religion, allied with political authority, and have had to define an ideological attitude toward the human rights claims upon society of the country's inhabitants; every religion is somewhere a minority religion, and has had to adapt to minority status; every religion has had to respond to the needs of its members in large, impersonal, developed (or developing), urban, industrial societies. Even Western religions, however, though they had had long experience with Caesar and the state, did not come ideologically prepared for the modern political-societal order. Their ideological attitudes to man's rights and duties vis-à-vis political authority have had an uncertain development and have taken different forms for different religions in different places and times. Often these attitudes depended on whether the religion was the state religion or a minority religion, whether political authority was theocratic, monarchic, republican or democratic, or, recently, totalitarian or authoritarian. To this day, religions have not developed a clear perspective on popular sovereignty and democracy, or on the idea of individual rights.

Today, religion and religious ideology embrace, indeed claim, the moral values underlying human rights. Religion and religious ideology espouse justice (including economic justice), reject torture and other inhuman treatment,* now oppose slavery, are committed to fair trial, insist on freedom of religion (at least for themselves), support participation in government. Even some religions that did not in the past, may now accept toleration if not equality for the outsider, are reexamining hierarchy and caste, are widening the roles of women. But ideolog-

---

* But some religions insist on, or accept, forms of punishment that are doubtless inhuman by international human rights standards.

ically, religion, even today, remains uncomfortable with the idea of rights. There is resistance to putting the individual front and center; to the idea of individual entitlement; of claims against society (which may include religious society); of limitations on the public good, including the religious good, in the name of individualism; of the individual "trumping" authority; of only limited limitations on rights; of narrow conceptions of public order. Religion also resists rights as an independent, secular ideology, based on a nontheological view of the nature of man and of society. Although religion may respond with sympathy to claims of economic-social rights, corresponding to the duty of charity, it may see the emphasis on the individual and the apotheosis of autonomy and freedom as hubris if not idolatry, inclining to materialism and hedonism. When human rights proclaims freedom of conscience and religion, religion may welcome that in respect of its own as a matter of God's law or natural rights, but it may also see the claim to freedom of religion as implying the equality of all religions (as well as of nonreligions, of atheism and agnosticism), as rejecting the true religion, perhaps as trivializing all religion. Religion is also sensitive to the emergence of rights as, plausibly, a response to the inadequacies of religion in the modern world.

Slowly, however, religion, religions—principal comprehensive spokesmen for an alternative vision of the Good—have themselves come to see the need for rights in the modern world: as societies develop; where society is pluralistic; in urban society, where the individual is lonely but where some loneliness is perhaps essential for individual dignity. Once, in homogeneous, hermetic societies, religion had offered a complete, sufficient image of the Good, based in order, communality, harmony. Without an idea of rights, the principles of religious morality reflecting the Golden Rule and reciprocity, and buttressed by commanded love and charity, promised and sometimes produced respectable versions of the good society, perhaps even of the good life. Even then, from our modern perspective, ideologically and usually in practice, religion provided the good society for the believer, not for the infidel; for the resident, not the stranger; for men, not for women; for masters, not slaves. Now, religions—at least some religions—increasingly recognize that the idea of human rights is needed to move religions—at least some religions—to reexamine ancient practices that may be less a matter of theological doctrine or other enduring values than relics of the sociology of societies long gone.

Religion will continue to reject human rights as a total ideology. It sees that human rights—cold rights—do not provide warmth, belonging, fitting, significance, do not exclude need for love, friendship, family, charity, sympathy, devotion, sanctity, or for expiation, atonement, forgiveness. But if human rights may not be sufficient, they are at least necessary. If they do not bring kindness to the familiar, they bring—as religions have often failed to do—respect for the stranger. Human rights are not a complete, alternative ideology, but rights are a *floor,* necessary to make other values—including religion—flourish. Human rights not only protect religion, but have come to serve religious ethics in respects and contexts where religion itself has sometimes proved insufficient. Human rights are, at least, a supplemental "theology" for pluralistic, urban, secular societies.* There, religion can accept if not adopt the human rights idea as an affirmation of its own values, and can devote itself to the larger, deeper areas beyond the common denominator of human rights. Religion can provide, as the human rights idea does not adequately, for the tensions between rights and responsibilities, between individual and community, between the material and the spirit.

I have spoken of religion principally as represented by so-called Western religions. The idea of rights has had a not-dissimilar reception and experience vis-à-vis Eastern religions, and other traditional indigenous cultures. By them— or, more accurately, by Western commentators on their behalf—the human rights idea has been challenged as a foreign, undigestible, unnecessary, disruptive manifestation of Western cultural imperialism. I think they are mistaken. It may indeed be that the spread of the idea of human rights was made possible and accelerated by Western rule and example. That is not to say, however, that it is an idea that is congenial only to the West, likely to flourish only in Western climate and soil.† Western thinkers developed the idea of rights as a principle of political theory expressing the proper relation of individual to organized authority in political society, but the moral assumptions and values that underlie the idea are to be found in the East as in the West, in Confucianism or Buddhism as in Judaism, Christianity, or Islam. The hard core of human rights, surely— rights to physical and psychic integrity of the person, basic autonomy, freedom from torture, from slavery, from arbitrary detention, autonomy in personal matters and equality before the law—are as dear to Eastern as to Western man. Contact between the human rights idea and traditional ideology has brought not conflict but accommodation, and a mutual transformation, the superimposition of a secular ideology on ancient religious ones, resulting in a variety of human rights ideologies. Now traditions are being reinterpreted in the light of the human rights idea.‡ The idea of rights, and its modest, essential content, not only respond to moral intuitions that are congenial to these cultures, but traditional societies have in fact been embracing them warmly. If not conclusive, it is surely relevant that the representatives of these societies—even official representatives who, as respondents to individual claims, have reason to resist the idea of rights—have uniformly and consistently espoused the idea and most of its content. Human rights have been enthusiastically received not only by earlier, Western-educated elites but by younger home-grown leaders, as, recently, in the

---

*Religion has been adapting to eclectic, secular justifications of human rights (or to no justifications at all); it has also found religious justifications for human rights in human equality, in man created in the image of God, in the common human ancestor.

†If Western thinkers gave the world the concept and vocabulary of rights, Western societies were as resistant to the idea as any others, and the worst violations of human rights in our day were committed in Western lands. See essay 1.

‡Resistance to the human rights idea on the ground that it is individualistic and breeds divisiveness is also misconceived. Americans, in particular, are sometimes misled by the tendency in our society to assert and insist on one's rights. But the rights idea is properly expressed not only—not particularly—in the assertion of one's own rights, but in recognition of, and respect and struggle for, the rights of others.

Organization of African Unity. When spokesmen for these societies claim priority for economic and social rights, they do not reject the idea of rights, but embrace it; they do not reject its political-civil content but assert the essential interdependence of all the recognized rights. When they claim the needs of development (discussed below) as a limitation on rights they are, of course, not invoking traditional values but a different set of imported, modern values.*

From reading I conclude that the idea of rights as presently understood was —is—unfamiliar as such to tribal societies as it was once—not long ago— unfamiliar in Western cultures. Traditional societies, too, whether on religious or near-religious grounds, have had conceptions of the good that exalted not the individual but some larger unity—life, the generational chain, the village, the tribe, the cosmic order. Some traditions have deemphasized individual life as we understand it—presently living individuals between birth and death. They too have tended to exalt order not freedom, harmony not adverse claims, not equality but authority and sometimes hierarchy and caste with mutual responsibility. Despite apologist protestations, however, it appears that authoritarianism, caste, and hierarchy did not commonly bring harmony, mutual respect and responsibility (any more than was generally the case—as was sometimes claimed—for American slavery). In most such societies, also, it was principally men who insisted that women found dignity and fulfillment in their allotted subservient traditional role under traditional mores. But basic underlying values—freedom from arbitrary killing or from torture, from slavery or unwarranted detention, notions of justice, fair trial (in local context)—are not generally foreign to them. If some ancient practices, involving cruelty, slavery or inequality, still remain, it is the *Zeitgeist,* reflecting not only Western but also developing indigenous ideas, that rejects them.

In the village perhaps, without any idea of rights, community and sympathy provided dignity and fulfillment, and an unusual person might find some freedom and autonomy in the realm of the spirit, or by moving elsewhere. But tribal societies are evolving, if not disintegrating, and it is hardly individualism and the human rights idea that have undermined them. Like traditional Western cultures, modernizing, developing, industrializing, urbanizing, pluralistic national societies in Asia, Africa, and Latin America are apparently looking to human rights to help protect not only personal dignity but also traditional culture against modern political power, and are adapting local ideas and ideology to the human rights idea.

SOCIALISM

Religion and tradition are old ideas that have been making their accommodation with the human rights idea; socialism is a modern ideology that is still

---

*Other contemporary political ideas—statehood, democracy, socialism—are also of Western origin, but are embraced by societies in all parts of the world.

developing its modus vivendi with human rights. Like some religions, it is sometimes seen as an exclusive ideology, and, by definition and hypothesis, one in which the individual is not central and individual rights are peripheral if not foreign.

There have been many socialisms and even more than one socialist idea; they have elements in common. Socialism worthy of the name would presumably include: a commitment to the welfare of the collective, to the interests of the society; to economic planning; to public ownership of "the means of production"; to a central concern for the laborer, the producer of goods; to limitations on the free market, on individual capital, on private economic enterprise, on accumulation of private property.

None of these commitments, I believe, is—or needs to be—inconsistent with the human rights idea. The commitment to the welfare of the collective need not preclude a hard core of respect for the individual; the human rights perspective —surely the contemporary international human rights perspective—accepts a right to own property and not be deprived of it arbitrarily, but does not preclude limitations on the kinds of property owned, on some uses of property, or on kinds of economic activity. Planning, some degree of societal intervention, I have suggested, is implied in the obligation of society to ensure rights, especially economic and social rights (see Introduction). Conflict between socialism and the idea of rights, then, is not inherent or inevitable, and some socialisms have combined socialist principles with deep attachment to individual rights.

Today, socialist societies exist in socialist states, although perhaps, in theory and in principle, they see themselves as on the road to a pure, stateless socialist society. Theories of socialism, even if called Marxist, have had to relate to actual socialist states in an international system which, whatever the inexorable laws of historical necessity, immediately reflects the iron law of national interest and power, of international politics and economics. Contemporary socialist states, with socialist theory far behind, have had to respond to the rise and the appeal of the idea of human rights. They have espoused the Universal Declaration of Human Rights, and (except China) have adhered to the principal international covenants. Successive socialist constitutions—proclamations of their faith to their own and to the world—have given increased attention to rights. The 1977 Constitution of the USSR devotes a chapter to the basic rights, freedoms and duties of citizens, and more than twenty of its articles deal with rights. The 1982 Constitution of the People's Republic of China puts the Fundamental Rights and Duties of Citizens near-front (in chapter 2) and contains some twenty articles devoted to rights.*

I have addressed the ideological attitudes of Communist states to the human

---

*I do not consider here accusations that adherence by these socialist states to international human rights instruments is cynical and hypocritical, and that the rights provisions of their constitutions are designed to deceive at home or abroad. I set aside, too, claims that in the implementation of their ideology, authorities in these states confuse the interests of socialism with those of the Russian (or Chinese) state, and the interest of the state with those of a particular regime. See essay 10.

rights idea, and the concept of rights as reflected in Communist constitutions (see essay 10). Contemporary Communist ideology has adopted the language of rights and has moved toward the human rights consensus, but it has not yet accepted and assimilated some basic implications of the idea. It does not take seriously enough the separateness of the individual; it sometimes forgets that its own raison d'être is the enrichment of *individual* life. In that ideology the individual has begun to count, but he does not yet count enough, and the recognized zone of individual autonomy and freedom remains too small and uncertain. The people is sovereign, but not wholly sovereign: notably, government is not effectively accountable and even the people is not permitted to move from socialism. The citizen can participate in government but does not significantly control or influence his or her government. Individuals are entitled to rights but only to the extent granted or acquiesced in by society; they do not have effective remedies to vindicate their claims and society does not provide other means to ensure them. Individual rights do not "trump" other public goods as perceived by political authority. The needs of socialism, as perceived by authority, are in effect seen as needs of "public order" permitting any limitation on rights. Individual autonomy, freedom, privacy, property, can apparently be sacrificed, virtually without limit, to the perceived good, present or future, of socialism, or of the particular socialist state.*

The idea of rights, then, has not yet been effectively assimilated into the ideology of socialism as represented by the principal socialist states of our time, the home of more than a billion people, a quarter—perhaps a third—of mankind, whose human rights are now universally recognized. Leninist-Stalinist theories that depreciated the individual and the idea of individual rights have still too much the aura of holy writ, and their reexamination still courts the dangers of heresy. But the idea of rights, I believe, has had to be faced and it is not beyond hope that the socialist states are moving toward an idea of socialism that has room for the idea of rights. If in the past some forms of socialism without individual rights may have provided the good life, somewhere, sometime, in older, smaller societies; if in the future Marx thought ineluctable the historical process might produce a different, socialist man in a different, socialist society who will need no rights; today, socialism without authentic rights does not work, does not bring dignity and fulfillment, for present man in present society, in a modernizing urbanizing world.

How authentic, how big a step toward socialism *cum* human rights will Gorbachev's Russia take? Will China and other socialist and near-socialist states follow?

---

*The conception of national security that some governments of socialist states have sometimes invoked as a basis for limiting rights is also extravagant, sometimes ludicrous, but I do not understand that to be necessarily part of the socialist ideology.

DEVELOPMENT

There is another "idea" that sometimes competes with human rights, and which, like socialism, looks ahead: I refer to development (see essay 10).

"Development" is commonly intoned but rarely defined. It sometimes refers to individual, sometimes to societal, development. It sometimes means economic development, sometimes also political-social development. Sometimes it is the equivalent of modernization, industrialization. Development is properly not an idea, at least not a single idea, but a set of contemporary values. Lacking an ideology, it has sometimes attached itself to socialism, but it is preached as well by societies and governments that are and proclaim themselves to be vigorously antisocialist. Development has also appropriated and attached itself to the human rights idea, proclaiming itself one of a young "generation" of human rights. It has linked itself to the people's right to sovereignty over its own natural resources and to economic self-determination which, at the insistence of the less-developed majority of states, have been incorporated into and placed at the head of the principal human rights covenants.[1] The attachment of development to the human rights idea is sometimes justified on the ground that it is "a people's right."[2] In 1986, the United Nations General Assembly adopted a Declaration on the Right of Development (G.A. Res. 41/128) as "an inalienable human right" (Art. 1).

"Development" is shorthand for important plans, programs, and attitudes. Principally, it connotes economic "growth" to raise the gross national product, to improve trade balance and magnify per capita earnings. Sometimes—especially for new underdeveloped states—development includes social and political development, the establishment of national institutions and a political ethos, raising the level of education and of cultural and scientific activity. Sometimes it implies also eliminating archaic vestiges—slavery, caste disabilities, the subjugation of women. The effort to achieve such development may entail sacrificing other values, including traditional values associated with life in ancient, small, homogeneous, hermetic communities. By its character and in its historical context the drive to development is revolutionary, and like other revolutions it is in a hurry. Often it is single-minded and prepared to sacrifice other values to its needs, and the present to the future. Development, then, is not universally and indisputably seen as an unmixed virtue; but it may be a necessity in the world as it has become.

The drive for development is deeply intertwined with the idea of rights. Development is often justified as necessary to make it possible to respect and insure individual rights. Political development is essential to assure the human right to participate in self-government in one's own country. Economic development will enable a country better to guarantee the economic and social rights of its inhabitants, will increase the resources available for that purpose and help achieve it more expeditiously. Societal development is essential for individual development which is necessary to enable individuals to know their rights, to claim them, to realize and to enjoy them and the human dignity they promise.

Some paths to development, however, have a less supportive relation to individual rights. In some countries the needs of development have been invoked as grounds for authoritarian or single-party government, brooking no political opposition; for regimentation, imposing various degrees of forced labor and denying freedom to choose one's place of residence or work; for economic planning that entails sacrificing the rights, including the basic human needs, of people today for the sake of the nation or of future generations.

Development is surely important but its importance, and the homage, the compliment, implied in its appropriation of the rights terminology, should not confuse us as to its relation to the human rights idea. Individual development, the growth of human capabilities and human dignity, are indeed goals of the rights idea, and the development of a society may contribute to its ability to promote individual development and dignity. But, in itself, the economic development of a society—modernization, growth, GNP—is not an individual right; and immediately, at least, it does not necessarily improve the lot, even the economic and social lot, of human beings today, and may even divert energies and resources that might be devoted to their basic human needs. The development of a society is a public good, but, under the rights ideology, there is a minimum, a floor, below which one cannot reduce individual rights for a public good however worthy. The sacrifice of rights today for an uncertain future surely denies rights today, while the future remains uncertain; in any event, it is inherent in the idea of rights that there is a limit to sacrificing the present for the future, the rights of living persons for those of generations to come. Development needs are not a temporary public emergency permitting derogation of rights. They are not, like the needs of national security or public order, special, occasional needs permitting limitations on individual rights at the margin. Development is a comprehensive, pervasive, long-term program in which individual rights have to be integrated, not one that can be used as a basis for disregarding them.

Development—whether seen as a societal goal or as a right—cannot be allowed to swallow up the human rights of the Universal Declaration. Development should not be allowed to appear to be in opposition to human rights. In fact, the common assumption that one must choose between societal development and individual rights has not been proven, or even examined. Torturing people, killing them, making them disappear, detaining them without trial, or punishing them for what cannot (consistently with the human rights idea) be made a crime—none of these feeds or educates any individual, or builds factories and highways. But it has not been proven either that economic development generally requires regimentation, invasion of privacy and "personhood," suppression of political freedom, of rights of assembly and association, trade union rights. It is not proven, even, that economic development requires a society to deny individual basic human needs and other economic and social rights today. On the contrary, thoughtful leaders committed to development are of Jan. 6, 1941, 87 *Cong. Rec.* 44, 46–47 (1941).

Italy, Feb. 10, 1947, T.I.A.S. No. 1648, 4 Bevans 311, 49
with Rumania, Feb. 10, 1947, 61 Stat. 1757, T.I.A.S. No.
N.T.S. 3.

ational Military Tribunal, 59 Stat. 1544. See Taylor, *Nürem-*
onciliation No. 450 (1959); T. Taylor, *Nüremberg and Viet-*
(Chicago: Quadrangle Books, 1970).

Georgia, 408 U.S. 328 (1972); *Gregg v. Georgia,* 428 U.S.

81 (1963); S.C. Res. 282 (1970), on South Africa.

T. Buergenthal, *International Protection of Human Rights*
l, 1973), pp. 750–51; John Carey, *UN Protection of Civil and*
.Y.: Syracuse University Press, 1970).

N Economic and Social Council authorized the Sub-Commis-
imination and Protection of Minorities "to appoint a working
ications "which appear to reveal a consistent pattern of gross
ons of human rights and fundamental freedoms." ECOSOC
SCOR Supp. 1A, U.N. Doc. E/4832/Add. 1 (1970). There
in ECSOC Resolution 1235, on the Question of Violations of
ental Freedoms, Including Policies of Racial Discrimination
theid, In All Countries, With Particular Reference to Colonial
ntries and Territories. ECOSOC Res. 1235, 42 ESCOR
(1967).

83 A through O (1979).

obs, *The European Convention on Human Rights* (Oxford:
lovis Morrisson, *The Developing European Law of Human*
67); A. H. Robertson, *Human Rights in Europe* (Manchester:
s, 2d ed., 1976); L. Mikaelsen, *European Protection of Human*
; Germantown, Md.: Sijthoff and Noordhoff, 1980).

"The Inter-American System for the Protection of Human
uman Rights in International Law (Oxford: Clarendon Press;
y Press, 1984).

Rights in Africa (Lagos: Nigerian Institute of International
frica and Regional Protection of Human Rights: A Study of the
nd Peoples' Rights: Its Effectiveness and Impact on the African

ONAL HUMAN RIGHTS

"Human Rights, Real and Supposed," in David D. Raphael,
Rights of Man (Bloomington: Indiana University Press,
W. Cranston, *What Are Human Rights?* (London: Bodley

nstitution contains only limitations on government, not posi-
and if affirmative obligations were to be constitutionally
system does not readily provide for remedies that would
y legislatures, say to appropriate adequate funds for educa-

on Economic, Social and Cultural Rights, which is written
See essay 1.
ational agreements have created institutions with interna-

of the view that development and human rights are symbiotic, not adversary. Development must be political and social as well as economic; it requires giving the villager as well as the city dweller a sense of personhood, worth, dignity; it requires more rather than less individualized rights. It is recognized that today there can be no freedom, no dignity without development; it is increasingly recognized that there can be no authentic development without freedom. (See essay 10.)

Human rights may have become the idea of our time in part because ours is the age of development, industrialization, urbanization, which in many parts of the world have helped undermine what religion and tradition long offered the individual. In this modern, modernizing world, the human rights idea may sometimes appear as an ideology competing with religion, as a threat to traditional societies, as an obstacle to totalitarian socialism or to development in a hurry. But the idea of rights is not a complete, all embracing ideology, is not in fact in competition with other ideologies. Religion explains and comforts, tradition supports, socialism cares, development builds; the human rights idea does none of these. In today's world—and tomorrow's—there may be no less need for what religion and tradition have promised and provided, what socialism strives for, what development will bring; the idea of rights is not inconsistent, not in competition with any of them. Rather, religion, traditional societies, socialism, developers, will find, I believe, that their values and goals, even along their particular path, depend on individual dignity and fulfillment, and in a modern world have to be firmly supported by the idea of human rights.

There is no agreement between the secular and the theological, or between traditional and modern perspectives, on man and the Universe. One cannot prove, or even persuade, whether a substantially free economy or substantial planning is more conducive to the good society or the good of individual man. But there is now a working consensus that every man and woman, between birth and death, counts, and has a claim to an irreducible core of integrity and dignity. In that consensus, in the world we have and are shaping, the idea of human rights is the essential idea.

4. Message to Congres

5. Treaty of Peace wit
U.N.T.S. 1; Treaty of Pea
1649, 4 Bevans 403, 42 U

6. Charter of the Inter
berg Trials, *International*
nam: An American Tragedy

7. See, e.g., *Furman v*
153 (1976).

8. See, e.g., S.C. Res.

9. See L. B. Sohn an
(Indianapolis: Bobbs-Merr
Political Rights (Syracuse,

10. Res. 1503 of the U
sion on Prevention of Discr
group" to consider commu
and reliably attested violat
Res. 1503 (XLVII), 48 E
was similar language earlie
Human Rights and Funda
and Segregation and of Apa
and Other Dependent Co
Supp.1, U.N. Doc. E/4393

11. E.g., G.A. Res. 33/

12. See Francis G. Ja
Clarendon Press, 1975); C
Rights (Leyden: Sijthoff, 19
Manchester University Pres
Rights (Alphen aan den Rij

13. See T. Buergentha
Rights," in T. Meron, ed.,
New York: Oxford Universi

14. See O. Eze, *Humar*
Affairs, 1984); N. Rembe,
African Charter on Human
States (Romai Leoni, 1985)

INTRODU

1. Ronald Dwo
worth, 1978), p. xi.

2. International
Covenant on Econo

3. *Ibid.,* Preamb

4. Preamble of t

5. UN Charter,

6. Universal De

7. *Ibid.,* Article

8. *Ibid.,* Article

9. *Ibid.,* Article

1. THE I
HUMAN

1. *Restatement,*
tion and chapter 2.

2. Hersch Laut
bia University Pres

3. Draper, "T
1949 and of the
Draper, *The Red C*

2. INTERNAT
AS "RIGHTS"

1. Maurice W. Cranston
ed., *Political Theory and th*
1967), pp. 43–53; Mauric
Head, 1973).

2. The United States Co
tive obligations upon them
imposed, the existing legal
mandate affirmative actions
tion. See essay 7.

3. Even in the Covenant
with the state as the subject.

4. Extraordinarily, inter

tional status and character independent of, and going beyond, obligations assumed by states in regard to them. Thus, the UN Organization, created by the UN Charter, is deemed to have status and character in the international system even in relation to states not party to the UN Charter. Compare the Advisory Opinion of the International Court of Justice in "The Bernadotte Case: Reparation for Injuries Suffered in the Service of the United Nations" (1949) I.C.J. 174.

5. Vienna Convention on the Law of Treaties, Article 36. The consent of the third state is required, but is ordinarily assumed. The treaty does not speak to rights for third "parties" which are not states.

6. See John Austin, *The Province of Jurisprudence Determined* (New York: Noonday Press, 1954 ed.).

7. See *Baker v. Carr,* 369 U.S. 186(1962); cf. *United States v. Richardson,* 418 U.S. 166 (1974). See generally Henkin, "Is There a 'Political Question' Doctrine?", 85 *Yale L. J.* 597 (1976).

8. See, for example, Henkin, *How Nations Behave: Law and Foreign Policy,* 2d ed. (New York: Columbia University Press, 1979), esp. chs. 3 and 4.

3. RIGHTS IN A WORLD OF STATES

1. International Covenant on Economic, Social and Cultural Rights, Article 2(1); International Convention on the Elimination of All Forms of Racial Discrimination, Articles 2 and 6.

2. In the Convention on the Prevention and Punishment of the Crime of Genocide, for example, states are obligated to bring to trial or to extradite persons charged with genocide. Article VII.

3. Universal Declaration of Human Rights, Article 14.

4. Article 2(1) of the Covenant on Civil and Political Rights extends coverage to persons "within its territory and subject to its jurisdiction," but a state is obligated to respect the rights of persons within its territory who may not be fully subject to its jurisdiction, e.g., foreign diplomats, as well as persons subject to its jurisdiction but not within its territory, e.g. nationals abroad. See Buergenthal, "To Respect and to Ensure: State Obligations and Permissible Derogations," in Louis Henkin, ed., *The International Bill of Rights: The Covenant on Civil and Political Rights* (New York: Columbia University Press, 1981), pp. 73–77.

5. Universal Declaration, Article 13(2).

6. See Article 33(1) of the Convention Relating to the Status of Refugees.

7. Universal Declaration, Article 13; International Covenant on Civil and Political Rights, Article 12(2).

8. Compare *Garcia-Mir v. Meese,* 788 F.2d 1446 (11th Cir.), cert. denied, 479 U.S. 889 (1986). See Henkin, "The Constitution and United States Sovereignty: A Century of *Chinese Exclusion* and Its Progeny," 100 *Harv. L. Rev.* 853 (1987).

4. HUMAN RIGHTS AND "DOMESTIC JURISDICTION"

1. See, e.g., Preuss, "Article 2, Paragraph 7 of the Charter of the United Nations and Matters of Domestic Jurisdiction," 74 *Recueil des Cours* 547–653 (1949–I); Gilmour, "The Meaning of 'Intervene' in Article 2, Paragraph 7," 5 *Ned. TIR* 348–65 (1958);

L. M. Goodrich, "The United Nations and Domestic Jurisdiction," 3 *Int. Org.* 14–28 (1949). See also bibliography in L. B. Sohn and T. Buergenthal, *International Protection of Human Rights* (Indianapolis: Bobbs-Merrill, 1973), pp. 594–96.

2. See bibliography in L. B. Sohn and T. Buergenthal.

3. Where the line lies between domestic and international jurisdiction is itself a question of international law, not one which any party can decide finally for itself. See the advisory opinion of the Permanent Court of International Justice in Tunis-Morocco Nationality Decrees Case, P.C.I.J. Ser. B., No. 4, 1 Hudson, World Ct. Rep. 143; Rights of Passage over Indian Territory Case, [1960] I.C.J. Rep. 33; Interpretation of Peace Treaties Case, [1950] I.C.J. 70–71; compare Publications of the European Court of Human Rights, Belgian Linguistic Case (preliminary objections), judgment of February 9, 1967, Series A. at 16–20. In rare circumstances a state may reserve to itself the right to determine whether a matter is within its domestic jurisdiction. See, e.g., the U.S. Declaration recognizing as compulsory the jurisdiction of the International Court of Justice, [1975–76] I.C.J.Y.B. 80.

4. See R. Higgins, *The Development of International Law Through the Political Organs of the United Nations* (Oxford: Oxford University Press, 1963), p. 4. But cf. Watson, "Autointerpretation, Competence, and the Continuing Validity of Article 2(7) of the U.N. Charter," 71 *Am. J. Int'l L.* 60 (1977).

5. See, generally, Ermacora, "Human Rights and Domestic Jurisdiction," 2 *Recueil des Cours* 371 (1968).

6. Much UN practice may be justified in part on the view that UN consideration does not constitute intervention within the meaning of Article 2(7), but there are innumerable indications that many members of the UN considered some alleged infringements of human rights to be violations of the UN Charter. See L. Sohn and T. Buergenthal, *International Protection of Human Rights,* pp. 505–997.

7. See, e.g., the first of many resolutions, Res. 721 (VIII), 8 December 1953, 8 GAOR, Supp. No. 17 (A/2630) at 67 (1953). See the materials collected in Sohn and Buergenthal, pp. 634–739.

8. The advisory opinion on the legal consequences for states of the continued presence of South Africa in Nambia, [1971] I.C.J. 16, para. 131, stated:

Under the Charter of the United Nations, the former Mandatory had pledged itself to observe and respect, in a territory having an international status, human rights and fundamental freedoms for all without distinction as to race. To establish instead, and to enforce, distinctions, exclusions, restrictions and limitations exclusively based on grounds of race, colour, descent or national or ethnic origin which constitute a denial of fundamental human rights is a flagrant violation of the purposes and principles of the Charter.

See Schwelb, "The International Court of Justice and the Human Rights Clauses of the Charter," 66 *Am. J. Int'l L.* 337 (1972).

9. ECOSOC Res. 1235 (XLII), 6 June 1967, 42 ESCOR, Supp. No. 1 (E/4393) at 17–18. See also ECOSOC Res. 1102 (XL), 4 March 1966, 40 ESCOR, Supp. No. 1 (2/4176) at 6.

10. ECOSOC Res. 1503 (XLVIII), 27 May 1970, 48 ESCOR, Supp. No. 1 A (E/4832/Add.1) at 8–9.

11. In 1974, the Commission on Human Rights sent a telegram to the government of Chile protesting violations of human rights. Later it established a group to investigate the violations. The General Assembly condemned Chile's violations, as well as her refusal to permit the investigation. See GA Res. 3219 (XXIX), 6 November 1974; GA Res. 32/124, 16 December 1976.

12. Case Concerning the Barcelona Traction, Light and Power Company, Ltd. [1970] I.C.J. paras. 33–34.

13. And "a serious breach on a widespread scale of such obligations" may constitute not merely an international delict but an international crime by the violating state. Article 19, subparagraph 3(c), and commentary, Report of the International Law Commission on the work of its twenty-eighth session, 3 May–23 July 1976, GAOR, Supp. No. 10 (A/31/10) pp. 226 et seq.

14. See Ermacora, "Human Rights and Domestic Jurisdiction." See *Restatement, Third, Foreign Relations Law of the United States* (1987) §702.

15. Schachter, "The Twilight Existence of Nonbinding International Agreements," 71 *Am. J. Int'l L.* 296 at 304 (1977).

16. See, for example, the Report of the International Law Commission above, n. 13 at 227–228, 265–270, and authorities citied therein. *Restatement, Third, Foreign Relations Law of the United States* (1987) § 902.

17. ". . . In particular, an essential distinction should be drawn between the obligation of a State towards the international community as a whole, and those arising vis-à-vis another State in the field of diplomatic protection. By their very nature the former are the concern of all States. In view of the importance of the rights involved, all States can be held to have a legal interest in their protection; they are obligations *erga omnes*.

Such obligations derive, for example, in contemporary international law, from the outlawing of acts of aggression, and of genocide, as also from the principles and rules concerning the basic rights of the human person, including protection from slavery and racial discrimination. Some of the corresponding rights of protection have entered into the body of general international law (Reservations to the Convention on the Prevention and Punishment of the Crime of Genocide, Advisory Opinion, *I.C.J. Reports 1951*, p. 23); others are conferred by international instruments of a universal or quasi-universal character."

Barcelona Traction Case, above n. 12, paras. 33–34; see also the Report of the International Law Commission, above n. 13.

18. The Allied Powers asserted their right to enforce the human rights provisions of World War II peace treaties. Compare the advisory opinion of the International Court of Justice, Interpretation of Peace Treaties with Bulgaria, Hungary and Romania, [1950] I.C.J. 65, 220.

19. Apparently, this general provision was accepted in lieu of an "International Court of Justice" clause (like that in the Genocide Convention), because it was feared that the court's unpopularity might discourage adherence to the covenant.

20. The same implication is to be found in the analogous Article 16 of the International Convention on the Elimination of All Forms of Racial Discrimination.

There is no contrary implication in the fact that state consent to being charged·before the Human Rights Committee of the Covenant, whether by other states or by private parties, is optional. (In the Convention on Racial Discrimination, submission to interstate complaint is not optional.) That is a kind of third-party adjudication which has generally required consent, as for the I.C.J.; by contrast, submission to ordinary diplomatic enforcement by the parties is inherent in the international legal system and requires no new consent.

One might argue that International Labor Organization (ILO) conventions were not intended to be enforceable between the parties; the agreements say nothing of disputes between parties, and ILO conventions are subject to an elaborate enforcement system linked to each ILO convention. Perhaps it can be argued, too, that remedies for violation of obligations rooted in the UN Charter were intended to be enforced only by the elaborate machinery established by the Charter.

21. To the extent that some human rights obligations are not based in international agreement but are deemed now part of customary law, perhaps no state could enforce them against another unless the particular obligation were also deemed to be universal, running to all states. Compare above n. 13.

22. South West Africa Cases (second phase), [1966] I.C.J. para. 32; compare paras. 34, 50. This may also be the import of an ambiguous dictum by the International Court of Justice in the Barcelona Traction Case. Having declared that some human rights violations may have become universal and enforceable *erga omnes* (see above n. 17), the court said elsewhere in the opinion: "However, on the universal level, the instruments which embody human rights do not confer on States the capacity to protect the victims of infringements of such rights irrespective of their nationality."

The court was apparently saying that the human rights agreements extant today do not create universal obligations enforceable by all states: it was not denying the right of parties to those agreements to enforce them by traditional means for the benefit of their intended beneficiaries.

23. Compare text, at n. 13.

24. It is a nice question whether substantial breach of a human rights agreement by another party, even by all other parties, justifies denunciation or suspension by an innocent party. Compare Vienna Convention on the Law of Treaties, Art. 60 (2)(b). Violation by one party surely does not warrant others "to retaliate" by violating human rights in turn. But in bilateral agreements, and others that are largely bilateral as between "two sides," is it permissible to threaten retaliation as to certain reciprocal provisions that implicate human rights, in order to deter or undo violations? For example, may State X exclude journalists of State Y if Y excludes her journalists?

25. "Where there is no domestic jurisdiction there is also no problem of intervention." Ermacora, "Human Rights and Domestic Jurisdiction," p. 431.

26. But cf. n. 20 above.

27. The West defeated efforts to dilute the domestic jurisdiction clause by replacing it with "internal affairs" or modifying it by "essentially" (which might have also given it a subjective cast).

28. Each succeeding clause is linked to the first by "accordingly," or "likewise:"

They will accordingly refrain from any form of armed intervention or threat of such intervention against another participating State.

They will likewise in all circumstances refrain from any other act of military, or of political, economic or other coercion designed to subordinate to their own interest the exercise by another participating State of the rights inherent in its sovereignty and thus to secure advantages of any kind.

Accordingly, they will, *inter alia,* refrain from direct or indirect assistance to terrorist activities, or to subversive or other activities directed towards the violent overthrow of the regime of another participating State.

29. L. F. L. Oppenheim, *International Law,* 8th ed., H. Lauterpacht, ed. (London: Longmans, 1955), p. 305; Ermacora, "Human Rights and Domestic Jurisdiction," p. 433. Despite efforts at Helsinki to broaden the sixth principle, the final text uses the legal term "intervention," rather than the broader "interference."

5. HUMAN RIGHTS AND UNITED STATES FOREIGN POLICY

1. 22 U.S.C. §§2151n(a), 2304.

2. United States Constitution, Article II, section 2, cl. 2.

3. Treaty of Peace with Bulgaria, Feb. 10, 1947, 61 Stat. 1915, T.I.A.S. No. 1650, 4 Bevans 429, 41 U.N.T.S. 21; Treaty of Peace with Hungary, Feb. 10, 1947, 61 Stat. 2065, T.I.A.S. No. 1651, 4 Bevans 453, 41 U.N.T.S. 135; Treaty of Peace with Italy, Feb. 10, 1947, T.I.A.S. No. 1648, 4 Bevans 311, 49 U.N.T.S. 1; Treaty of Peace with Romania, Feb. 10, 1947, 61 Stat. 1757, T.I.A.S. No. 1649, 4 Bevans 403, 42 U.N.T.S. 3.

4. See n. 1.

5. 22 U.S.C. §262d and §262d–1.

6. Section 301(a), P.L. 94–329, 1976, 22 U.S.C. §§ 2151n, 2304, 2384 (1976).

7. *Ibid.,* at §116(a), 22 U.S.C. §2151n.

8. Chile: Military and Economic Assistance Restrictions, International Security Assistance and Arms Export Control Act of 1976. P.L. 94–329, §406, 22 U.S.C. §2370 note (Supp. II 1978) (as amended by International Security Assistance Act of 1978, P.L. 95–

384, §§10(b)(5), 12(c)(5), 92 Stat. 735, 737) (repealed, 1981). Argentina: Foreign Assistance Restrictions, Foreign Assistance Act of 1961, P.L. 87–195. §620B, 22 U.S.C. §2372 (Supp. II 1978) (repealed, 1981). South Korea: Restrictions on Military Assistance, Foreign Assistance Act of 1974, P.L. 93–559, §26, 88 Stat. 1809 (repealed, 1981). Uganda: Import Restrictions, Bretton Woods Agreements Act Amendments, 1978, P.L. 95–435, §§5(a), (c), (e), 22 U.S.C. §2151 note (1979) (repealed, 1979). Uganda: Export Restrictions, Export Administration Act of 1969, §4(m), 50 U.S.C. app. §2403m (Supp II. 1979) (repealed, 1979).

9. Guatemala: International Security and Development Cooperation Act of 1985, §703, P.L. 99–83, 99 Stat. 239; Nicaragua: International Security and Development Cooperation Act of 1981, §724, P.L. 97–113. 95 Stat. 1552–53.

10. Comprehensive Anti-Apartheid Act of 1986, P.L. 99–440, 22 U.S.C. §§5001 et seq. (1986). The purpose of the chapter "is to set forth a comprehensive and complete framework to guide the efforts of the United States in helping to bring an end to apartheid in South Africa and lead to the establishment of a nonracial, democratic form of government." 22 U.S.C. §5002.

11. Foreign Assistance Act of 1961, §502B(e), 22 U.S.C. §2151n(b).

12. 22 U.S.C. §§2304(a)(2), and (e).

13. Foreign Assistance and Related Programs Appropriations Act of 1978, §507, 22 U.S.C. §262d–1 (Supp. II 1978).

14. The Reagan administration succeeded in using quiet diplomacy to free Kim Dae Jung in South Korea; it publicly endorsed the *Rikhoto* decision by the courts in South Africa, doubtless helping to persuade the South African parliament not to overturn the decision; and the failure to certify Chile as eligible for aid in 1983 apparently led the Pinochet regime to permit some exiles to return. See *Failure: The Reagan Administration's Human Rights Policy in 1983*. Americas Watch, Helsinki Watch, Lawyers Committee for International Human Rights, January 1984.

15. United States Constitution, Article II, section 3.

16. Henkin, Pugh, Schachter and Smit, eds., *International Law: Cases and Materials* 192–93 (2d ed. 1987).

17. *Restatement, Third, Foreign Relations Law of the United States*, §702.

18. *Restatement, Third,* §702, Reporters' note 1; *The Paquete Habana*, 175 U.S. 677 (1900).

19. *Filartiga v. Pena-Irala*, 630 F. 2d 876 (2d Cir. 1980).

20. *Rodriguez-Fernandez v. Wilkinson*, 505 F. Supp. 787 (D. Kan. 1980), *aff'd*, 654 F.2d 1382 (10th Cir. 1981). In *Garcia-Mir v. Meese*, 788 F.2d 1446 (11th Cir.), cert. denied, 479 U.S. 889 (1986), the lower court, as well as the Court of Appeals, accepted that there had been a violation of international law, but concluded that the courts could not order the Attorney General to follow that law.

21. For example, the Supreme Court has held that education and welfare are not fundamental rights as to which state regulations and classifications are subject to strict judicial scrutiny. *San Antonio Independent School Dist. v. Rodriguez*, 411 U.S. 1 (1973); *Dandridge v. Williams*, 397 U.S. 471 (1970). The Court might perhaps hold otherwise if the United States adhered to international agreements that recognize these to be fundamental rights.

22. See, e.g., Henkin, *Foreign Affairs and the Constitution* (Mineola, N.Y.: Foundation Press, 1972), pp. 140–56; Henkin, "The Constitution, Treaties, and International Human Rights," 116 *U. Pa. L. Rev.* 1012 (1968); Henkin, "The Treaty Makers and the Law Makers: The Law of the Land and Foreign Relations," 107 *U. Pa. L. Rev.* 903, 930–36 (1959).

23. A principal section would have provided that a treaty could not become law in the United States except by act of Congress that would have been valid in the absence of the treaty. See S.J. Res. 1, 83d Cong., 1st sess., 99 Cong. Rec. 6777 (1953); Treaties and Executive Agreements, Hearings before a Subcommittee on S.J. Res. 1 & S.J. Res. 43, 83d Cong., 1st sess. (1953); S. Rep. No. 412, 83d Cong., 1st sess. (1953).

24. T. Paine, *The Rights of Man* (Collins ed. 1969) p. 223 (emphasis in original).

25. In a famous address Franklin Roosevelt proclaimed Four Freedoms to the world —Freedom of Expression, Freedom of Religion, Freedom from Want and Freedom from Fear. See Address to Congress, January 6, 1941, 87 *Cong. Rec.* 44, 46–47 (1941).

6. THE IDEA OF RIGHTS AND THE UNITED STATES CONSTITUTION

1. Some early Supreme Court Justices toyed with deriving additional limitations on government from "natural rights" but that suggestion did not flourish. See Justice Chase, in *Calder v. Bull,* 3 U.S. (3 Dall.) 386 (1798); Justice Marshall, in *Fletcher v. Peck,* 10 U.S. (6 Cranch) 87 (1810).

2. *Bute v. Illinois,* 333 U.S. 640, 651 (1948).

3. T. Paine, *The Rights of Man* (Collins ed. 1969), p. 93.

4. 1 *Messages and Papers of the Presidents* 309, 311 (J. Richardson ed. 1897).

5. Compare *The Federalist* Nos. 47, 48, 51, 84; Justice Brandeis, dissenting in *Myers v. U.S.,* 272 U.S. 52, 293 (1926).

6. *Marbury v. Madison,* 5 U.S. (1 Cranch) 137, 177 (1803) ("It is emphatically the province and duty of the judicial department to say what the law is.").

7. Probably the most quoted statement in constitutional jurisprudence. See *McCulloch v. Maryland,* 17 U.S. (4 Wheat.) 316, 407 (1819).

8. *Piqua Branch of the State Bank of Ohio v. Knoop,* 57 U.S. (16 Howard) 369, 392 (1850). Earlier, the Court frequently referred to the Social Compact, e.g., Justice Chase, in *Calder v. Bull,* n. 1 *supra,* at 388; see also, e.g., *Dartmouth College v. Woodward,* 17 U.S. (4 Wheat.) 518, 588 (1819); *Satterlee v. Matthewson,* 27 U.S. (2 Pet.) 627 (1829); *Livingston v. Moore,* 32 U.S. (7 Pet.) 469 (1833). Also *The Federalist* No. 40 (Madison).

9. 5 *The Writings of Thomas Jefferson* 121 (P. Ford ed. 1894).

10. *Reynolds v. Sims,* 377 U.S. 533 (1964); *Wesberry v. Sanders,* 376 U.S. 1 (1964).

11. *Bolling v. Sharpe,* 347 U.S. 497 (1954).

12. "The government of the Union . . . is emphatically, and truly, a government of the people. In form and in substance it emanates from them. Its powers are granted by them. . . ." See *McCulloch v. Maryland, supra* n. 7, at 404–405.

13. In 1905, the Supreme Court declared: "Although the Preamble indicated the general purposes for which the people ordained and established the Constitution, it has never been regarded as the source of any substantive power conferred on the Government of the United States or on any of its Departments." See *Jacobson v. Massachusetts,* 197 U.S. 11, 22 (1905). Nor have the references in the Preamble to "liberty" and "justice" been held to serve as prohibitions or limitations on governmental authority. However, the Court, and individual justices, have sometimes invoked the purposes of the Constitution declared in the Preamble to support particular constitutional interpretations. See, e.g., *Garrison v. Louisiana,* 379 U.S. 64, 83 (1969); *Schlesinger v. Reservists,* 418 U.S. 208, 233 (1974); *Equal Employment Opportunity Commission v. Wyoming* 460 U.S. 226, 267 (1983); *Wayte v. United States,* 470 U.S. 598, 618 (1985); *Roe v. Wade,* 410 U.S. 179, 210–11 (1973) (Justice Douglas, concurring).

14. Thorpe, 3 *Federal and State Constitutions* 1893 (1909).

15. Beginning in the nineteenth century, the courts have held that the powers of government over immigration and the exclusion and deportation of aliens are not subject to the Bill of Rights. That conclusion, I believe, is without foundation and is inconsistent with the basic Jeffersonian conception of universal, inherent, unalienable rights. See also Henkin, "The Constitution and United States Sovereignty: A Century of *Chinese Exclusion* and its Progeny," 100 *Harv. L. Rev.* 853 (1987).

of the view that development and human rights are symbiotic, not adversary. Development must be political and social as well as economic; it requires giving the villager as well as the city dweller a sense of personhood, worth, dignity; it requires more rather than less individualized rights. It is recognized that today there can be no freedom, no dignity without development; it is increasingly recognized that there can be no authentic development without freedom. (See essay 10.)

Human rights may have become the idea of our time in part because ours is the age of development, industrialization, urbanization, which in many parts of the world have helped undermine what religion and tradition long offered the individual. In this modern, modernizing world, the human rights idea may sometimes appear as an ideology competing with religion, as a threat to traditional societies, as an obstacle to totalitarian socialism or to development in a hurry. But the idea of rights is not a complete, all embracing ideology, is not in fact in competition with other ideologies. Religion explains and comforts, tradition supports, socialism cares, development builds; the human rights idea does none of these. In today's world—and tomorrow's—there may be no less need for what religion and tradition have promised and provided, what socialism strives for, what development will bring; the idea of rights is not inconsistent, not in competition with any of them. Rather, religion, traditional societies, socialism, developers, will find, I believe, that their values and goals, even along their particular path, depend on individual dignity and fulfillment, and in a modern world have to be firmly supported by the idea of human rights.

There is no agreement between the secular and the theological, or between traditional and modern perspectives, on man and the Universe. One cannot prove, or even persuade, whether a substantially free economy or substantial planning is more conducive to the good society or the good of individual man. But there is now a working consensus that every man and woman, between birth and death, counts, and has a claim to an irreducible core of integrity and dignity. In that consensus, in the world we have and are shaping, the idea of human rights is the essential idea.

Notes

INTRODUCTION

1. Ronald Dworkin's term; see Dworkin, *Taking Rights Seriously* (London: Duckworth, 1978), p. xi.

2. International Covenant on Civil and Political Rights, Article 1, and International Covenant on Economic, Social and Cultural Rights, Article 1.

3. *Ibid.*, Preambles.

4. Preamble of the Universal Declaration and the Covenants.

5. UN Charter, Article 55.

6. Universal Declaration, Article 21(3).

7. *Ibid.*, Article 17.

8. *Ibid.*, Article 23; Covenant on Economic, Social and Cultural Rights, Article 6.

9. *Ibid.*, Articles 8, 9; Universal Declaration, Article 25.

1. THE INTERNATIONALIZATION OF HUMAN RIGHTS

1. *Restatement, Third, Foreign Relations Law of the United States,* part VII, Introduction and chapter 2.

2. Hersch Lauterpacht, *An International Bill of the Rights of Man* (New York: Columbia University Press, 1945), pp. 104–7.

3. Draper, "The Implementation and Enforcement of the Geneva Conventions of 1949 and of the Two Additional Protocols," 164 *Recueil des Cours* 1 (1979); G. I. Draper, *The Red Cross Conventions* (London: Stevens, 1958).

4. Message to Congress of Jan. 6, 1941, 87 *Cong. Rec.* 44, 46–47 (1941).

5. Treaty of Peace with Italy, Feb. 10, 1947, T.I.A.S. No. 1648, 4 Bevans 311, 49 U.N.T.S. 1; Treaty of Peace with Rumania, Feb. 10, 1947, 61 Stat. 1757, T.I.A.S. No. 1649, 4 Bevans 403, 42 U.N.T.S. 3.

6. Charter of the International Military Tribunal, 59 Stat. 1544. See Taylor, Nüremberg Trials, *International Conciliation* No. 450 (1959); T. Taylor, *Nüremberg and Vietnam: An American Tragedy* (Chicago: Quadrangle Books, 1970).

7. See, e.g., *Furman v. Georgia,* 408 U.S. 328 (1972); *Gregg v. Georgia,* 428 U.S. 153 (1976).

8. See, e.g., S.C. Res. 181 (1963); S.C. Res. 282 (1970), on South Africa.

9. See L. B. Sohn and T. Buergenthal, *International Protection of Human Rights* (Indianapolis: Bobbs-Merrill, 1973), pp. 750–51; John Carey, *UN Protection of Civil and Political Rights* (Syracuse, N.Y.: Syracuse University Press, 1970).

10. Res. 1503 of the UN Economic and Social Council authorized the Sub-Commission on Prevention of Discrimination and Protection of Minorities "to appoint a working group" to consider communications "which appear to reveal a consistent pattern of gross and reliably attested violations of human rights and fundamental freedoms." ECOSOC Res. 1503 (XLVII), 48 ESCOR Supp. 1A, U.N. Doc. E/4832/Add. 1 (1970). There was similar language earlier in ECSOC Resolution 1235, on the Question of Violations of Human Rights and Fundamental Freedoms, Including Policies of Racial Discrimination and Segregation and of Apartheid, In All Countries, With Particular Reference to Colonial and Other Dependent Countries and Territories. ECOSOC Res. 1235, 42 ESCOR Supp.1, U.N. Doc. E/4393 (1967).

11. E.g., G.A. Res. 33/183 A through O (1979).

12. See Francis G. Jacobs, *The European Convention on Human Rights* (Oxford: Clarendon Press, 1975); Clovis Morrisson, *The Developing European Law of Human Rights* (Leyden: Sijthoff, 1967); A. H. Robertson, *Human Rights in Europe* (Manchester: Manchester University Press, 2d ed., 1976); L. Mikaelsen, *European Protection of Human Rights* (Alphen aan den Rijn; Germantown, Md.: Sijthoff and Noordhoff, 1980).

13. See T. Buergenthal, "The Inter-American System for the Protection of Human Rights," in T. Meron, ed., *Human Rights in International Law* (Oxford: Clarendon Press; New York: Oxford University Press, 1984).

14. See O. Eze, *Human Rights in Africa* (Lagos: Nigerian Institute of International Affairs, 1984); N. Rembe, *Africa and Regional Protection of Human Rights: A Study of the African Charter on Human and Peoples' Rights: Its Effectiveness and Impact on the African States* (Romai Leoni, 1985).

2. INTERNATIONAL HUMAN RIGHTS AS "RIGHTS"

1. Maurice W. Cranston, "Human Rights, Real and Supposed," in David D. Raphael, ed., *Political Theory and the Rights of Man* (Bloomington: Indiana University Press, 1967), pp. 43–53; Maurice W. Cranston, *What Are Human Rights?* (London: Bodley Head, 1973).

2. The United States Constitution contains only limitations on government, not positive obligations upon them; and if affirmative obligations were to be constitutionally imposed, the existing legal system does not readily provide for remedies that would mandate affirmative actions by legislatures, say to appropriate adequate funds for education. See essay 7.

3. Even in the Covenant on Economic, Social and Cultural Rights, which is written with the state as the subject. See essay 1.

4. Extraordinarily, international agreements have created institutions with interna-

tional status and character independent of, and going beyond, obligations assumed by states in regard to them. Thus, the UN Organization, created by the UN Charter, is deemed to have status and character in the international system even in relation to states not party to the UN Charter. Compare the Advisory Opinion of the International Court of Justice in "The Bernadotte Case: Reparation for Injuries Suffered in the Service of the United Nations" (1949) I.C.J. 174.

5. Vienna Convention on the Law of Treaties, Article 36. The consent of the third state is required, but is ordinarily assumed. The treaty does not speak to rights for third "parties" which are not states.

6. See John Austin, *The Province of Jurisprudence Determined* (New York: Noonday Press, 1954 ed.).

7. See *Baker v. Carr,* 369 U.S. 186(1962); cf. *United States v. Richardson,* 418 U.S. 166 (1974). See generally Henkin, "Is There a 'Political Question' Doctrine?", 85 *Yale L. J.* 597 (1976).

8. See, for example, Henkin, *How Nations Behave: Law and Foreign Policy,* 2d ed. (New York: Columbia University Press, 1979), esp. chs. 3 and 4.

3. RIGHTS IN A WORLD OF STATES

1. International Covenant on Economic, Social and Cultural Rights, Article 2(1); International Convention on the Elimination of All Forms of Racial Discrimination, Articles 2 and 6.

2. In the Convention on the Prevention and Punishment of the Crime of Genocide, for example, states are obligated to bring to trial or to extradite persons charged with genocide. Article VII.

3. Universal Declaration of Human Rights, Article 14.

4. Article 2(1) of the Covenant on Civil and Political Rights extends coverage to persons "within its territory and subject to its jurisdiction," but a state is obligated to respect the rights of persons within its territory who may not be fully subject to its jurisdiction, e.g., foreign diplomats, as well as persons subject to its jurisdiction but not within its territory, e.g. nationals abroad. See Buergenthal, "To Respect and to Ensure: State Obligations and Permissible Derogations," in Louis Henkin, ed., *The International Bill of Rights: The Covenant on Civil and Political Rights* (New York: Columbia University Press, 1981), pp. 73–77.

5. Universal Declaration, Article 13(2).

6. See Article 33(1) of the Convention Relating to the Status of Refugees.

7. Universal Declaration, Article 13; International Covenant on Civil and Political Rights, Article 12(2).

8. Compare *Garcia-Mir v. Meese,* 788 F.2d 1446 (11th Cir.), cert. denied, 479 U.S. 889 (1986). See Henkin, "The Constitution and United States Sovereignty: A Century of *Chinese Exclusion* and Its Progeny," 100 *Harv. L. Rev.* 853 (1987).

4. HUMAN RIGHTS AND "DOMESTIC JURISDICTION"

1. See, e.g., Preuss, "Article 2, Paragraph 7 of the Charter of the United Nations and Matters of Domestic Jurisdiction," 74 *Recueil des Cours* 547–653 (1949–I); Gilmour, "The Meaning of 'Intervene' in Article 2, Paragraph 7," 5 *Ned. TIR* 348–65 (1958);

L. M. Goodrich, "The United Nations and Domestic Jurisdiction," 3 *Int. Org.* 14–28 (1949). See also bibliography in L. B. Sohn and T. Buergenthal, *International Protection of Human Rights* (Indianapolis: Bobbs-Merrill, 1973), pp. 594–96.

2. See bibliography in L. B. Sohn and T. Buergenthal.

3. Where the line lies between domestic and international jurisdiction is itself a question of international law, not one which any party can decide finally for itself. See the advisory opinion of the Permanent Court of International Justice in Tunis-Morocco Nationality Decrees Case, P.C.I.J. Ser. B., No. 4, 1 Hudson, World Ct. Rep. 143; Rights of Passage over Indian Territory Case, [1960] I.C.J. Rep. 33; Interpretation of Peace Treaties Case, [1950] I.C.J. 70–71; compare Publications of the European Court of Human Rights, Belgian Linguistic Case (preliminary objections), judgment of February 9, 1967, Series A. at 16–20. In rare circumstances a state may reserve to itself the right to determine whether a matter is within its domestic jurisdiction. See, e.g., the U.S. Declaration recognizing as compulsory the jurisdiction of the International Court of Justice, [1975–76] I.C.J.Y.B. 80.

4. See R. Higgins, *The Development of International Law Through the Political Organs of the United Nations* (Oxford: Oxford University Press, 1963), p. 4. But cf. Watson, "Autointerpretation, Competence, and the Continuing Validity of Article 2(7) of the U.N. Charter," 71 *Am. J. Int'l L.* 60 (1977).

5. See, generally, Ermacora, "Human Rights and Domestic Jurisdiction," 2 *Recueil des Cours* 371 (1968).

6. Much UN practice may be justified in part on the view that UN consideration does not constitute intervention within the meaning of Article 2(7), but there are innumerable indications that many members of the UN considered some alleged infringements of human rights to be violations of the UN Charter. See L. Sohn and T. Buergenthal, *International Protection of Human Rights,* pp. 505–997.

7. See, e.g., the first of many resolutions, Res. 721 (VIII), 8 December 1953, 8 GAOR, Supp. No. 17 (A/2630) at 67 (1953). See the materials collected in Sohn and Buergenthal, pp. 634–739.

8. The advisory opinion on the legal consequences for states of the continued presence of South Africa in Namibia, [1971] I.C.J. 16, para. 131, stated:

Under the Charter of the United Nations, the former Mandatory had pledged itself to observe and respect, in a territory having an international status, human rights and fundamental freedoms for all without distinction as to race. To establish instead, and to enforce, distinctions, exclusions, restrictions and limitations exclusively based on grounds of race, colour, descent or national or ethnic origin which constitute a denial of fundamental human rights is a flagrant violation of the purposes and principles of the Charter.

See Schwelb, "The International Court of Justice and the Human Rights Clauses of the Charter," 66 *Am. J. Int'l L.* 337 (1972).

9. ECOSOC Res. 1235 (XLII), 6 June 1967, 42 ESCOR, Supp. No. 1 (E/4393) at 17–18. See also ECOSOC Res. 1102 (XL), 4 March 1966, 40 ESCOR, Supp. No. 1 (2/4176) at 6.

10. ECOSOC Res. 1503 (XLVIII), 27 May 1970, 48 ESCOR, Supp. No. 1 A (E/4832/Add.1) at 8–9.

11. In 1974, the Commission on Human Rights sent a telegram to the government of Chile protesting violations of human rights. Later it established a group to investigate the violations. The General Assembly condemned Chile's violations, as well as her refusal to permit the investigation. See GA Res. 3219 (XXIX), 6 November 1974; GA Res. 32/124, 16 December 1976.

12. Case Concerning the Barcelona Traction, Light and Power Company, Ltd. [1970] I.C.J. paras. 33–34.

13. And "a serious breach on a widespread scale of such obligations" may constitute not merely an international delict but an international crime by the violating state. Article 19, subparagraph 3(c), and commentary, Report of the International Law Commission on the work of its twenty-eighth session, 3 May–23 July 1976, GAOR, Supp. No. 10 (A/31/10) pp. 226 et seq.

14. See Ermacora, "Human Rights and Domestic Jurisdiction." See *Restatement, Third, Foreign Relations Law of the United States* (1987) §702.

15. Schachter, "The Twilight Existence of Nonbinding International Agreements," 71 *Am. J. Int'l L.* 296 at 304 (1977).

16. See, for example, the Report of the International Law Commission above, n. 13 at 227–228, 265–270, and authorities cited therein. *Restatement, Third, Foreign Relations Law of the United States* (1987) § 902.

17. ". . . In particular, an essential distinction should be drawn between the obligation of a State towards the international community as a whole, and those arising vis-à-vis another State in the field of diplomatic protection. By their very nature the former are the concern of all States. In view of the importance of the rights involved, all States can be held to have a legal interest in their protection; they are obligations *erga omnes*.

Such obligations derive, for example, in contemporary international law, from the outlawing of acts of aggression, and of genocide, as also from the principles and rules concerning the basic rights of the human person, including protection from slavery and racial discrimination. Some of the corresponding rights of protection have entered into the body of general international law (Reservations to the Convention on the Prevention and Punishment of the Crime of Genocide, Advisory Opinion, *I.C.J. Reports 1951,* p. 23); others are conferred by international instruments of a universal or quasi-universal character."

Barcelona Traction Case, above n. 12, paras. 33–34; see also the Report of the International Law Commission, above n. 13.

18. The Allied Powers asserted their right to enforce the human rights provisions of World War II peace treaties. Compare the advisory opinion of the International Court of Justice, Interpretation of Peace Treaties with Bulgaria, Hungary and Romania, [1950] I.C.J. 65, 220.

19. Apparently, this general provision was accepted in lieu of an "International Court of Justice" clause (like that in the Genocide Convention), because it was feared that the court's unpopularity might discourage adherence to the covenant.

20. The same implication is to be found in the analogous Article 16 of the International Convention on the Elimination of All Forms of Racial Discrimination.

There is no contrary implication in the fact that state consent to being charged before the Human Rights Committee of the Covenant, whether by other states or by private parties, is optional. (In the Convention on Racial Discrimination, submission to interstate complaint is not optional.) That is a kind of third-party adjudication which has generally required consent, as for the I.C.J.; by contrast, submission to ordinary diplomatic enforcement by the parties is inherent in the international legal system and requires no new consent.

One might argue that International Labor Organization (ILO) conventions were not intended to be enforceable between the parties; the agreements say nothing of disputes between parties, and ILO conventions are subject to an elaborate enforcement system linked to each ILO convention. Perhaps it can be argued, too, that remedies for violation of obligations rooted in the UN Charter were intended to be enforced only by the elaborate machinery established by the Charter.

21. To the extent that some human rights obligations are not based in international agreement but are deemed now part of customary law, perhaps no state could enforce them against another unless the particular obligation were also deemed to be universal, running to all states. Compare above n. 13.

22. South West Africa Cases (second phase), [1966] I.C.J. para. 32; compare paras. 34, 50. This may also be the import of an ambiguous dictum by the International Court of Justice in the Barcelona Traction Case. Having declared that some human rights violations may have become universal and enforceable *erga omnes* (see above n. 17), the court said elsewhere in the opinion: "However, on the universal level, the instruments which embody human rights do not confer on States the capacity to protect the victims of infringements of such rights irrespective of their nationality."

The court was apparently saying that the human rights agreements extant today do not create universal obligations enforceable by all states: it was not denying the right of parties to those agreements to enforce them by traditional means for the benefit of their intended beneficiaries.

23. Compare text, at n. 13.

24. It is a nice question whether substantial breach of a human rights agreement by another party, even by all other parties, justifies denunciation or suspension by an innocent party. Compare Vienna Convention on the Law of Treaties, Art. 60 (2)(b). Violation by one party surely does not warrant others "to retaliate" by violating human rights in turn. But in bilateral agreements, and others that are largely bilateral as between "two sides," is it permissible to threaten retaliation as to certain reciprocal provisions that implicate human rights, in order to deter or undo violations? For example, may State X exclude journalists of State Y if Y excludes her journalists?

25. "Where there is no domestic jurisdiction there is also no problem of intervention." Ermacora, "Human Rights and Domestic Jurisdiction," p. 431.

26. But cf. n. 20 above.

27. The West defeated efforts to dilute the domestic jurisdiction clause by replacing it with "internal affairs" or modifying it by "essentially" (which might have also given it a subjective cast).

28. Each succeeding clause is linked to the first by "accordingly," or "likewise:"

They will accordingly refrain from any form of armed intervention or threat of such intervention against another participating State.

They will likewise in all circumstances refrain from any other act of military, or of political, economic or other coercion designed to subordinate to their own interest the exercise by another participating State of the rights inherent in its sovereignty and thus to secure advantages of any kind.

Accordingly, they will, *inter alia,* refrain from direct or indirect assistance to terrorist activities, or to subversive or other activities directed towards the violent overthrow of the regime of another participating State.

29. L. F. L. Oppenheim, *International Law,* 8th ed., H. Lauterpacht, ed. (London: Longmans, 1955), p. 305; Ermacora, "Human Rights and Domestic Jurisdiction," p. 433. Despite efforts at Helsinki to broaden the sixth principle, the final text uses the legal term "intervention," rather than the broader "interference."

5. HUMAN RIGHTS AND UNITED STATES FOREIGN POLICY

1. 22 U.S.C. §§2151n(a), 2304.

2. United States Constitution, Article II, section 2, cl. 2.

3. Treaty of Peace with Bulgaria, Feb. 10, 1947, 61 Stat. 1915, T.I.A.S. No. 1650, 4 Bevans 429, 41 U.N.T.S. 21; Treaty of Peace with Hungary, Feb. 10, 1947, 61 Stat. 2065, T.I.A.S. No. 1651, 4 Bevans 453, 41 U.N.T.S. 135; Treaty of Peace with Italy, Feb. 10, 1947, T.I.A.S. No. 1648, 4 Bevans 311, 49 U.N.T.S. 1; Treaty of Peace with Romania, Feb. 10, 1947, 61 Stat. 1757, T.I.A.S. No. 1649, 4 Bevans 403, 42 U.N.T.S. 3.

4. See n. 1.

5. 22 U.S.C. §262d and §262d–1.

6. Section 301(a), P.L. 94–329, 1976, 22 U.S.C. §§ 2151n, 2304, 2384 (1976).

7. *Ibid.,* at §116(a), 22 U.S.C. §2151n.

8. Chile: Military and Economic Assistance Restrictions, International Security Assistance and Arms Export Control Act of 1976. P.L. 94–329, §406, 22 U.S.C. §2370 note (Supp. II 1978) (as amended by International Security Assistance Act of 1978, P.L. 95–

384, §§10(b)(5), 12(c)(5), 92 Stat. 735, 737) (repealed, 1981). Argentina: Foreign Assistance Restrictions, Foreign Assistance Act of 1961, P.L. 87–195. §620B, 22 U.S.C. §2372 (Supp. II 1978) (repealed, 1981). South Korea: Restrictions on Military Assistance, Foreign Assistance Act of 1974, P.L. 93–559, §26, 88 Stat. 1809 (repealed, 1981). Uganda: Import Restrictions, Bretton Woods Agreements Act Amendments, 1978, P.L. 95–435, §§5(a), (c), (e), 22 U.S.C. §2151 note (1979) (repealed, 1979). Uganda: Export Restrictions, Export Administration Act of 1969, §4(m), 50 U.S.C. app. §2403m (Supp II. 1979) (repealed, 1979).

9. Guatemala: International Security and Development Cooperation Act of 1985, §703, P.L. 99–83, 99 Stat. 239; Nicaragua: International Security and Development Cooperation Act of 1981, §724, P.L. 97–113. 95 Stat. 1552–53.

10. Comprehensive Anti-Apartheid Act of 1986, P.L. 99–440, 22 U.S.C. §§5001 et seq. (1986). The purpose of the chapter "is to set forth a comprehensive and complete framework to guide the efforts of the United States in helping to bring an end to apartheid in South Africa and lead to the establishment of a nonracial, democratic form of government." 22 U.S.C. §5002.

11. Foreign Assistance Act of 1961, §502B(e), 22 U.S.C. §2151n(b).

12. 22 U.S.C. §§2304(a)(2), and (e).

13. Foreign Assistance and Related Programs Appropriations Act of 1978, §507, 22 U.S.C. §262d–1 (Supp. II 1978).

14. The Reagan administration succeeded in using quiet diplomacy to free Kim Dae Jung in South Korea; it publicly endorsed the *Rikhoto* decision by the courts in South Africa, doubtless helping to persuade the South African parliament not to overturn the decision; and the failure to certify Chile as eligible for aid in 1983 apparently led the Pinochet regime to permit some exiles to return. See *Failure: The Reagan Administration's Human Rights Policy in 1983*. Americas Watch, Helsinki Watch, Lawyers Committee for International Human Rights, January 1984.

15. United States Constitution, Article II, section 3.

16. Henkin, Pugh, Schachter and Smit, eds., *International Law: Cases and Materials* 192–93 (2d ed. 1987).

17. *Restatement, Third, Foreign Relations Law of the United States,* §702.

18. *Restatement, Third,* §702, Reporters' note 1; *The Paquete Habana,* 175 U.S. 677 (1900).

19. *Filartiga v. Pena-Irala,* 630 F. 2d 876 (2d Cir. 1980).

20. *Rodriguez-Fernandez v. Wilkinson,* 505 F. Supp. 787 (D. Kan. 1980), aff'd, 654 F.2d 1382 (10th Cir. 1981). In *Garcia-Mir v. Meese,* 788 F.2d 1446 (11th Cir.), cert. denied, 479 U.S. 889 (1986), the lower court, as well as the Court of Appeals, accepted that there had been a violation of international law, but concluded that the courts could not order the Attorney General to follow that law.

21. For example, the Supreme Court has held that education and welfare are not fundamental rights as to which state regulations and classifications are subject to strict judicial scrutiny. *San Antonio Independent School Dist. v. Rodriguez,* 411 U.S. 1 (1973); *Dandridge v. Williams,* 397 U.S. 471 (1970). The Court might perhaps hold otherwise if the United States adhered to international agreements that recognize these to be fundamental rights.

22. See, e.g., Henkin, *Foreign Affairs and the Constitution* (Mineola, N.Y.: Foundation Press, 1972), pp. 140–56; Henkin, "The Constitution, Treaties, and International Human Rights," 116 *U. Pa. L. Rev.* 1012 (1968); Henkin, "The Treaty Makers and the Law Makers: The Law of the Land and Foreign Relations," 107 *U. Pa. L. Rev.* 903, 930–36 (1959).

23. A principal section would have provided that a treaty could not become law in the United States except by act of Congress that would have been valid in the absence of the treaty. See S.J. Res. 1, 83d Cong., 1st sess., 99 Cong. Rec. 6777 (1953); Treaties and Executive Agreements, Hearings before a Subcommittee on S.J. Res. 1 & S.J. Res. 43, 83d Cong., 1st sess. (1953); S. Rep. No. 412, 83d Cong., 1st sess. (1953).

24. T. Paine, *The Rights of Man* (Collins ed. 1969) p. 223 (emphasis in original).

25. In a famous address Franklin Roosevelt proclaimed Four Freedoms to the world —Freedom of Expression, Freedom of Religion, Freedom from Want and Freedom from Fear. See Address to Congress, January 6, 1941, 87 *Cong. Rec.* 44, 46–47 (1941).

6. THE IDEA OF RIGHTS AND THE UNITED STATES CONSTITUTION

1. Some early Supreme Court Justices toyed with deriving additional limitations on government from "natural rights" but that suggestion did not flourish. See Justice Chase, in *Calder v. Bull,* 3 U.S. (3 Dall.) 386 (1798); Justice Marshall, in *Fletcher v. Peck,* 10 U.S. (6 Cranch) 87 (1810).

2. *Bute v. Illinois,* 333 U.S. 640, 651 (1948).

3. T. Paine, *The Rights of Man* (Collins ed. 1969), p. 93.

4. 1 *Messages and Papers of the Presidents* 309, 311 (J. Richardson ed. 1897).

5. Compare *The Federalist* Nos. 47, 48, 51, 84; Justice Brandeis, dissenting in *Myers v. U.S.,* 272 U.S. 52, 293 (1926).

6. *Marbury v. Madison,* 5 U.S. (1 Cranch) 137, 177 (1803) ("It is emphatically the province and duty of the judicial department to say what the law is.").

7. Probably the most quoted statement in constitutional jurisprudence. See *McCulloch v. Maryland,* 17 U.S. (4 Wheat.) 316, 407 (1819).

8. *Piqua Branch of the State Bank of Ohio v. Knoop,* 57 U.S. (16 Howard) 369, 392 (1850). Earlier, the Court frequently referred to the Social Compact, e.g., Justice Chase, in *Calder v. Bull,* n. 1 *supra,* at 388; see also, e.g., *Dartmouth College v. Woodward,* 17 U.S. (4 Wheat.) 518, 588 (1819); *Satterlee v. Matthewson,* 27 U.S. (2 Pet.) 627 (1829); *Livingston v. Moore,* 32 U.S. (7 Pet.) 469 (1833). Also *The Federalist* No. 40 (Madison).

9. 5 *The Writings of Thomas Jefferson* 121 (P. Ford ed. 1894).

10. *Reynolds v. Sims,* 377 U.S. 533 (1964); *Wesberry v. Sanders,* 376 U.S. 1 (1964).

11. *Bolling v. Sharpe,* 347 U.S. 497 (1954).

12. "The government of the Union . . . is emphatically, and truly, a government of the people. In form and in substance it emanates from them. Its powers are granted by them. . . ." See *McCulloch v. Maryland, supra* n. 7, at 404–405.

13. In 1905, the Supreme Court declared: "Although the Preamble indicated the general purposes for which the people ordained and established the Constitution, it has never been regarded as the source of any substantive power conferred on the Government of the United States or on any of its Departments." See *Jacobson v. Massachusetts,* 197 U.S. 11, 22 (1905). Nor have the references in the Preamble to "liberty" and "justice" been held to serve as prohibitions or limitations on governmental authority. However, the Court, and individual justices, have sometimes invoked the purposes of the Constitution declared in the Preamble to support particular constitutional interpretations. See, e.g., *Garrison v. Louisiana,* 379 U.S. 64, 83 (1969); *Schlesinger v. Reservists,* 418 U.S. 208, 233 (1974); *Equal Employment Opportunity Commission v. Wyoming* 460 U.S. 226, 267 (1983); *Wayte v. United States,* 470 U.S. 598, 618 (1985); *Roe v. Wade,* 410 U.S. 179, 210–11 (1973) (Justice Douglas, concurring).

14. Thorpe, 3 *Federal and State Constitutions* 1893 (1909).

15. Beginning in the nineteenth century, the courts have held that the powers of government over immigration and the exclusion and deportation of aliens are not subject to the Bill of Rights. That conclusion, I believe, is without foundation and is inconsistent with the basic Jeffersonian conception of universal, inherent, unalienable rights. See also Henkin, "The Constitution and United States Sovereignty: A Century of *Chinese Exclusion* and its Progeny," 100 *Harv. L. Rev.* 853 (1987).

16. As originally presented by Madison, the Ninth Amendment suggested that the rights enumerated were no more important than those retained, but that some were "inserted merely for greater caution."

17. *Barron v. Baltimore,* 32 U.S. (7 Pet.) 243 (1883); *Adamson v. California, infra* n. 19.

18. Before he became a Justice, Professor Frankfurter called for an end to "substantive due process." "The Red Terror of Judicial Reform," *New Republic* (Oct. 1, 1924). Later he advised the framers of the Indian Constiution not to include a due process clause. See B. N. Rau, *India's Constitution in the Making* (London: Longmans, 1960), p. 218.

19. Justice Black dissenting in *Adamson v. California,* 332 U.S. 46, 75–8 (1947), and in *Griswold v. Connecticut,* 381 U.S. 479, 511–13 (1965).

20. See, for example, *Roe v. Wade,* 410 U.S. 113 (1973).

21. Henkin, "Privacy and Autonomy," 74 *Colum. L. Rev.* 1410 (1970).

22. *Nebbia v. New York,* 291 U.S. 502 (1934).

23. *Allgeyer v. Louisiana,* 165 U.S. 578, 589 (1897); *Meyer v. Nebraska,* 262 U.S. 390, 399 (1923).

24. *Kent v. Dulles,* 357 U.S. 116 (1958); *Roe v. Wade, supra* n. 20.

25. *Bolling v. Sharpe, supra* n. 11, at 500.

26. See, for example, the right to marry, *Zablocki v. Redhail,* 434 U.S. 374 (1978); the right of parents to withhold their children from public school to protect religious values, *Pierce v. Society of Sisters,* 268 U.S. 510 (1925); the right to be convicted only on proof beyond a reasonable doubt, *In re Winship,* 397 U.S. 358 (1970); the freedom to travel, *Kent v. Dulles, supra* n. 24.

27. *Paul v. Davis,* 424 U.S. 693 (1976).

28. *Ingraham v. Wright,* 430 U.S. 651 (1977).

29. Centuries earlier, localities in England had succeeded to the Church's responsibility for the poor. E. M. Leonard, *The Early History of English Poor Relief,* viii–x (London: F. Cass, 1965); An Act of Relief of the Poor, 43 Eliz. ch. 2, reprinted in E. Bott, *A Collection of Decisions upon the Poor's Laws,* (New York: Garland, 1978).

30. *Dandridge v. Williams,* 397 U.S. 471 (1970); *San Antonio Indep. School District v. Rodriguez,* 411 U.S. 1 (1973); *Lindsey v. Normet,* 405 U.S. 56 (1972); *Massachusetts Bd. of Retirement v. Murgia,* 427 U.S. 307 (1976).

31. *Civil Rights Cases,* 109 U.S. 3 (1883).

32. Once, indeed—in a lonely case—the Supreme Court held that a state would be taking an individual's property without due process of law if it abolished a remedy for tort. *Truax v. Corrigan,* 257 U.S. 312 (1921).

33. E.g., *Consolidated Edison Co. v. Public Service Commission,* 447 U.S. 530, 540 (1980) (invalidating order prohibiting public utility from enclosing with its bills inserts discussing public issues); *Korematsu v. United States,* 323 U.S. 214 (1944) (upholding Japanese relocation during Second World War); also *Loving v. Virginia,* 388 U.S. 1 (1967) (statute preventing interracial marriage violates the Fourteenth Amendment). See, generally, Henkin, "Infallibility Under Law: Constitutional Balancing," 78 *Colum. L. Rev.* 1022 (1978).

34. I refer to judicial requirements of standing, ripeness, concreteness, and justiciability; see generally, G. Gunther, *Constitutional Law* (11th ed., Mineola, N.Y.: Foundation Press, 1985) pp. 1532–1633.

7. CONSTITUTIONAL RIGHTS— 200 YEARS LATER

1. See Henkin, "Constitutional Fathers, Constitutional Son," 60 *Minn. L. Rev.* 1113 (1976).

2. Charles and Mary Beard characterized the result as "the mosaic of their second choices." *The Rise of American Civilization* (rev. ed., New York: Macmillan, 1935), p. 317.

3. See, e.g., *The Federalist* Nos. 47, 48, 51, 84 (Madison); G. Wood, *The Creation of the American Republic* 539–40, 547–53 (New York: Norton 1969); Brandeis J., dissenting in *Myers v. U.S.*, 272 U.S. 52, 293 (1926); "The Bill of Rights and the Constitution," address by Justice John M. Harlan at the dedication of Bill of Rights Room, U.S. Sub-Treasury Building, New York, Aug. 9, 1964.

4. See Henkin, "Infallibility Under Law: Constitutional Balancing," 78 *Colum. L. Rev.* 1022 (1978).

5. In 1989 the Supreme Court confirmed that there is no enforceable constitutional obligation for a state to protect an individual against his neighbor. *DeShaney v. Winnebago County*, 109 S. Ct. 998 (1989).

6. *Barron v. City of Baltimore*, 32 U.S. (7 Pet.) 243 (1833).

7. See generally J. M. Smith, *Freedom's Fetters* (Ithaca: Cornell University Press, 1956).

8. See, e.g., *Dartmouth College v. Woodward*, 17 U.S. (4 Wheat.) 518 (1819); *Charles River Bridge v. Warren Bridge*, 36 U.S. (11 Pet.) 420 (1837). In the twentieth century, too, the Contract clause is commonly invoked by companies, e.g., *Home Building & Loan Ass'n v. Blaisdell*, 290 U.S. 398 (1934); *United States Trust Co. v. New Jersey*, 431 U.S. 1 (1977).

9. *Scott v. Sandford*, 60 U.S. (19 How.) 393 (1857).

10. *Slaughter-House Cases*, 83 U.S. (16 Wall.) 36 (1873).

11. *Civil Rights Cases*, 109 U.S. 3 (1883). And see the decision upholding the denial to women of the right to practice law, n. 14 below. Compare the limited interpretation of the due process clause by the Supreme Court and its "bad guess" about the equal protection clause: "We doubt very much whether any action of a State not directed by way of discrimination against the negroes as a class, or on account of their race, will ever be held to come within the purview of this provision." *Slaughter-House Cases, supra* n. 10, at 81.

12. Compare *Strauder v. Virginia*, 100 U.S. 303 (1880) (exclusion of blacks from jury), and *Yick Wo v. Hopkins*, 118 U.S. 356 (1886) (denial to Chinese of right to operate laundry), with *Plessy v. Ferguson* (racial segregation), n. 13 *infra*, and the cases refusing to apply the Amendment to discrimination that was held not to involve state action, e.g., *Civil Rights Cases* (discrimination by railroads, inns), n. 11 *supra*.

13. *Plessy v. Ferguson*, 163 U.S. 537 (1896), *overruled, Brown v. Board of Education*, 347 U.S. 483 (1954), n. 30 *infra*.

14. *Bradwell v. State*, 83 U.S. (16 Wall.) 130 (1873).

15. See *Lochner v. New York*, 198 U.S. 45 (1905); *Hammer v. Dagenhart*, 247 U.S. 251 (1918); *Carter v. Carter Coal Co.*, 298 U.S. 238 (1936). The Court also invalidated a progressive income tax. *Pollock v. Farmers' Loan and Trust Co.*, 157 U.S. 429 (1895).

16. *Schenck v. United States*, 249 U.S. 47 (1919); *Debs v. United States*, 249 U.S. 211 (1919); *Abrams v. United States*, 250 U.S. 616 (1919); *Gitlow v. New York*, 268 U.S. 652 (1926).

17. See *Duncan v. Louisiana*, 391 U.S. 145, 147–49 (1968), and the cases collected there. Incorporation rendered rights against the federal and state governments identical. See *Apodaca v. Oregon*, 406 U.S. 404 (1972); *Williams v. Florida*, 399 U.S. 78 (1970).

18. *South Carolina v. Katzenbach*, 383 U.S. 301 (1966); *Katzenbach v. Morgan*, 384 U.S. 641 (1966). See the various United States civil rights acts, now in 18 U.S.C. §§ 241–42; 42 U.S.C. §§ 1981–85 as interpreted; also the statutes cited in n. 42 *infra*.

19. *Brandenburg v. Ohio*, 395 U.S. 444 (1969) (Constitution protects even "advocacy" of violence, as distinguished from "incitement to imminent lawless action"); *Collin v. Smith*, 578 F.2d 1197 (7th Cir.), cert. denied, 439 U.S. 916 (Nazi demonstrations); compare *Beauharnais v. Illinois*, 343 U.S. 250 (1952), a case upholding group libel laws, its authority now questioned; *Thornhill v. Alabama*, 310 U.S. 88 (1940) (labor picketing);

Virginia State Board of Pharmacy v. Virginia Citizens Consumer Council, Inc., 425 U.S. 748 (1976) (invalidating prohibition of advertising of prescription drug prices); *Zauderer v. Office of Disciplinary Counsel,* 471 U.S. 626 (1985) (professional advertising); *Memoirs v. Massachusetts,* 383 U.S. 413 (1966) (requiring prosecution for obscenity to prove materials "utterly without redeeming social value"); also *Miller v. California,* 413 U.S. 15 (1973) (obscene materials are not protected by the First and Fourteenth Amendments and may be regulated by the states).

20. *Tinker v. Des Moines School District,* 393 U.S. 503 (1969); but compare *United States v. O'Brien,* 391 U.S. 367 (1968) (conviction for burning draft-card upheld); *Buckley v. Valeo,* 424 U.S. 1 (1976) (invalidating limitations on political contributions).

21. Compare *New York Times v. Sullivan,* 376 U.S. 254 (1964); *Curtis Publishing Co. v. Butts,* 388 U.S. 130 (1967); *Gertz v. Robert Welch, Inc.,* 418 U.S. 323 (1974); *Time, Inc. v. Hill,* 385 U.S. 374 (1967).

22. *Hague v. CIO,* 307 U.S. 496 (1939) (parks); *Cox v. Louisiana,* 379 U.S. 536 (1965) (street demonstrations); *Richmond Newspapers, Inc. v. Virginia,* 448 U.S. 555 (1980) (right of press to attend criminal trial); *Houchins v. KQED, Inc.,* 438 U.S. 1 (1978) (press access to jails).

23. *Talley v. California,* 362 U.S. 60 (1960) (invalidating prohibition of anonymous leaflets); *Sweezy v. New Hampshire,* 354 U.S. 234 (1957) (rejecting inquiry into content of professor's lecture); *Miami Herald Pub. Co. v. Tornillo,* 418 U.S. 241 (1974) (right not to publish).

24. *NAACP v. Alabama,* 357 U.S. 449 (1958); *Shelton v. Tucker,* 364 U.S. 479 (1960); *Abood v. Detroit Board of Education,* 431 U.S. 209 (1977) (right not to join trade union or contribute to its ideological programs); *Roberts v. United States Jaycees,* 468 U.S. 609 (1984); *Gibson v. Florida Legislative Investigation Comm.,* 372 U.S. 539 (1963); *DeGregory v. New Hampshire Attorney General,* 383 U.S. 825 (1966) (legislative investigation); *Baird v. State Bar of Arizona,* 401 U.S. 1 (1971) (right of association prohibits exclusion from profession on grounds of membership in particular political organization).

25. *Sherbert v. Verner,* 374 U.S. 398 (1963); *Everson v. Board of Education,* 330 U.S. 1 (1947); *School District of Abington v. Schempp,* 374 U.S. 203 (1963); *Lemon v. Kurtzman,* 403 U.S. 602 (1971). Also *Estate of Thornton v. Caldor, Inc.,* 472 U.S. 703 (1985); *Edwards v. Aguillard,* 482 U.S. 578 (1987).

26. *Berger v. New York,* 388 U.S. 41 (1967); *Katz v. United States,* 389 U.S. 347 (1967); *Camara v. Municipal Court,* 387 U.S. 523 (1967); but see *Wyman v. James,* 400 U.S. 309 (1971) (refusal to allow visit by social worker may support denial of welfare benefits).

27. *Weeks v. United States,* 232 U.S. 383 (1914); *Mapp v. Ohio,* 367 U.S. 643 (1961) (exclusion of unlawfully obtained evidence); *Gideon v. Wainwright,* 372 U.S. 335 (1963) (counsel); *Malloy v. Hogan,* 378 U.S. 1 (1964); cf. *Griffin v. California,* 380 U.S. 609 (1965) (privilege against self-incrimination). See also *Miranda v. Arizona,* 384 U.S. 436 (1966) (obligation to inform person in custody of right not to respond to interrogation). In addition, old laws and accepted official practices, and legislative delegations that lend themselves to official abuse, are no longer tolerated: crimes such as loitering and vagrancy are now void for vagueness, because the activities are essentially inoffensive and give too much power and discretion to officials, too little warning to the putative offender. Overbroad laws are invalidated or narrowed to prevent them from "chilling" and discouraging the exercise of important freedoms. Penological assumptions and practices have acquired a constitutional dimension: a person cannot be punished for a condition—being intoxicated or under the influence of drugs—that he or she was unable to resist; punishment that is excessive in relation to the crime is forbidden as "cruel and unusual"; the death penalty, in particular, may not be imposed lightly, and not to protect values other than life, e.g., for rape. See *Thompson v. Louisville,* 362 U.S. 199 (1960) (loitering); *Robinson v. California,,* 370 U.S. 660 (1962) (addict); *Weems v. United States,* 217 U.S. 349 (1910) (excessive punishment); *Coker v. Georgia,* 433 U.S. 584 (1977) (capital punishment for rape); see also *Enmund v. Florida,* 458 U.S. 782 (1982).

28. *Bolling v. Sharpe,* 347 U.S. 497 (1954).

29. *Smith v. Texas,* 311 U.S. 128, 132 (1940) (exclusion of blacks from Grand Jury is unconstitutional "whether such discrimination was accomplished ingeniously or ingenuously"); also *Lane v. Wilson,* 307 U.S. 268, 275 (1939) (Constitution prohibits "sophisticated as well as simple-minded modes of discrimination").

30. *Brown v. Board of Education,* 347 U.S. 483 (1954), *overruling Plessy v. Ferguson, supra* n. 13.

31. *Reed v. Reed,* 407 U.S. 71 (1971); *Frontiero v. Richardson,* 411 U.S. 677 (1973); *Craig v. Boren,* 429 U.S. 190 (1976); *Mississippi University for Women v. Hogan,* 458 U.S. 718 (1983).

32. *Griffin v. Illinois,* 351 U.S. 12 (1956); *Boddie v. Connecticut,* 401 U.S. 371 (1971); but cf. *United States v. Kras,* 409 U.S. 434 (1973); *Kadrmas v. Dickinson Public Schools,* 108 S. Ct. 2481 (1988).

33. *Graham v. Richardson,* 403 U.S. 365 (1971); *In re Griffith,* 413 U.S. 717 (1973) (practice of law by aliens); *Sugarman v. Dougall,* 413 U.S. 634 (1973) (civil service); but cf. *Foley v. Connelie,* 435 U.S. 291 (1978); *Ambach v. Norwick,* 441 U.S. 68 (1979) (state may exclude aliens from posts in which they would be exercising "governmental functions"); *Levy v. Louisiana,* 391 U.S. 68 (1968); but cf. *Mathews v. Lucas,* 427 U.S. 495 (1976) (illegitimate children).

34. *Cruz v. Beto,* 405 U.S. 319 (1972) (religious rights of prisoners); cf. *Turner v. Safley,* 482 U.S. 78 (1987) (right of prisoner to marry or to communicate with other inmates); cf. *Goldman v. Weinberger,* 475 U.S. 503, 106 S. Ct. 1310 (1986) (limiting religious rights of military officer); *O'Connor v. Donaldson,* 422 U.S. 563 (1975) (mental patients); *City of Cleburne v. Cleburne Living Center,* 473 U.S. 432 (1985) (discrimination against mentally retarded); *Goss v. Lopez,* 419 U.S. 565 (1975) (procedural rights of high school students); *Bellotti v. Baird,* 443 U.S. 622 (1979) (abortion for minors); cf. Douglas, J., in *Wisconsin v. Yoder,* 406 U.S. 205, 241 (1972).

35. *Kent v. Dulles,* 357 U.S. 116 (1958); but cf. *Regan v. Wald,* 468 U.S. 222 (1984) (upholding restrictions on travel to Cuba); *Shapiro v. Thompson,* 394 U.S. 618 (1969) (invalidating durational residence requirement for eligibility for welfare assistance); *Dunn v. Blumstein,* 405 U.S. 330 (1972) (durational residence requirement for voting); *Memorial Hospital v. Maricopa County,* 415 U.S. 250 (1974); but cf. *Sosna v. Iowa,* 419 U.S. 393 (1975) (residence requirement for divorce action).

36. *Griswold v. Connecticut,* 381 U.S. 479 (1965); *Roe v. Wade,* 410 U.S. 113 (1973); *Stanley v. Georgia,* 394 U.S. 557 (1969).

37. *Pierce v. Society of Sisters,* 268 U.S. 510 (1925); cf. *Wisconsin v. Yoder,* 406 U.S. 205 (1972) (compulsory high school attendance law violates Amish parent's freedom of religion).

38. *Wesberry v. Sanders,* 376 U.S. 1 (1964); *Reynolds v. Sims,* 377 U.S. 533 (1964).

39. *Nebbia v. New York,* 291 U.S. 502 (1934).

40. *Hirabayashi v. United States,* 320 U.S. 81 (1943); *Korematsu v. United States,* 323 U.S. 214 (1944).

41. *Heart of Atlanta Motel v. United States,* 379 U.S. 241 (1964); *Katzenbach v. McClung,* 379 U.S. 294 (1964).

42. See the Civil Rights Act of 1964, 78 *Stat.* 241, 42 U.S.C. §2000 (a) (1970); Voting Rights Act of 1965, 79 *Stat.* 437, 42 U.S.C. §1973 (1970). And see nn. 18 and 43.

43. *Jones v. Alfred H. Mayer Co.,* 392 U.S. 409 (1968); *Runyon v. McCrary,* 427 U.S. 160 (1976). The interpretation reflected in those cases was reaffirmed but limited in *Patterson v. McLean Credit Union,* 109 S. Ct. 2363 (1989).

44. See n. 15.

45. See *Lynch v. Donnelly,* 465 U.S. 668 (1984) (permitting creche on public grounds); *Bowers v. Hardwick,* 478 U.S. 186 (1986) (upholding state law prohibiting homosexual activity). See generally V. Blasi, *The Burger Court: The Counter-Revolution That Wasn't* (New Haven: Yale University Press, 1983).

46. In *United States v. Salerno,* 481 U.S. 739, 107 S. Ct. 2095 (1987), the Supreme Court upheld legislative provisions requiring courts to order detention prior to trial of persons charged with certain serious felonies if the government demonstrates by "clear and convincing evidence" that no conditions for release will reasonably assure the safety of the community.

47. See also the decision to reexamine the interpretation of the Civil Rights Acts, n. 43 *supra.*

48. See Henkin, "The Constitution and United States Sovereignty: A Century of *Chinese Exclusion* and its Progeny," 100 *Harv. L. Rev.* 853 (1987); see essay 8.

49. See n. 21 *supra.*

50. See *Collin v. Smith* and *Beauharnais v. Illinois,* n. 19.

51. *Regents of University of California v. Bakke,* 438 U.S. 265 (1978); *Fullilove v. Klutznick,* 448 U.S. 448 (1980); *Local No. 93, International Association of Firefighters v. City of Cleveland,* 478 U.S. 501 (1986); cf. *Wygant v. Jackson Board of Education,* 476 U.S. 267 (1986).

52. For one recent "correction," see the Civil Rights Restoration Act of 1987, P.L. 100–259, correcting *Grove City College v. Bell,* 465 U.S. 555 (1984). Compare the Court's "correction" of its own interpretation, n. 43 *supra.*

8. THE CONSTITUTION AS COMPACT AND AS CONSCIENCE

1. See *Plyler v. Doe,* 457 U.S. 202 (1982).

2. See *Sanchez-Espinoza v. Reagan,* 568 F. Supp. 596 (D.D.C. 1983); *Greenham Women Against Cruise Missiles v. Reagan,* 591 F. Supp. 1332 (S.D.N.Y. 1984), *aff'd,* 755 F.2d 34 (2d Cir. 1985); *United States v. Tiede,* 86 F.R.D. 227 (U.S. Ct. Berlin 1979).

3. *Jean v. Nelson,* 727 F.2d 957 (11th Cir. 1984) (en banc), *aff'd on other grounds,* 472 U.S. 846 (1985); *Bertrand v. Sava,* 684 F.2d 204 (2d Cir. 1982); *Rodriguez-Fernandez v. Wilkinson,* 654 F.2d 1382 (10th Cir. 1981).

4. See Exec. Order No. 12,324, 46 Fed. Reg. 48,109 (1981), reprinted in 8 U.S.C. § 1182 at 992–93 (1983); Proclamation No. 4865, 46 Fed. Reg. 48,107 (1981), reprinted in 8 U.S.C. § 1182 at 993 (1983); see also *Haitian Refugee Center v. Gracey,* 600 F. Supp. 1396 (D.D.C. 1985), dismissed for lack of standing, 809.F.2d 794 (1987) (unsuccessful challenge to Haitian Interdiction Program).

5. *Jean v. Nelson, supra* n. 3; *Fernandez-Roque v. Smith,* 734 F.2d 576 (11th Cir. 1984); 600 F. Supp. 1500 (N.D. Ga. 1985); 622 F. Supp. 887 (N.D. Ga. 1985), *aff'd sub nom.* Garcia-Mir v. Meese, 788 F.2d 1446 (11th Cir. 1986), cert. denied, 479 U.S. 889 (1986). Cf. *Shaughnessy v. United States ex rel. Mezei,* 345 U.S. 206, 215–16 (1953) (detention on Ellis Island without actual entry into United States, pursuant to statutory authorization), discussed later, this chapter at notes 42 and 43.

6. Cf. *Galvan v. Press,* 347 U.S. 522 (1954) (deportation on grounds of Communist Party membership); Harisiades v. Shaughnessy, 342 U.S. 580 (1952) (same).

7. See, e.g., *Nishimura Ekiu v. United States,* 142 U.S. 651, 659 (1892); *The Chinese Exclusion Case,* 130 U.S. 581, 585 (1889).

8. 118 U.S. 356 (1886); 140 U.S. 453 (1891); 130 U.S. 581 (1889).

9. Act of Mar. 26, 1790, ch. 3, 1 Stat. 103, *repealed by* Act of Jan. 29, 1795, ch. 20, 1 Stat. 414. Congress quickly drew a line between citizens and aliens, however, when it enacted the Alien Enemies Acts. Act of June 25, 1798, ch. 58, 1 Stat. 570; Act of July 6, 1798, ch. 66, 1 Stat. 577. See generally J. Smith, *Freedom's Fetters* (Ithaca: Cornell University Press, 1956), pp. 1–155.

10. Va. Const. Art. I, § 6.

11. 118 U.S. 356 (1886).

12. *Ibid.*, at 369.

13. See, e.g., *Wong Wing v. United States*, 163 U.S. 228 (1896) (holding that the Constitution precludes punishment of an alien for being in the United States unlawfully except pursuant to trial in accordance with the Fifth and Sixth Amendments); *Russian Volunteer Fleet v. United States*, 282 U.S. 481 (1931) (holding that the property of friendly aliens may not be taken for public purposes without just compensation). Aliens also are entitled to the equal protection of the laws implied in the concept of due process. See *Hampton v. Mow Sun Wong*, 426 U.S. 88, 100 (1976): See *Restatement, Third, Foreign Relations Law of the United States* (1987) § 722 and Comment a.

14. *Bernal v. Fainter*, 467 U.S. 216 (1984) (notary public); *In re* Griffiths, 413 U.S. 717 (1973) (practice of law); *Sugarman v. Dougall*, 413 U.S. 634 (1973) (classified civil service); *Graham v. Richardson*, 403 U.S. 365 (1971) (welfare benefits).

15. *Foley v. Connelie*, 435 U.S. 291, 296 (1978) (state trooper); see also *Cabell v. Chavez-Salido*, 454 U.S. 432 (1982) (deputy probabtion officer); *Ambach v. Norwick*, 441 U.S. 68 (1979) (public school teacher).

16. See *Hampton v. Mow Sun Wong*, 426 U.S. 68, 101 n. 21, 104, (1976); *Mathews v. Diaz*, 426 U.S. 67, 78–80 (1976); *Hines v. Davidowitz*, 312 U.S. 52, 62–69 (1941); *The Chinese Exclusion Case*, 130 U.S. 581, 606–09 (1889).

17. *Mathews v. Diaz*, at 79 n. 12; *National City Bank v. Republic of China*, 348 U.S. 356, 363 (1955); see *United Continental Tuna Corp. v. United States*, 550 F.2d 569 (9th Cir. 1977); *Westfal-Larsen & Co. v. United States*, 41 F.2d 550 (N.D. Cal. 1930). Statutes containing reciprocity provisions include 10 U.S.C. § 7435(a) (1982) (National Petroleum Reserves Act), 28 U.S.C. § 2502 (1982) (Tucker Act (claims)), and 46 U.S.C. § 785 (1982) (Public Vessels Act). For other reciprocity provisions see Henkin. "The Treaty Makers and the Law Makers: The Law of the Land and Foreign Relations," 107 *U. Pa. L. Rev.* 903, 921 n. 41 (1959).

18. See *Mathews v. Diaz, supra* n. 16; *Restatement, supra* n. 13.

19. 140 U.S. 453 (1891).

20. *Ibid.*, at 464.

21. *Ross* in effect was overruled in 1957 by *Reid v. Covert*, 354 U.S. 1 (1957).

22. *Balzac v. Porto Rico*, 258 U.S. 298 (1922); *Dorr v. United States*, 195 U.S. 138 (1904); *Hawaii v. Mankichi*, 190 U.S. 197 (1903); *Downes v. Bidwell*, 182 U.S. 244 (1901).

23. *Downes v. Bidwell*, at 343 (J. White, concurring).

24. Pursuant to a joint resolution of Congress, the United States relinquished its last extraterritorial ("capitulation") rights in 1956. See Act of Aug. 1, 1956, ch. 807, 70 Stat. 773 (1956) (repealing 22 U.S.C. §§ 141–43, 145–75, 176–81, 183).

25. Cf. *Madsen v. Kinsella*, 343 U.S. 341 (1952) (upholding criminal conviction of U.S. civilian by courts of U.S. military occupation authorities in Germany).

26. The United States still has the authority of an occupying power for some purposes in Germany today. See Quadripartite Agreement on Berlin, Sep. 3, 1971, 24 U.S.T. 283, T.I.A.S. No. 7551. For an exercise of such authority, see *United States v. Tiede*, 86 F.R.D. 227 (U.S. Ct. Berlin 1979).

27. See Agreement Between the Parties of the North Atlantic Treaty Regarding the Status of Their Forces, June 19, 1951, 4 U.S.T. 1792, T.I.A.S. No. 2846, 199 U.N.T.S. 67.

28. 354 U.S. 1 (1957), *rev'g* Kinsella v. Krueger, 351 U.S. 470 (1956), and *Reid v. Covert*, 351 U.S. 487 (1956). A similar case, involving the wife of a United States Army officer who was tried and convicted for her husband's murder by a military court in Japan, was consolidated with this case on appeal.

29. 354 U.S. at 5–9 (footnotes omitted).

30. *Ibid.*, at 12.

31. In *United States v. Belmont*, the Supreme Court acknowledged that "our Constitution, laws and policies have no extraterritorial operation, unless in respect of our own

citizens." 301 U.S. 324, 332 (1937) (citations omitted). In context, however, the Court was asserting merely that our Constitution, laws, and policies do not govern the acts of *other governments*.

32. See, e.g., *United States v. Hensel,* 699 F.2d 18 (1st Cir.), cert. denied, 461 U.S. 958, cert. denied, 464 U.S. 823, cert. denied, 464 U.S. 824 (1983); *United States v. Williams,* 617 F.2d 1063 (5th Cir. 1980); *United States v. Cadena,* 585 F.2d 1252 (5th Cir. 1978). See generally Henkin, "The Constitution at Sea," 36 *Me. L. Rev.* 201 (1984).

33. *Ramirez de Arellano v. Weinberger,* 745 F.2d 1500, 1505 (D.C. Cir. 1984) (en banc), *rev'g* 724 F.2d 143 (D.C. Cir. 1983), *vacated mem.,* 471 U.S. 1113 (1985).

34. 500 F.2d 267 (2d Cir. 1974).

35. See, e.g., *United States v. Demanett,* 629 F.2d 862, 866 (3d Cir. 1980).

36. *United States v. Tiede,* 86 F.R.D. 227 (U.S. Ct. Berlin 1979).

37. *Greenham Women Against Cruise Missiles v. Reagan,* 591 F. Supp. 1332 (S.D.N.Y. 1984), *aff'd,* 755 F.2d 34 (2d Cir. 1985).

38. 130 U.S. 581 (1889).

39. See Head Money Cases, 112 U.S. 580 (1884).

40. The Court explicitly held the Constitution inapplicable abroad two years later in *In re Ross,* 140 U.S. 453 (1891), *overruled, Reid v. Covert,* 354 U.S. 1, 12 (1957).

41. 8 U.S.C. § 1182(a)(28) (1928); see *Kleindienst v. Mandel,* 408 U.S. 753 (1972); *Harisiades v. Shaughnessy, supra* n. 6; *United States ex rel. Knauff v. Shaughnessy,* 338 U.S. 537 (1950); see also *Shaughnessy v. United States ex rel. Mezei, supra* n. 5 (exclusion based on "information of a confidential nature, the disclosure of which would be prejudicial to the public interest").

42. *Mezei;* see also *United States ex rel. Knauff v. Shaughnessy* (upholding a decision, based on confidential information, to deny entry to the wife of an American serviceman).

The Court had an opportunity in 1985 to reconsider and disown *Mezei* but only the dissenting justices seized it. See *Jean v. Nelson,* 472 U.S. 846, 868–882 (1985) (Marshall and Brennan, J J., dissenting).

43. *Galvan v. Press, Harisiades v. Shaughnessy,* n. 6.

44. Cf. Jean v. Nelson, 727 F.2d 957 (11th Cir. 1984) (en banc), *aff'd on other grounds,* 472 U.S. 846 (1985); *Fernandez-Roque v. Smith,* F.2d 576 (11th Cir. 1984); 600 F. Supp. 1500 (N.D. Ga. 1985); 622 F. Supp. 887 (N.D. Ga. 1985), *affirmed sub nom. Garcia-Mir v. Meese,* 788 F.2d 1446 (11th Cir. 1986), certiorari denied, 479 U.S. 889 (1986). But see *Jean v. Nelson* at 868, n. 8 (Marshall, J., dissenting) (citing *Augustin v. Sava,* 735 F.2d 32 (2d Cir. 1984), *Yiu Sing Chung v. Sava,* 708 F.2d 869 (2d Cir. 1983), and *Rodriguez-Fernandez v. Wilkinson,* 654 F.2d 1382 (10th Cir. 1981)).

45. *Haitian Refugee Center v. Gracey,* n. 4. For an indication of the issues raised by the Program, see Henkin, "The Constitution at Sea," 36 *Me. L. Rev.* 201, 216–18 (1984).

46. *Bugajewitz v. Adams,* 228 U.S. 585, 591 (1913).

47. *Galvan v. Press* 347 U.S. at 530.

48. The Immigration and Nationality Act of 1952 abolished the "national origins" system of the Act of 1924, and gave every country at least a modest quota, but the differences in the quotas themselves may suggest ethnic and racial considerations. See Immigration and Nationality Act, ch. 477, 66 Stat. 163, 175–78 (1952). The 1965 Amendment to the Act of 1952 abolished all quotas and gave preferences for immigration purposes on other grounds, such as concern for family reunification and needed skills. See Act of Oct. 3, 1965, Pub. L. No. 89–236, 79 Stat. 911, 911–12.

49. See generally Henkin, "The Constitution and United States Sovereignty: A Century of *Chinese Exclusion* and its Progeny," 100 *Harv. L. Rev.* 853 (1987).

50. Whether an alien abroad has access to the courts of the United States is a different question. No reasons exist why an alien held by United States authorities abroad should not have the right to bring a writ of habeas corpus in a United States court, or seek compensation through our courts for any taking of property by the United States government. But see *Johnson v. Eisentrager,* 339 U.S. 763 (1950) (denying alien enemies access

to courts in time of war). Whether a nonresident alien has a remedy under a particular statute depends upon statutory interpretation. See, e.g., *Constructiones Civiles de Centroamerica, S.A. v. Hannah,* 459 F.2d 1183, 1190 (D.C. Cir. 1972).

See also *Berlin Democratic Club v. Rumsfeld,* 410 F. Supp. 144 (D.D.C. 1976), in which the court denied access to an Austrian national who was a co-plaintiff with United States nationals challenging United States Army wiretapping in Europe. The court declared a general rule denying access to United States courts for aliens resident abroad subject to three possible exceptions. According to the court, none of these exceptions applied to a plaintiff who had "no contact with the United States other than his meetings with private United States citizens and his alleged electronic surveillance by United States Army personnel." *Ibid.,* at 153. The basis for the court's general rule is unclear, and its application to deny a remedy in that particular situation is open to question. Even applying the court's own rule, an alien who had been subjected to government surveillance seemingly had sufficient "contact with the United States."

51. See *Hampton v. Mow Sun Wong,* 426 U.S. 88, 103–05 (1976) (national interests may justify congressional exclusion of aliens from Civil Service employment); *Mathews v. Diaz,* 426 U.S. 67, 80 (1976).

52. Va. Const. art. 1, § 6.

9. RIGHTS: AMERICAN AND HUMAN

1. The power later given to Congress to implement the Civil War Amendments applies only to the rights protected by those Amendments and only against violations by the states. See *Civil Rights Cases,* 109 U.S. 3 (1883).

2. But the Civil Rights Act would presumably apply to a federal official who conspired with a state official to violate rights. See *Hampton v. Hanrahan,* 600 F.2d 600, 623 (7th Cir. 1979); *Kletschka v. Driver,* 411 F.2d 436, 448–49 (2d Cir. 1969). Compare *District of Columbia v. Carter,* 409 U.S. 418, 424–25 (1973), with *Adickes v. Kress & Co.,* 398 U.S. 144, 152 (1970). And see note 8 *infra.*

3. *Heart of Atlanta Motel v. United States,* 379 U.S. 241 (1964); *Katzenbach v. McClung,* 379 U.S. 294 (1964).

4. *Harris v. McRae,* 448 U.S. 297 (1980); *Maher v. Roe,* 432 U.S. 464 (1977).

5. Art. 2(1) of the International Covenant on Civil and Political Rights. See T. Buergenthal, "To Respect and to Ensure," in L. Henkin, ed., *The International Bill of Rights* (New York: Columbia University Press, 1981), ch. 3.

6. *Ibid.,* Art. 6(1).

7. See A. Beveridge, *Life of John Marshall* (Boston: Houghton, Mifflin, 1919), pp. 177–78.

8. In some cases, however, the courts have provided a remedy for constitutional violations on their own authority. E.g., *Bivens v. Six Unknown Named Agents of Fed. Bureau of Narcotics,* 403 U.S. 388 (1971). See also *Davis v. Passman,* 442 U.S. 228 (1979).

9. Compare *Dandridge v. Williams,* 397 U.S. 471 (1970).

10. But the Court in effect orders the spending of money when it enjoins a county from terminating a school system to avoid desegregating the schools, or directs it to provide counsel to an indigent criminal defendant, or to improve the quality of prisons. E.g., *Griffin v. County School Board,* 377 U.S. 218 (1964); *Gideon v. Wainwright,* 377 U.S. 355 (1963); *U.S. ex rel. Wolfish v. United States,* 428 F.Supp. 333 (S.D.N.Y. 1977), *rev'd* 441 U.S. 520 (1979).

11. E.g., 18 U.S.C. §§241–242 (1976); 42 U.S.C. §§1981–1983, 1985 (1976).

12. E.g., *Jones v. Alfred H. Mayer Co.,* 392 U.S. 409 (1968). See essay 7, n. 43.

13. Covenant on Civil and Political Rights, Art. 2(2).

14. *Ibid.,* Art. 9(5).
15. *Wesberry v. Sanders,* 376 U.S. 1 (1964); *Reynolds v. Sims,* 377 U.S. 533 (1964).
16. Covenant on Civil and Political Rights, Art. 20(2), discussed later this chapter at n. 36.
17. Article 17, Universal Declaration of Human Rights. See *Restatement, Third, Foreign Relations Law of the United States,* §702, Comment *k.*
18. Covenant on Civil and Political Rights, Art. 7.
19. *Ingraham v. Wright,* 430 U.S. 651 (1977).
20. Art. 6(5), Covenant on Civil and Political Rights.
21. United States Constitution, Amendment V; Covenant on Civil and Political Rights, Art. 14(7); *Abbate v. United States,* 359 U.S. 187 (1959); *Bartkus v. Illinois,* 359 U.S. 121 (1959).
22. Covenant on Civil and Political Rights, Art. 10(2).
23. *Ibid.,* Art. 10(3).
24. *Ibid.,* Art. 17; *Paul v. Davis,* 424 U.S. 693 (1976).
25. *Bolling v. Sharpe,* 347 U.S. 497 (1954).
26. See *Dandridge v. Williams,* 397 U.S. 471 (1970); also *San Antonio Ind. School Dist. v. Rodriguez,* 411 U.S. 1 (1973), cited in essay 6, n. 30.
27. *Regents of University of California v. Bakke,* 438 U.S. 265 (1978). See also other cases cited in essay 7, n. 51.
28. See, e.g., International Covenant on Civil and Political Rights, Arts. 2(1), 3, 4(1), 20, 24, 25, 26; International Covenant on Economic, Social and Cultural Rights, Arts. 2(2), 3, 7(a)(i), 10(3).
29. International Covenant on Economic, Social and Cultural Rights, Art. 2(1).
30. International Covenant on Civil and Political Rights, Art. 4.
31. Universal Declaration of Human Rights, Art. 29(1).
32. E.g., Constitution of the USSR, Art. 59.
33. See Henkin, *The Rights of Man Today* (Boulder: Westview Press, 1978), Ch. 2.
34. For example, the Supreme Court has held that education and welfare are not fundamental rights as to which state regulations and classifcations are subject to strict judicial scrutiny. *San Antonio Independent School Dist. v. Rodriguez,* 411 U.S. 1 (1973); *Dandridge v. Williams,* 397 U.S. 471 (1970). The Court might hold otherwise if the United States adheres to international agreements which recognize these to be fundamental rights.
35. Art. 20 of the International Covenant on Civil and Political Rights.
36. *Brandenburg v. Ohio,* 395 U.S. 444 (1969).
37. For example, the United States Senate gave consent to U.S. ratification of the Genocide Convention in 1987, but controversy over implementing legislation delayed ratification until late in 1988. For arguments against a disposition to render treaties "non-self-executing" and requiring implementing legislation, see *Restatement,* n. 17 *supra,* §111, Reporters' note 5.
38. Letter of Submittal from the Department of State to the President (Dec. 17, 1977), *reprinted in* "Message from the President of the United States Transmitting Four Treaties Pertaining to Human Rights, S. Executives C, D, E & F," 95th Cong., 2d Sess. vi (1978).
39. The Supreme Court held that the Constitution permits capital punishment for an offense committed by a person sixteen years of age, Stanford v. Kentucky, 109 S.Ct. 2969 (1989), but not by a person fifteen yers old, *Thompson v. Oklahoma,* 108 S.Ct. 2687 (1988).
40. Henkin, "The Treaty Makers and the Law Makers: The Law of the Land and Foreign Relations," 107 *U. Pa. L. Rev.* 903, 936 (1959).
41. See, e.g., Q. McC. H. Hailsham, *The Dilemma of Democracy* (London: Collins, 1978); L. Scarman, *English Law—The New Dimension* (London: Stevens, 1974); L. Scarman, "Fundamental Rights—The British Scene," 78 *Colum. L. Rev.* 1575 (1978).

10. RIGHTS: HERE AND THERE

1. Compare Rousseau, *The Social Contract,* Book I, ch. VI, in *The Essential Rousseau* (L. Bair trans. 1974).

2. Declaration of the Rights of Man and of the Cititzen, Article 6.

3. *Ibid.,* Articles 5, 7, 10, 11.

4. Constitution of 1791, tit. 1 (Fr.), reprinted in F. Anderson, *The Constitutions and other Select Documents Illustrative of the History of France 1789–1907,* at 58, 62 (New York: Russell & Russell, 1967); Constitution of 1793, Arts. 21, 22 (Fr.), reprinted in Anderson, at 171, 173.

5. See M. Cappelletti and W. Cohen, *Comparative Constitutional Law* (Indianapolis: Bobbs-Merrill, 1979), pp. 34–41.

6. Constitution of 1946, preamble (Fr.)(incorporated by reference in the preamble of the current French constitution).

7. *Ibid.*

8. 1958 Constitution Art. 34 (Fr.).

9. The United States Supreme Court invalidated a state law that gave a tax deduction for tuition paid to private schools (including parochial schools) but upheld a state law that permits all parents a tax deduction for educational expenses. Compare *Committee for Public Education v. Nyquist,* 413 U.S. 756 (1973), with *Mueller v. Allen,* 463 U.S. 388 (1983).

10. 1958 Constitution, Art. 16.

11. Konstitutsiia (Constitution) Arts. 39–58 (USSR) (official trans). In this section I draw on L. Henkin, *The Rights of Man Today* (Boulder: Westview Press, 1978), ch. 2, and my essay in Edwards, Henkin, and Nathan, *Human Rights in Contemporary China* (New York: Columbia University Press, 1986).

12. See generally Przetacznik, "The Socialist Concept of Human Rights: Its Philosophical Background and Political Justification," *Revue Belge de Droit International* (1977), p. 239.

13. Konstitutsiia (Constitution) preamble (USSR).

14. Konstitutsiia (Constitution) of 1936 Art. 12 (USSR), reprinted in *Constitutions of the Communist Party-States,* at 37, 38 (J. Triska ed. 1968).

15. Konstitutsiia (Constitution) Art 14 (USSR).

16. Konstitutsiia (Constitution) Art. 58 (USSR).

17. Const. Art. 13 (Libya); Const. Art. 26 (Iraq).

18. International Covenant on Economic, Social and Cultural Rights Art. 2(1), G.A. Res. 2200, 21 U.N. GAOR, Supp. (No. 16) 49, 52, U.N. Doc. A/6316 (1966), reprinted in *Human Rights—A Compilation of International Instruments,* at 3, U.N. Doc. ST/HR/1/ Rev. 1 (1978).

19. [1955–1957] Y.B. Eur. Conv. on Human Rights 4 (Eur. Comm'n on Human Rights), reprinted in A. Robertson, *Human Rights in Europe,* at 294 (2d ed. 1976).

20. Constitution of the Federal Republic of Nigeria, 1979, §41(2).

21. Const. § 42(4) (b)(i) (Nigeria).

22. C. Pratt, *The Critical Phase in Tanzania, 1945–1968* (New York: Cambridge University Press, 1976).

23. The Arusha Declaration pt. 1, reprinted in J. Nyerere, *Ujamaa—Essays on Socialism,* at 13, 14 (1968).

24. Newspaper Ordinance Act, ch. 229, § 21A (1968), quoted in R. Martin, *Personal Freedom and the Law in Tanzania,* at 93–94 (1974). See also Penal Code, 1945 cap. 16, § 51, cited in R. Martin, at 94.

25. Preventive Detention Act, ch. 490, § 2 (1962), quoted in R. Martin *supra* n. 24, at 87–88.

26. French Declaration, preamble.

27. Quoted in Collins, Introduction to T. Paine, *Rights of Man,* at 47 (H. Collins ed. 1969).

EPILOGUE: HUMAN RIGHTS AND COMPETING IDEAS

1. See International Covenant on Economic, Social and Cultural Rights, Article 1; International Covenant on Civil and Political Rights, Article 1.

2. Compare the African Charter on Human and Peoples' Rights, Articles 20–22.

Index